[in context of both pieces & "Did they cross the line? If so, were they right?"

195-271

1) Dec. 1 final
— 5 questions about issues raised in class, discussion, presentation, etc.

1995 best newspaper writing

— 1 question on Fallows, short essay

WINNERS: THE AMERICAN SOCIETY OF NEWSPAPER EDITORS COMPETITION

- 2 or 3 questions (choose 2) essay type response on

- Equivalent to a drill. Facts → fashion a news story

EDITED BY CHRISTOPHER SCANLAN

The Poynter Institute
and
Bonus Books, Inc.

98   97   96   95   94   5   4   3   2   1

International Standard Book Number: 1–56625–046–3
International Standard Serial Number: 0195–895X

The Poynter Institute for Media Studies
801 Third Street South
St. Petersburg, Florida 33701

Bonus Books, Inc.
160 East Illinois Street
Chicago, Illinois 60611

Printed in the United States of America

Book design and production by Billie M. Keirstead

Cover illustration by Phillip Gary Design, St. Petersburg,
Florida

Photos for cover illustration courtesy of the Associated Press
and AP photographers Jean-Marc Bouju (Rwanda), Doug
Mills (White House plane crash), Dennis Cook (Nixon
funeral), Mark Lennihan (New York subway bomb victims),
and Denis Paquin (Oksana Baiul)

For the victims—in Rwanda, New York, Oklahoma City, and elsewhere—and for the journalists who chronicle their pain.

About this series

The Poynter Institute for Media Studies proudly publishes the 17th volume of its series *Best Newspaper Writing,* valued since 1979 by students, teachers, and professionals as an indispensable text on clear, effective, and graceful newswriting.

As in past years, *Best Newspaper Writing* is a joint venture of the Institute and the American Society of Newspaper Editors. In 1978, ASNE made the improvement of newspaper writing one of its primary goals. The Society inaugurated a contest to select the best writing from newspapers in the United States and Canada, and to reward the winning writers with monetary prizes. The Institute volunteered to spread the gospel of good writing by publishing the winning entries along with notes, commentaries, and interviews. That first volume, *Best Newspaper Writing 1979,* sold out long ago and has become a collector's item.

Best Newspaper Writing 1995 is edited by Christopher Scanlan, an experienced newspaper reporter and writing coach, who is the director of Poynter's writing programs.

This year, the ASNE Writing Awards Competition was augmented by the introduction of the Jesse Laventhol Prizes for Deadline Reporting for individual and team reporting. David Laventhol, editor-at-large for the Times-Mirror Co., endowed the prizes in honor of his father, a longtime Philadelphia newspaperman. Laventhol said he wanted to encourage and recognize high quality in this key component of newspaper reporting: "While much of the journalistic world's prizes tend to focus on investigative reporting, special projects, and analysis and explanation, the fact is that more than half of what appears in most newspapers each day is based on events that occurred in the last news cycle before publication."

The 1994 award categories are deadline reporting (individual and team categories), non-deadline writing, commentary, editorial writing, and sports writing. A committee of 14 judges, chaired by David Lawrence Jr., publisher of *The Miami Herald,* judged this year's entries:

John Carroll, *Baltimore Sun*

Roy Peter Clark, The Poynter Institute

Michael Fancher, *The Seattle Times*

Gregory Favre, *Sacramento Bee*; ASNE president

William Hillard, retired from the *Portland Oregonian*

Deborah Howell, Newhouse News Service, Washington, D.C.

Pamela Johnson, *Arizona Republic*

Beverly Kees, Freedom Forum, Oakland, Calif.

David Laventhol, Times-Mirror Co.

Tim McGuire, *Star Tribune,* Minneapolis

Geneva Overholser, former editor, *Des Moines Register*

Paul Tash, *St. Petersburg Times*

Don Wycliff, *Chicago Tribune*

The Institute congratulates the winners and finalists of the ASNE Distinguished Writing Awards, and thanks the judges for their fine work and dedication to good writing.

* * *

Founded in 1975 by the late Nelson Poynter, chairman of the *St. Petersburg Times* and its Washington affiliate, *Congressional Quarterly,* the Institute was bequeathed Poynter's controlling stock in the Times Publishing Company in 1978. It invests its dividends in educational activities in four areas of print and broadcast journalism: writing, reporting, and editing; visual journalism; management; and ethics. The faculty teaches beginning and midcareer professionals as well as news executives, publishes teaching tools such as this book, and conducts educational and research projects, all of which seek the same goal: to raise levels of excellence in newspapers and the communications media generally, so that journalists can fulfill their responsibility to empower citizens by informing them.

Robert J. Haiman, President
The Poynter Institute

Acknowledgments

Production of this book depends, as do all the activities at The Poynter Institute for Media Studies, on a staff and faculty that dedicates itself to teaching and inspiring journalists and media leaders. Thank you all for your encouragement, inspiration, and spirit.

It also relied heavily on the creativity and commitment of Billie M. Keirstead, the Institute's publications manager, and a network of Institute friends that reaches far beyond St. Petersburg, Florida. Among them: Kevin Kerrane of the University of Delaware; G. Stuart Adam of Canada's Carleton University; Vicki Krueger and Joyce Olson; Elise Burroughs; the American Society of Newspaper Editors; David Laventhol; and Chuck Zoeller at the Associated Press photo library.

Thanks to all the writers who shared of themselves during Poynter seminars by writing personal essays and, in several cases, contributed their observations about the process. Editors who publish the form shared their insights, including Lary Bloom, Mary Jane Park, and Evelynne Kramer.

A special thanks to Roy Peter Clark for indispensable backup and inspiration, and to Don Murray for his readiness to abandon his own work to make this volume better, and to my wife, Kathy Fair, and our daughters, Michaela, Lianna, and Caitlin, for their love and patience.

Finally, my thanks and congratulations to the newspapers, editors, visual journalists, and writers whose work made this collection possible. Special thanks to the finalists for their illuminating essays on the writing lessons they learned, and to the winners of this year's Distinguished Writing and Jesse Laventhol Awards for their willingness to explore the way they write.

As always, this is their book.

Contents

The clock ticks: Writing on deadline with grace

Outside the village of Musha, Rwanda, Mark Fritz, a foreign correspondent for the Associated Press, crouches in the dirt and strains to read by the light of his laptop screen the notes he has taken after interviewing villagers who admitted they took part in the slaughter of their neighbors. He has less than two hours to write his story and beam it via satellite in the East Indian Ocean in order to beat the other news organizations competing for space in America's morning newspapers.

In a suburban home in East Greenwich, Rhode Island, Brian Dickinson writes a column for the *Providence Journal-Bulletin* even though he is paralyzed by amyotrophic lateral sclerosis, the crippling and fatal illness known best by the baseball hero who succumbed to it 50 years ago, Lou Gehrig. Using a computer that he controls with one thumb, Dickinson selects his words carefully, one word, sometimes one letter, at a time. To finish, it will take him 15 hours.

Minutes after a firebomb explodes on a crowded New York City subway train, injuring scores of commuters a few days before Christmas, more than 30 reporters and editors at *New York Newsday* begin their own race against time: how to make sense of chaos in the hours before their deadline.

In Lillehammer, Norway, George Vecsey, sports columnist for *The New York Times,* watches Oksana Baiul of the Ukraine win the gold medal in figure skating from the favorite, American Nancy Kerrigan. He has less than 30 minutes to write an 800-word piece that will add meaning to an event already watched by millions on television.

In Boston, Susan Trausch emerges from the morning meeting of the editorial board of *The Boston Globe.* A freighter has sunk in the Baltic. Hundreds are dead. By mid-afternoon she must write a 400-word editorial that will make sense of the senseless. She picks up a notepad and begins making a list of her thoughts. Lunch at her desk again.

In Westerly, Rhode Island, Gerald Carbone of the *Providence Journal-Bulletin* has a two-week deadline to produce a narrative reconstruction of a dramatic operation that saved a state trooper wounded by a suspect's gunfire. But his editors push his deadline up a week after they learn he has secured a detailed interview with the surgeon.

For these journalists, and their counterparts in newsrooms around the world, the clock ticks. This book is proof that these writers rose to the challenge.

What follows is a collection of articles, editorials, and columns honored by the American Society of Newspaper Editors as the best writing published in American newspapers in 1994. Two of the writers, Mark Fritz and Ron Suskind, a finalist in the non-deadline category, also received the Pulitzer Prize for their work.

The winning entries in this year's Distinguished Writing Awards competition are a reflection of today's news and enduring themes. They catalogue the front-page disasters and deliverances as well as the private moments of tragedy and triumph that today's newspaper writers bring to their readers every day. Rwandan massacres. The Tonya-Nancy-Oksana saga. The New York City subway firebombing. One man's battle against disability.

Since 1979, the *Best Newspaper Writing* series has used benchmarking, a surveyor's term for a point of reference, to document the journalism profession's best practices.

Like their predecessors, these stories will serve as benchmarks for other writers and editors, a measure for their own work. Interviews with the winning writers and essays by the finalists also allow readers to learn how the best produce the best.

This volume marks the first appearance of two new awards to recognize excellence in deadline reporting. The Jesse Laventhol Prizes, each worth $10,000, honor deadline reporting by a single writer and by a team. They were endowed by David Laventhol, editor-at-large of The Times-Mirror Company, in memory of his father, Jesse

Laventhol. The elder Laventhol was a reporter for the highly competitive Philadelphia newspapers of the 1930s, scoring many exclusives on his crime, government, and politics beats.

It was David Laventhol's hope that an award that emphasizes writing as well as reporting might also be a spur for journalists "to do even better than they already do."

More than 100 entries in the deadline category fulfilled the prediction of Gregory Favre, executive editor of the *Sacramento Bee* and ASNE president in 1994, that the substantial cash awards (the other ASNE writing awards carry a $2,500 prize) would generate interest in "the very heart of journalism—the day-to-day work done under deadline pressure."

Interviewing the winning writers over the past several months, I was struck by the way the spirit of Jesse Laventhol and the deadline news reporters of his time seem to loom over the ASNE Distinguished Writing Awards this year. For no matter what the category, each writer was on a deadline of one kind or another. In the age of instantaneous transmission of information, the journalist must still work with skill and efficiency to achieve that combination of timeliness and timelessness that has marked the ASNE awards since their inception. This book is an exploration of the strategies, techniques, and attitudes that enabled these distinguished writers to achieve that elusive goal.

LESSONS FROM THE WINNERS

By focusing on individual victims and their killers, Mark Fritz of the Associated Press makes the mass horror of African genocide understandable in a series of chilling dispatches from Rwanda written under conditions that challenged a reporter's ingenuity and heart.

KARUBAMBA, RWANDA (AP)—Nobody lives here any more.

Not the expectant mothers huddled outside the maternity clinic, not the families squeezed into the church, not the man who lies rotting in a schoolroom beneath a chalk-board map of Africa.

Everybody here is dead. Karubamba is a vision from hell, a flesh-and-bone junkyard of human wreckage, an obscene slaughter-house that has fallen silent save for the roaring buzz of flies the size of honeybees.

With silent shrieks of agony locked on decaying faces, hundreds of bodies line the streets and fill the tidy brick buildings of this village, most of them in the sprawling Roman Catholic complex of classrooms and clinics at Karubamba's stilled heart.

Karubamba is just one breathtakingly awful example of the mayhem that has made beautiful little Rwanda the world's most ghastly killing ground.

Fritz says it was the time he spent before deadline—scouring databases, reading the clips and references works—that enabled him to explain the forces behind one of the most bizarre massacres in human history.

"In a country like Rwanda you have absolutely no opportunity to do research; it's just logistically impossible," he says. "So it is critical to do as much background as possible and to take reams of boiler plate with you and try to absorb as much as you can, so you can give some historical foundation to the story. It is critical to be prepared to do a lot of homework so you can evoke what is happening, but also keep it in historical context and give an explanation for why something incredible happened."

* * *

After a firebomb exploded at 1:34 p.m. on December 21, 1994, on a crowded New York City subway train, a team of *New York Newsday* reporters, columnists, and editors had just several hours to piece together a dramatic, comprehensive account. The package of stories in the next day's edition are remarkable for their completeness, complexity, and attention to detail, as in this reconstruction of the first moments of horror.

It was lunch time, and the fifth car of the southbound No. 4 express train was crowded— so crowded that Bennett Fischthal had to walk back and board the car right behind it when he transferred from a local train at 14th Street.

Fischthal, a 27-year-old Brooklyn Law School grad who had been studying for his bar exam, put on his Sony Walkman and was listening to Peter Gabriel's "Biko." His fellow passengers—an off-duty transit police officer among them—were a typical melting pot of New Yorkers.

At 1:34 p.m., their routine was shattered by a wall of flame.

Many of those on the *Newsday* team were veterans of disaster coverage: "Three plane crashes, a subway derailment, the World Trade Center bombing," recalled Deborah Henley, the editor who supervised the firebombing coverage. Among its hallmarks: attention to detail and commitment to storytelling and teamwork.

"Everyone becomes a police reporter," says reporter Wendell Jamieson, one of the first on the scene. "You want to cover every possible angle, and every little detail. And you do this massive sweep to get everything you possibly can. And then it gets molded into a story."

* * *

Veteran journalist and sports columnist George Vecsey writes literate and provocative sports columns that speak to amateurs who read sports pages for more than the scores. Among his winning entries is a tough-minded but compassionate piece about Mickey Mantle's alcoholism, the Fellini-esque antics of the coach of Italy's World Soccer Cup team, and a memorable deadline account of the Olympic figure skating competition.

...She was in pain from a dreadful collision in practice on Thursday, but Oksana Baiul is no stranger to pain.

She began to skate and the entire audience gazed at her, and so did the nine judges, even though all nine of them had just voted Nancy Kerrigan first, up to that moment. She skated, and within the Olympic Amphitheater of Hamar, the mystery of art asserted itself over the practicality of science. She made everybody stop and think that maybe Nancy Kerrigan's by-the-numbers, totally competent performance was not enough.

...Five judges felt the gifted young woman from Odessa had skated the best last night, and so did I. This takes nothing away from Nancy Kerrigan's grace under pressure in these last two ugly months, but the young woman from Odessa also had courage, and she had genius besides.

In the fast-paced world of sports reporting, Vecsey may be in the middle of writing his column when the sports desk calls with news of a breaking story, such as Michael Jordan's return to basketball, and wants his special take on it—in two hours. Vecsey remembers writing his winning column about Oksana Baiul in less than 30 minutes. But he had been thinking about her qualities as an athlete for months. That kind of advance thinking is what enables him to produce thoughtful commentary on a moment's notice. Whether the subject is tonight's big game or the City Council's vote on a new sewage treatment plant, says Vecsey, "You have to do your thoughtfulness way in advance."

* * *

Gerald Carbone's presence in this book will furnish hope to reporters across America. He is the winner of the non-deadline writing award, but he is not a project reporter. He is a one-person bureau in Westerly, Rhode Island. He captures readers with gripping tales that represent the story-telling art at its most engaging. He recreates a harrowing rescue effort on a snowbound New Hampshire mountain, sketches a fascinating mystery about the disappearance of a cross-dressing heiress, and had ASNE judges gasping for breath with the suspenseful reconstruction of a touch-and-go surgery to save a wounded state trooper.

But with the kidney out and clamped, the stomach holes stapled, and the liver tied off, the bleeding still will not stop.

Every time that Leadbetter [the surgeon] gets involved with something—packing the hole in the back muscles, stapling the stomach, reaching (for a third time) to clamp the aorta, blood wells up around Lemont's spleen.

Leadbetter suctions off the blood, looks away, and there it is again pooling around the spleen. The spleen is a delicate organ, a little bigger than a baseball, reddish brown like the liver, but rounder. It's an important organ in that it filters impurities from the vast net of lymph nodes that transport fluids throughout the body, and it helps fight certain kinds of organisms, especially a bacterial pneumonia.

As far as Leadbetter knows, the bullet did not damage the spleen, but a blood puddle keeps forming there—a pint every 15 minutes. Perhaps, Leadbetter suggests, it is an "iatrogenic injury" to the spleen—that is, an injury caused by the surgeon. He has, by necessity, been pretty rough on the organs, flopping over the intestines to get at the kidney, poking his fingers up into Lemont's chest.

There is only one way to rule out the spleen as the cause of all this bleeding—take it out. So Leadbetter takes a half-hour to cut out the spleen; and still the hemorrhaging continues.

It was during his interview with Carbone that the surgeon Leadbetter used a term Carbone had never heard before: "iatrogenic injury."

"Whoa! Time out. What's that ten-dollar word you just threw past me?" Carbone recalls asking.

The doctor's confession that he feared he had hurt the patient he was trying to save made Carbone's story more dramatic and richer, not the black-and-white treatment of standard journalism but a story with shades of gray that is more real and infinitely more powerful. By paying attention, he got his story. "It is better," he says, "to get as much as you can while you can the first time when you are writing on deadline."

* * *

Editorials can make you choke with rage, sputter with disbelief, rail with indignation. Rarely do they make you laugh or bring a lump to your throat. That's how Susan Trausch's uncommon voice stands out. Whether the subject is Columbus Day, frivolous lawsuits against pick-your-own orchards, or the search for Nazi war criminals, her wise and often witty editorials on *The Boston Globe*'s editorial page lead readers to a new vision of their world.

America's obsession with chic bottled water is getting worse. Moving way beyond "Perrier with a twist," the truly trendy are seeking the ultimate H_2O experience from big-name fashion designers, who give away private-label stock as a promotional item in their stores.

Buy a $1,500 Donna Karan original and take home a bottle of DKNY water to drink while wearing it. Talk about a fashion statement. At those prices they should be handing out Dom Perignon.

Water "just seems so right," Patti Cohen, public relations executive for Donna Karan, told *The Wall Street Journal.* "Water is international. It's real. It's part of you."

It's also becoming a pain in the glass.

...Enough! Bring back the days when water was boring, when a person could go into a restaurant and order it straight from the kitchen for free and when people did not discuss the relative merits of glaciers versus natural springs.

When Trausch sits down to write, she doesn't turn to her computer keyboard like most of her

Globe colleagues. Instead, she picks up a pen and a legal pad. Before she can tell editorial page readers what to think on a given subject, she first has to find out what her own thoughts are.

The notes she makes in those first moments make sense of the jumbled thoughts in her head. They will drive her reporting, plan her structure, make connections—all in rehearsal for the writing to come. "Then I turn to the screen, and somewhere in that list is a lead," she says. "And then you fire away and don't stop. The trouble with writing is it is always threatening to stop, and you have got to keep pushing."

* * *

Brian Dickinson's two year battle with Lou Gehrig's disease has left him speechless and virtually paralyzed, but has not kept him from writing the poignant columns that celebrate life, love, and the power of words to triumph over adversity. Most of Dickinson's winning columns focus on the lessons the disease has taught him and about the family whose love and devotion sustain him. One column does not mention his disease at all. But its shadow makes the advice he gives even more powerful.

Seize the moment. Make it your own. One never has quite enough moments, although we don't know this when we are young. Then, if we look ahead, we see an endless stream full of moments, so many that we could never count them, and all of them ours for the taking. Before we know it, though, the stream has shrunk dramatically and the available moments are growing scarce; and we wish that we had gone after them more assiduously when the stream was full.

So, we say again: Seize the moment— while you can.

As long as you are seizing moments, use the opportunity to divest yourself of all that residual guilt you are carrying around. Guilt gives us warts and yellow teeth, among other things, and never did anyone any good. Gather up your guilt, wrap with care and send it Federal Express to my cousin Pearl in Bayonne, who can never get enough of the stuff.

Forgive. Smile. Walk. (Oh, do walk when you can.) Share. Reach. Laugh. Teach. Learn. Run. Believe. Lift. Climb. Understand. Explore. Give. Appreciate. And, since you can never do it all, savor the small moments that, aggregated, become great. Stay in the game—oh, and do remember to look after the birds.

It takes Dickinson hours to write sentences like these, his wife Barbara reports. "Brian may say he writes for himself, but I think he writes for a universal person, that inner core in everybody who is out there reading, the 'myself' in all of us."

Asked for his advice to other writers during the interview for this book, which was conducted via America Online, Dickinson also speaks to the aspiring writer in all of us.

"Read, read, read. Write one true sentence, as Hemingway advised, then chew it over and make it better. Say your sentence aloud the better to feel cadence, rhythm, stress. Play around with different genres of writing. Take some risks. Stretch your working vocabulary. Believe in yourself."

A NOTE ABOUT THIS EDITION

The discussions with most of the ASNE winners in this book are based on tape-recorded interviews, conducted by telephone, that lasted between four and eight hours. For reasons of clarity or pacing, I reorganized some questions and answers, and in some cases, inserted additional questions. The edited transcripts were reviewed for accuracy and, in some instances, revised slightly by the subjects.

The ASNE judges selected Molly Ivins, columnist for the *Fort Worth Star-Telegram,* as the finalist in the commentary category. Biographical information and other materials for this book were not provided.

Christopher Scanlan
June 1995

1995 best newspaper writing

Mark Fritz

Deadline Reporting

Mark Fritz was the West African correspondent for the Associated Press, stationed in Abidjan, the Ivory Coast, when he was assigned in the spring of 1994 to cover the ethnic massacre in Rwanda. He also covered the U.S. mission in Somalia for the news cooperative. Fritz joined the AP in Detroit in 1984 after working at the *Kalamazoo* (Mich.) *Gazette.* He was a correspondent in Grand Rapids, Mich., and a newsman on the international desk in New York before transferring in 1990 to East Berlin, where he covered the fall of communism and the reunification of Germany before moving to Africa in 1993. Fritz is a native of Detroit and a graduate of Wayne State University. In addition to winning the first Jesse Laventhol Award for Deadline Reporting, his stories from Rwanda earned him the Pulitzer Prize for international reporting. He is now a national writer based in New York.

Foreign correspondence is often a confusing blend of alien names and even stranger situations, comprehensible perhaps to the reporter on the scene, but a puzzle to the average reader. Fritz writes stories that are brilliant examples of deadline storytelling. They take us to someplace foreign and make it as understandable as our own hometown. Even while he is describing the complex power struggles behind warring tribes, Fritz never loses sight of the people whose individual stories allow readers to bridge the gap between their own experience and those on another continent. Reporting and writing under harrowing conditions and brutal time constraints, he uses the reporter's tools —curiosity, observation, and empathy—and the writer's techniques—analogy, metaphor, and unforgettable imagery—to convey the human as well as the historical dimension of an unfathomable horror.

No hard feelings: Villagers defend motives for massacres

MAY 14, 1994

MUSHA, Rwanda (AP)—Juliana Mukankwaya is the mother of six children and the murderer of two, the son and daughter of people she knew since she herself was a child.

Last week, Mukankwaya said, she and other women rounded up the children of fellow villagers they perceived as enemies. With gruesome resolve, she said, they bludgeoned the stunned youngsters to death with large sticks.

"They didn't cry because they knew us," said the woman. "They just made big eyes. We killed too many to count."

Wearing a black shawl and a blank expression, the slightly built 35-year-old said she was doing the children a favor, since they were now orphans who faced a hard life. Their fathers had been butchered with machetes and their mothers had been taken away to be raped and killed, she said.

Mukankwaya is a member of the Interahamwe, the name for the innumerable Hutu tribal militias that have been blamed for slaughtering an estimated 100,000 to 200,000 people since April 6, when a mysterious plane crash killed the Hutu presidents of Rwanda and neighboring Burundi.

Most of the victims have been members of the minority Tutsi tribe and Hutus perceived as opponents of the government.

Mukankwaya was among 30 peasants from around Kigali, the capital, rounded up in recent days by the Rwandan Patriotic Front, the Tutsi-dominated rebel army that has captured large chunks of the country since the carnage began.

The people are being held in a former village community center at a small rebel base in Musha, 20 miles northeast of Kigali, the site of fierce artillery battles between the rebels and the government army backed by the Hutu militias.

The rebel commander of this strategic outpost north of Kigali agreed to let the Associated Press interview the militia members. All appeared healthy and there was no evidence of mistreatment.

Lt. Vincent Anyakarundi, a rebel officer, said the captives were being "re-educated" rather than punished because they were exhorted and coerced into killing their neighbors. The instigators, he said, were the government, local officials and army soldiers, who the prisoners said supplied them with weapons ranging from clubs to grenades.

"They are peasants," he said. "They are just puppets of the government."

In areas where rebels have seized control, they have appointed political officers to urge people not to listen to exhortations of violence against Tutsis or Hutu foes of the government. The "re-educators" have been preaching national unity and the official party line is no reprisals, no revenge and no punishment.

"People who would carry out such massacres, especially against children, are less than animals," said Tito Rutaremara, 49, a former party coordinator and leading political influence in the rebel movement. "You have to teach people to forgive and forget. It's like the Nazis. Most people were behind the Nazis, but you can't punish all the people."

Although individual acts of revenge likely have taken place, there have been no independently confirmed instances of mass reprisals.

In Musha, captives gave detailed accounts of the horrors they helped to carry out in their villages, when one part of the community suddenly rose up and destroyed another part.

Virtually all of the prisoners recounted their horrific deeds in dull, emotionless voices, their faces a collection of impassive masks.

Mukankwaya blithely mentioned the names of the parents of the two children she killed during the killing spree that she said left hundreds dead in her village of Nyatovu, just north of Kigali.

Potato and sorghum farmer Alfred Kirukura, 29, said he joined in the murderous orgy in his village of Muhazi, 30 miles north of Kigali, on May 9. He said he took a machete to three child-hood pals—one a Tutsi and the others Hutus branded by the locals as anti-government agitators.

As he killed them, "They said, 'We are friends! We shared the same classroom!'" he said.

Maria-Devota Mukazitoni, 24, said she didn't kill anybody in her village of Rutonde, just north of Kigali, but organized the looting of homes after hundreds of people in her town were massacred.

Sixteen-year-old Kitazigurwa—who said he had no first name—said his job was to spy on people saying bad things about the government. People he named were killed.

Joseph Rukwavu, 74, said he was too old to kill anybody but acted as the key authority in his vil-lage of Mwuma on people who claimed to be Hutu but whose parents or grandparents were, in fact, Tutsi.

"Two hundred were killed in my sector, even my wife, because she would not join Intera-hamwe," he said in a dull monotone, his face un-moving even as he mentioned his wife's death.

"The militia gathered everybody up near a big hole," he said. "They were weeping, even the men. Even the week before we killed them they were weeping in fear."

He said the army supplied the villagers with the necessary killing tools and oversaw the slaughter.

"They (the victims) said, 'Oh, we are the same people, we are your neighbors. Instead of hiding us you are killing us.'"

Boniface Gasana, 52, said he invited 15 people on the local hit list into his home on the pretense of hiding them, then tipped the village killers of their whereabouts when the massacre began. A woman near him shouted that he also took part.

Even as they spoke, the evening air brought the stench of rotting corpses from the gentle hills around Musha, a common odor throughout the country.

At Kiramuruz, 60 miles northeast of Kigali, 20 bodies lay in a neat row in the woods just outside the seemingly sedate and bustling village.

Resident Vitali Rudasingwa said the people were killed by Hutu militias two weeks ago, even though rebels were in control of the town.

"These militias are still killing people," he said. "But now they are hiding in the corners."

Writers' Workshop

Talking Points

1) Fritz is an acute observer who notices the inherent tensions in the experience of a person or a place. He often builds a lead around such tensions. In this story we learn that Juliana Mukankwaya is both a "mother of six" and "the murderer of two," a tension that is emphasized by alliteration. In another story, we see a young boy singing in spite of the horrible deaths of his parents. Discuss the effect of this technique on readers. Look for other examples of this ironic juxtaposition in Fritz's stories.

2) The organization that Fritz employs is simple but elegant. He begins with an anecdotal lead about one of the killers and then shifts quickly to give the reader necessary background about the massacres in Rwanda. He then sets the scene for his story, spatially and psychologically, by placing the reader at the scene of the prison and by explaining the rebel leader's surprisingly compassionate attitude toward the killers. The bulk of the story is a long section, beginning at paragraph 15, where five of the killers recount their actions. Finally, the story shifts away from the prison camp to another village where "20 bodies lay in a neat row in the woods."
   Why is this structure so effective? Could the story be organized differently?

3) Fritz reports that the killers he interviewed at the rebel camp where they were held captive "all appeared healthy and there was no evidence of mistreatment." Consider why Fritz would want to convey that information. Is it necessary? Is it sufficiently explained?

4) Confronted with tales of mass killings, a reader might naturally wonder whether victims' survivors had sought revenge. Effective stories anticipate such readers' questions. Notice how Fritz reports that, "Although individual acts of revenge likely have taken place, there have been no independently confirmed instances of mass reprisals."

Assignment Desk

1) To learn more about story organization and planning, reduce this story to an outline. Rearrange the sections to see how the story would change. Devise one or more alternative structures that you think might be more effective.

2) Detecting patterns, however contradictory, is one of the important ways that journalists help readers make sense of their world. As you report and write, stay attuned, as Fritz does, to the tensions that exist in people, situations, and events. Write leads that embody these tensions.

3) Before you turn in your next story, ask yourself, "What questions might the reader have about this story? Does the story answer them?" If you are an editor, pose the same question of stories you are editing.

Only human wreckage is left in village of Karubamba

MAY 12, 1994

KARUBAMBA, Rwanda (AP)—Nobody lives here any more.

Not the expectant mothers huddled outside the maternity clinic, not the families squeezed into the church, not the man who lies rotting in a schoolroom beneath a chalkboard map of Africa.

Everybody here is dead. Karubamba is a vision from hell, a flesh-and-bone junkyard of human wreckage, an obscene slaughterhouse that has fallen silent save for the roaring buzz of flies the size of honeybees.

With silent shrieks of agony locked on decaying faces, hundreds of bodies line the streets and fill the tidy brick buildings of this village, most of them in the sprawling Roman Catholic complex of classrooms and clinics at Karubamba's stilled heart.

Karubamba is just one breathtakingly awful example of the mayhem that has made beautiful little Rwanda the world's most ghastly killing ground.

Karubamba, 30 miles northeast of Kigali, the capital, died April 11, six days after Rwandan President Juvenal Habyarimana, a member of the Hutu tribe, was killed in a plane crash whose cause is still undetermined.

The paranoia and suspicion surrounding the crash blew the lid off decades of complex ethnic, social and political hatreds. It ignited a murderous spree by extremists from the majority Hutus against rival Tutsis and those Hutus who had opposed the government.

This awesome wave of remorseless mayhem has claimed 100,000 to 200,000 lives, say U.N. and other relief groups. Many were cut down while cowering in places traditionally thought safe havens: churches, schools, relief agencies.

One stroll past the bleached skulls, ripped limbs and sunbaked sinews on the blood-streaked streets of Karubamba gives weight to those estimates.

Almost every peek through a broken window or splintered door reveals incomprehensible horror. A schoolboy killed amid tumbling desks and benches. A couple splattered against a wall beneath a portrait of a serene, haloed Jesus Christ.

Peer into the woods every few hundred feet along the red-clay road to Karubamba and see piles of bodies heaped in decaying clumps.

News from Rwanda has been dominated by accounts of the carnage in Kigali or of millions of refugees living in mud and filth in vast encampments just outside the border. But what happened in Karubamba has happened—and is still happening—in villages across this fertile green nation of velvety, terraced hills.

Survivors from Karubamba say when early word came of the Hutu rampage, people from surrounding towns fled to the seemingly safe haven of the Rukara Parish complex here.

On the night of April 11, the killers swarmed among the neat rows of buildings and began systematically executing the predominantly Tutsi population with machetes, spears, clubs and guns.

"They said, 'You are Tutsi, therefore we have to kill you,'" said Agnes Kantengwa, 34, who was among dozens holed up inside the yellow-brick church.

"We thought we were safe in church. We thought it was a holy place."

It wasn't.

Her husband and four children were butchered amid the overturned pews. Bodies stretched to the ornately carved hardwood altar beneath a large crucifix.

Somewhere amid the stinking human rubble is the Rev. Faustin Kagimbura, "who tried to protect us," Kantengwa said.

Down the road, outside the maternity clinic next to the hospital, about 25 bodies lie beneath a cluster of shade trees; most appear to be women, but it is difficult now to be sure.

"They were women waiting to have babies," Kantengwa said. "The killers made them go outside and kneel down, then cut them in the head with machetes and spears. They said, 'You are Tutsi.'"

Mrs. Kantengwa, her 6-year-old son and 6-month-old daughter survived with a mosaic of machete wounds. They share one hospital bed in nearby Gahini, a larger town that breathes bustling life as easily as Karubamba exudes the suffocating stench of month-old death.

At the primary school midway between the maternity clinic and the church, a man lies prone beneath a meticulously drawn blackboard sketch of Africa, the capitals of each nation listed alongside.

Serena Mukagasana, 16, said the man was teacher Matthias Kanamugire.

The girl also was in the church when the slaughter began. By the time it was over, she was an orphan.

"All my family was killed," she said. She fled outside during the slaughter and watched from the bushes.

"They just killed and killed," she said.

The Tutsi-dominated Rwandan Patriotic Front that has been battling the government since 1991 has made huge gains in the countryside since the rampage began.

Their secured areas are relatively stable and well-policed, though scores of villages remain empty and thousands of people line the roads looking for safe places to stop. More than 1.3 million people in this nation of 8 million are displaced.

The rebels took Gahini and set up a base just days after the massacre at Karubamba. It is one of the staging areas for what is believed to be an imminent rebel assault on Kigali, where guerrillas are battling government troops backed by Hutu militias.

Capt. Diogene Mugenge, the rebel commander in Gahini, said an estimated 1,500 to 2,000 people died in the carnage at Karubamba. The only sign of human life in the area is a lone sentry posted roughly where the fresh air begins.

When asked about the massacre, and the fact that mutilated, battered bodies remain frozen in the moment of agonizing death just a few miles from his base, Mugenge shrugs.

"It's happening everywhere," he said.

Writers' Workshop

Talking Points

1) Sometimes less is more. The short sentence carries a powerful emotional punch. Consider Fritz's lead: "Nobody lives here any more." Five words. Discuss their effect.

2) Good reporters explain complicated issues to readers, and few issues are as complicated as the strife between the Hutus and the Tutsis in Rwanda. Analyze how Fritz defines this conflict in each of his stories. Pay attention to how much space he uses and where in the story this background appears.

3) Consider the emotional problems of having to cover such a story: the confrontation with death and physical suffering; concern for your own health and safety; the pressure to do justice to the story on deadline. Discuss the sources of strength that you would draw from if confronted with this assignment.

4) Fritz writes detailed, concrete prose that conveys the horror of Karubamba without flinching. At other times, he relies on metaphoric language. "Mrs. Kantengwa, her 6-year-old son and 6-month-old daughter survived with a *mosaic* of machete wounds." "But what happened in Karubamba has happened—and is still happening—in villages across this fertile green nation of *velvety,* terraced hills." [Italics added.] What is the effect of such language?

5) Too often, it has been argued, Western culture portrays Africa as a dark primitive place filled with savage people. The term "darkest Africa" was a common phrase through the 1950s. Discuss these stories with that criticism in mind. To add texture to your debate, read Joseph Conrad's novella *Heart of Darkness.* You might want to contrast press coverage of Rwanda with coverage of the democracy movement in South Africa.

6) To give a broad sense of the horror, Fritz will at times use statistics as evidence: "More than 1.3 million people in this nation of 8 million are displaced." It is sometimes argued that journalists are "innumerate," that they fail to use

numbers well. Study Fritz's use of numbers and discuss its effect on both narrative and explanation.

7) "No one wants to write a story that offends readers or viewers," Melvin Mencher writes in his textbook *News Reporting And Writing.* "But how do we draw the line? How does a reporter or an editor decide which words and what subject matter are offensive or essential?" Consider Mencher's comment in light of Fritz's graphic descriptions of the Rwanda massacres in the story from Karubamba. Would you eliminate or tone down any descriptions? Who draws the line? What role does the reader play in determining taste?

Assignment Desk

1) Write the lead of your next two stories in fewer than 10 words, the fewer the better.

2) Try this test of Fritz's effectiveness in conveying the origins and natures of the Rwandan massacres. After reading all of his stories, sit down and try to write a paragraph explaining the origins of this historical conflict.

3) Try an experiment to test your own ability to observe and report. Sit in a busy or chaotic environment: a train station, crowded restaurant, sports stadium, emergency room waiting area, or student union. With a notebook ready, watch intensely and record your impressions. If you were writing a description of this place, which people would stand out? Which details would bring the place to life for your reader? Now write several descriptive paragraphs.

4) Study how you presented statistics and other numbers in your last five stories. Read the sentences and paragraphs aloud. Keep in mind this advice from William Blundell's *The Art and Craft of Feature Writing:* "Numbers, especially big numbers and comparative sets of numbers densely packed in consecutive paragraphs, (are) cyanide to reader interest." Rewrite these passages, using more concrete descriptions (for example, "There are two firefighters in town for every 10,000 residents"). Try to avoid numbers bumping up against each other.

5) Fritz writes with impressive economy, compressing events with as few words as possible. Study this example from paragraph 25: "The girl also was in the church when the slaughter began. By the time it was over she was an or-

phan." Look for examples of such telescoping of time in other stories. Try to reduce a time-driven element in one of your own stories to a two-sentence summary, as in this hypothetical example: "The City Council began debating the new property tax proposal before lunch. By dinner, it had decided to ask homeowners to increase their tax contributions by 20 percent."

Death by design: Planning for the apocalypse

MAY 21, 1994

BYUMBA, Rwanda (AP)—They were trained, armed and programmed to explode, a human dooms-day device designed to detonate on command.

The extremist Hutu militias responsible for many of the 200,000 deaths in Rwanda were forged more than a year ago as a chilling final solution to ancient ethnic animosities and modern political pressures, former government officials say.

These secret civilian armies—which the government purportedly claimed at one point were being trained as park rangers—were the creation of Hutu President Juvenal Habyarimana, who continued to arm them even as he negotiated peace with his Tutsi-dominated enemies.

When he died in a mysterious plane crash on April 6, his murder machine thundered to terrifying life in every corner of this crowded little country, killing minority Tutsis and Hutus deemed opponents of the government.

The switch has yet to be shut off.

"We warned the international community that this was happening, that these people were being trained and armed to kill great numbers of people," said former Finance Minister Marc Rugenera, one of the Social Democrats Habyarimana had been pressured to include in his Cabinet.

Holly Burkhalter, Washington director of Human Rights Watch, said it was well known that the massacres were carried out by people "armed and trained by the Rwandan army." She said the army training had gone on "for a couple of years and there were many, many reports that it was very organized."

The Rwanda massacres came at a time when post-Cold War pressures for multiparty democracy collided horribly with ingrained ethnic animosities and internal power struggles.

The majority Hutus were traditionally farmers whose dominance by the tall cattle herders known as the Tutsi—also known as the Watutsi—dates back centuries.

Belgium, which took control of the country after World War I, favored the Tutsis with better educations and jobs for 40 years, fanning the fires of the 1959 Hutu revolt that toppled the Tutsi government and led to bloody reprisals against the minority.

In 1990, Tutsi exiles led a well-equipped rebel army into the county from Uganda. Many of them had become high-ranking soldiers in the army of former Ugandan dictator Idi Amin and the guerrilla army that put current Ugandan President Yoweri Museveni in power.

Habyarimana, a Hutu hardliner, came under international pressure to make peace with the rebels and open his government to opposition parties.

After bitter negotiations, Habyarimana gave 10 Cabinet posts to opposition parties in April 1992 and three months later opened talks with the rebel Rwandan Patriotic Front in Arusha, Tanzania.

The 34 months of negotiations were disrupted by repeated broken cease-fires, sporadic fighting, threats and acrimonious meetings, but ultimately resulted in a power-sharing agreement.

But the last year also marked the recruitment, training and arming of extremist Hutus from virtually every village, Rugenera said.

During one breakdown in peace talks in Arusha a year ago, Rugenera said opposition figures got an inkling of what was to come from a comment made by Col. Theoneste Bagosora of the elite presidential guard, which reputedly ignited the massacres.

"He said he was going back to Kigali to prepare for the apocalypse," Rugenera said.

There were numerous other threats by Hutu hardliners that Tutsis would be killed and float back to their ethnic homeland via the Kagera River, a warning borne out by the bodies that now fill Rwanda's waterways.

Opposition figures said they complained nearly a year ago that Hutu extremists were being trained at secret sites at the Kagera National Park in the northeast and the town of Gisenyi near the Zairean border.

Rugenera said at one point the government said the militias were learning to be park rangers.

"We knew something would happen. But we didn't know the day or the scope," said Joseph Nsengimana, 43, a member of the governing board of the opposition Liberal Party.

"Habyarimana said repeatedly that if the RPF were to take power, they would find their families dead."

Sporadic killings of Tutsis by terror groups broke out in mid-1993 and escalated in early 1994, including a massacre of hundreds in January.

Rwandans will debate for generations whether or how Habyarimana intended to use the militias had he lived. Rugenera believes they would have been used to disrupt multiparty elections or bring havoc if the opposition won an election or the rebels won the war.

Opposition parties and the rebels deny shooting down or blowing up the plane carrying Habyarimana, and contend that he was instead killed by his own people to thwart the Arusha accord he had signed.

"Habyarimana was caught in his own trap," contended Denis Polisi, a rebel spokesman. "He had to keep arming his militias and he had to accept democratic reforms, but he couldn't do both."

But while the rebels and opposition leaders say they had no reason to kill Habyarimana, they also paradoxically cite the militias as proof that he had no intention of honoring the power-sharing accord with the RPF.

Whoever killed him, his death plunged Rwanda into one of history's most incomprehensible series of massacres.

"The presidential guard began it when they went to kill the (opposition party) government ministers," Rugenera said. "First they killed their kids and wives."

Rugenera is a Hutu member of the Social Democrats and not affiliated with the Tutsi-dominated rebels. He was one of the few ministers who lived in his own house, rather than an official residence, and said he managed to escape to the home of a German neighbor.

He fled Kigali, taking advantage of the chaos when the rebels moved close to the city.

Militias, many of them operating in their own villages, pulled out their lists of names of Tutsis and anti-government Hutus and began separating women, men and children and killing them with guns, grenades, special knobby clubs, machetes, spears, bows and arrows and at least one sharpened umbrella.

"It was a plan of genocide that had been prepared a long time," said Polisi. "We warned the embassies, the (Roman Catholic) church, the EC (European Community) months before, but nobody listened."

Nsengimana, 43, a former university art professor, said he had a routine meeting with an RPF official inside the parliament building in Kigali when Habyarimana died. He said he was trapped inside while massacres erupted, followed by fighting between the approaching rebels and regular army soldiers.

"In the morning we were informed that important persons had been killed," he said. "I called my wife and she said her brother had been killed with all of his family."

Rebels took the parliament building and Nsengimana was escorted to Byumba, the rebel-held town north of Kigali where most of the opposition ministers now live.

Nsengimana said he is still waiting for word on his wife and children, who were at home.

"I asked the RPF to look at my home. It was empty. When they went to the house next door, it was filled with cadavers," he said, his face twisting into tears. "I have asked them to look again."

Writers' Workshop

Talking Points

1) Metaphors are figures of speech that apply a word or phrase to a person, idea, or object that is not literally accurate. Writers use them because they know metaphors are an effective means to link two ideas in readers' minds, heightening their understanding. Using the metaphor of the doomsday device, Fritz tells the story behind the massacre in Rwanda, the chilling final solution that kicked into action following the April 6 plane crash that killed the Hutu president. Discuss how, with masterful economy, he makes sense of the senseless, giving the historical, political, and ethnic causes behind Africa's worst massacre in history.

2) Alliteration is the repetition of initial consonant sounds. For example, Fritz describes the Hutu militias as "a human doomsday device designed to detonate on command." Three paragraphs later he writes "his murder machine thundered to terrifying life in every corner of this crowded little country...." Discuss the effects of this word play, especially in such gruesome stories. Examine your own stories to find examples of this technique, even if they were unintentional.

3) In this story, Fritz uses the phrase "final solution" to describe the ethnic violence and hatred in Rwanda. If you don't recognize the historical allusion in that phrase, try to discover it. Is it an appropriate comparison for what is happening in Rwanda? Should Fritz have explained it?

4) Even while he is describing the complex power struggles behind warring factions, he never loses sight of the human dimension. You read this history lesson, understand how this massacre came to be, and then in two poignant paragraphs come face to face with a survivor still hoping against hope that the cadavers in the house beside his home do not include his wife and children. How would the story change if the ending became the lead?

5) Effective organization is a key to clear writing. Fritz begins with an easily understandable metaphor—a human doomsday device—and then sets forth the history that explains its creation. Outline this story to see how Fritz as-

sembled the various elements. Discuss the effectiveness of the story's structure.

Assignment Desk

1) Examine your own stories for use of metaphors. In your next story, employ the device to help your reader better understand.

2) Consult a historical dictionary, such as the *Oxford English Dictionary,* to find the exact meaning of the word "apocalypse." Discuss its meaning in this story.

3) Look in your reporting and writing for ways to convey the human dimension of the news you are covering. Ask whether a person's experiences could provide a vehicle to amplify the news event or issues you are reporting. Experiment with leads and endings that employ the personal to convey the universal aspects of your stories.

Rwandan children search for new meaning of 'family'

MAY 25, 1994

KIBUNGO, Rwanda (AP)—Dad was drowned in a cattle dip and mom was taken away by a man with a machete. But 14-year-old Donata Nyinshimiye was singing as she walked to get water with her new family.

Twelve kids from different towns and ethnic backgrounds clanged their containers and their voices together as they trooped down main street toward the water pump in the center of this town 70 miles southeast of Kigali.

Singing, they walked to a mass grave sealed over with red soil by a yellow bulldozer—a single left arm reaching out from the ground.

Singing, they walked past the homes of the dead, ransacked by fanatical militias still looking for some reminder of their enemies to destroy.

They were children being children, oblivious for the moment to the signs of carnage around them and the ghastly personal losses they each suffered.

The massacres that broke out after President Juvenal Habyarimana died in an unexplained plane crash on April 6 have left few families intact among the minority Tutsis and anti-government Hutus who were targeted for slaughter.

Entire villages and neighborhoods were wiped out in the days that followed, their inhabitants killed with guns and hand grenades or hacked and clubbed to death by extremist Hutu militias bent on avenging the death of their president.

The remnants of tens of thousands of shattered families are frantically trying to reunite, wandering great distances in search of blood links. In some cases children themselves are building desperate little units without parents to watch over them.

Rose Kayumba, who runs an orphanage in Byumba, said nearly every day small groups of children show up at the gate, without parents or siblings, only each other.

Jennifer Wibabara, a reporter for a radio station run by the rebel Rwandan Patriotic Front, puts people on the air who are desperate to find somebody from the family.

"They say 'It's me, I'm alive,'" she said. "But rarely do people come forward."

In Gahini, about 45 miles northeast of Kigali, the Bwakeyebute family now only consists of father Benoit and 6-year-old son David. Bwakeyebute watched as militias cut the throat of his wife four weeks ago. He tried to flee, but the killers hacked at his face and arms and then left him for dead.

"An old woman with a goat found me," said Bwakeyebute, his right arm in a cast and his left arm and face tattooed with wounds.

His son, spared by the killers, was standing nearby when he regained consciousness.

The 12 young people walking in a tight little knot down the main street of Kibungo ranged in age from 5-year-old Francine Mahoro, a wide-eyed waif in dirty white dress, to 17-year-old Cesare Nyirabashumba, a rail-thin woman who stood more than 6 feet tall.

"I'm the leader," Nyirabashumba, a Tutsi, said of her charges, who were both Hutu and Tutsi.

Some came from this town, where survivors say at least 1,000 people were massacred in the local Roman Catholic Church on April 17, loaded into trucks and buried in a pit atop one of the green hills nestling the city.

Others walked from as far away as Rusumo and Sake, towns near the Burundi border 50 miles away, to escape the militias.

All came together at a nearby hospital that was turned into a refugee camp. Asked how many had lost one or both parents, eight of the 12 raised their hands.

Donata Nyinshimiye was from Rusumo, where she had the living nightmare of watching men grab her cattle herder father, drag him into the deep trench of chemicals used to cure cattle of parasites, and hold him under until the bubbles stopped.

"I'm alone," she said.

Prosper Rudasingwa, 10, who comes from Kibungo, said he's the only male member of his family left alive. His three brothers and father were killed, and his mother is missing. He was with his two little sisters.

Kibungo, a modern-looking town of neat brick buildings, a post office and large electrical power plant that supplied power nationwide, was seized by rebels of the Rwandan Patriotic Front on April 20.

The Tutsi-dominated rebels have been battling the Hutu-led government they blame for inflicting the carnage across this nation the size of Maryland. Aid agencies say most of the massacres were carried out by the Interahamwe, the government-backed civilian militias that attacked in nearly every village.

The children said they have a deep fear of the Interahamwe. During their mile-long walk for water, a group of men they believed were militia members shouted obscenities at them.

"We're always worried they will finish us off," said Nyirabashumba, wearing a baseball cap with a BMW logo.

The raggedy youngsters then walked on down the road to fill their odd assortment of plastic containers. Trudging along, they started singing again.

Writers' Workshop

Talking Points

1) This story is a vignette, a French term meaning "little vine," from the vinelike decorations in early manuscripts and books. It now refers to a sketch or other brief piece of writing noteworthy for the precision of phrasing and emotional impact. In this vignette, Fritz tells the larger story of the Rwandan massacres through its most vulnerable victims, children left orphaned and still living in fear. Study how Fritz uses this encounter and balances it against the news event he is covering.

2) Journalists traffic in details. Their observations, clearly conveyed, draw pictures in readers' minds that place them on the scene of news stories a continent away. Discuss the effect of the following details, drawn from this and other stories by Fritz:

A young refugee "wearing a baseball cap with a BMW logo."

A list of weapons including "one sharpened umbrella."

A corpse beneath "a meticulously drawn blackboard sketch of Africa."

3) Notice in these stories from Rwanda how Fritz regularly uses analogies that make it possible to bridge the gap between American readers and an African nation most have not seen. "Dad was drowned in a cattle dip and mom was taken away by a man with a machete." Why is the analogy, which is based on a partial similarity of features that allow a comparison to be based, such an effective device?

4) Fritz uses this brave, tattered troop of children to open and close his story, almost as bookends. Discuss why such a structure is effective.

Assignment Desk

1) On your next reporting assignment, collect vignettes—scenes, snatches of dialogue (two or more people talking to each other as opposed to quotes from a single speaker)—and incorporate them into your story. Discuss the challenges of such reporting and writing.

2) Look for examples of analogies in your own stories and in the work of Fritz and others. Use an analogy to describe an aspect of a story you're working on.

3) Plan to use the bookend device in one of your next stories: begin and end with the same elements the way Fritz does with the children in this story.

A conversation with

Mark Fritz

CHRISTOPHER SCANLAN: Congratulations, Mark. You're the first winner of the Jesse Laventhol Prize for deadline reporting. What was your reaction?

MARK FRITZ: I was happy personally, and I was happy for the AP. The people who work for the AP usually toil in anonymity, and they don't always get the recognition they deserve.

In most cases, especially if you're overseas, it is a deadline every minute. You're competing against virtually everybody, internationally and nationally. Our bosses, and I think our members, expect us to be faster than Reuters and have the conceptual sweep of *The New York Times* and get it out before either of them.

You have to produce, and you have to overcome a lot of logistical hurdles, and maybe the sun is going down and you haven't written a word and you've already advertised a digest line back in New York. Sometimes you have a half-hour, 45 minutes to write and send it.

It's like finding a muscle you didn't know you had. You just develop this ability to squeeze it our real fast.

What is that muscle?

Practice. I don't think it's written anywhere that the longer you take, the better something is. You just force yourself to do it quicker.

You may cringe over the wording, or some cliché or trite phrase, but you have to get it out fast, and you learn little tricks: writing it in your head, jotting a transition. You break it down into its raw essentials. It may sound formulaic, but I don't think it really is. Things become pieces as you're reporting them, and you think, "Ah, there's my lead."

I'll scribble along the side and I'll circle something, or put an asterisk, or write a little note next to it. I'll underline it three times. I'll write in block letters "LEAD."

Sometimes after I've talked to somebody, maybe it's an element, or a particular person that is the best way to get the reader into the story, and I'll write the lead on the spot in the notebook or flip open the laptop and type it in.

Let's look at the lead from Musha: "Juliana Mukankwaya is the mother of six children and the murderer of two." Do you remember when that line came to you?

I don't remember. That's another story that I wrote in, like, 40 minutes, at the end of the day. We had just found these people, and it was a classic panic attack. I was with the photographer, and he had his own schedule to meet. We spent the day getting from here to there. We heard about these people, and we wanted to talk to them, and we had to go through various hurdles; and then we talked to them. Then you open the truck, pull out the satellite dish, gas up the generator, find the coordinates for the satellite in the East Indian Ocean, and then plug your laptop into the generator, because the battery has been dead all day, and then just pound it out.

The material was so dramatic that I just tried to stay out of the way and let it flow. Then I think probably a half-hour after I sent it, it was out on the wire.

In Rwanda, I traveled with a photographer named Jean-Marc Bouju. I had three trips to Rwanda, and we hooked up on each. We rented a Mitsubishi four-wheel drive van in Uganda, and we hired a driver who would take people on safaris in peacetime. He was very savvy. He wasn't a member of any particular ethnic group that would have caused problems.

There weren't a lot of journalists going in at that point. There was a lot of attention on the refugee camps in Tanzania at that time. Jean-

Marc and I wanted to just hit the villages and the back roads, and stay away from the other reporters and just see if we could find out what was going on on the real basic fundamental level.

Why did you want to do that?

That's the kind of reporting I think is most satisfying, to stay away from the main roads and from the groups where the other journalists are, because I think you'll lose something. You really have to find out how the most typical person caught up in your story is living it.

We wanted to cover that country's psyche on a deadline basis. And I think Jean-Marc got some good photos out of it, too. [Photographs taken of the Rwandan massacres by Bouju and three other AP photographers won the Pulitzer Prize for feature photography.]

Tell me about your background.

I grew up in the Midwest, was born in East Chicago, Ind. My father worked for an oil company and then had different kinds of civil service jobs with the defense department. We lived in Cleveland and Dayton and Detroit, which I considered my hometown. I spent a good part of my teenage years and then my career in college at Western Michigan University and Wayne State in Detroit.

I studied business at Western Michigan for two years. I took a journalism class my last semester there. I'd taken some journalism in high school and I felt I had a knack for it, and teachers encouraged me to pursue it. I transferred to Wayne State to study journalism.

I got an internship at *The Detroit News* and worked there for three-and-a-half months. They let me work the weekend police beat. That's when I first covered human tragedy, because Detroit was then the murder capital of the world. You just had these horrible things happening every day.

Once, on a slow Sunday, there was a missing kid in one of the bedroom communities. A kid was at a park, and he'd gone out chasing after his dog, and the parents couldn't find him. There was a manhunt that lasted all day. At 9 o'clock at night they found the kid had slid down a river bank and drowned. One of the desk guys called me up and said, "Call the father. Get some quotes." And that was the first time I had to do something like that. I thought, "Jesus. Call the father? Come on."

I called the father, and he was obviously grief stricken; but people sometimes in those situations just talk and talk and talk. And he was talking about the kid, the dog. I wrote the story, and of course, the desk loved it; but the editor called me back and said, "What's the dog's name?" I said, "What?" "Call the father back and get the name of the dog. Always, always get the name of the dog."

This was my first hard lesson: Always get the name of the dog.

Then I went to work at the *Kalamazoo Gazette,* and had a great editor there whose name was C. Lane Wick. He used to say, "Keep it short. Don't write long. There are only two stories that require more than 20 inches: the Second Coming and a great fishing feature." And he was right. It always stayed with me. Too many stories are just over-written.

I worked there for five years. It was during the recession, the job freezes. I tried desperately to go somewhere. Everyone was trying to move in the industry, and nobody was moving, and people were getting laid off. Things started softening up a little bit, and I was always intrigued by the AP reporter who would sometimes wander into the newsroom in southwest Michigan, and he seemed to have this incredible amount of freedom and autonomy, and they were always showing up for the big story and stealing our stuff.

So I applied to the Detroit bureau. I went in there and I took a test, and they hired me. That was in 1984.

In your Rwandan pieces, you bring this sense of history and humanity that made a bridge

between people we've never seen and a country we can't even imagine. What do you think it is about you that enables you to do this?

I don't know if I have any special talents at all. It's just hard work. You just try to grab this sense of a country's history. People live their history, and in a country like Rwanda, you can trace it back to when the two ethnic groups were growers and herders fighting over land.

How did you get backgrounded?

In East Africa, we had a lot of reference books about the continent, and I looked at those, and there wasn't very much about Rwanda. There was a huge reference book on Africa that comes out once a year. It had Rwanda as this promising beacon that could bloom in the coming years, and it was all completely off-base. So there was a real dearth of stuff.

I read a lot of our stories. Our East Africa bureau did a good job of writing about the history of the country, and I basically read everything they wrote about it, and what we had in our books, and took it from there. And I discovered a gold mine in a small book shop in Uganda. It was a book by a Rwandan historian called *Rwanda, The Roots of Conflict*. It went up to about 1993; and it went back to as far as the 15th century, talking about the conflict between the Hutus and Tutsis. It was an invaluable resource. At the end of this book there were the first hints about militias being trained in the forest for this Doomsday.

How long were you in Rwanda?

I was in and out in two- or three-week stretches for eight or nine weeks.

After the two presidents died in the plane crash, the East African-based reporters rushed in. Then, they started killing Belgians and Europeans and everybody rushed out. Everybody who looked European was in danger of dying. It was a panic.

You had to get out of the country. There was this vacuum period, where everyone was sort of like, "Whoa, stand back." And then people started sticking a toe back in. Once these massacres started, reports were coming out of people dying, 10,000, 15,000, 20,000, rippling like a red wave across the countryside. Then there became this urgency to get people back into that country.

That's when they called me. They said, "We've got to send someone in. Do you want to go?" They don't really demand that you go in a place like that. We've buried too many people at the AP these last few years, especially out of that bureau. We've lost two people in the last three years out of that region. And someone kidnapped a woman in Somalia.

What was your emotional reaction when you got the call?

Different things go through your mind. "Wow, this is a heck of a story," or "Gee, I could get killed," or "Gee, my wife probably wouldn't want me to go," and "Gee, I wonder when the next flight is." Meanwhile, you're picking up the phone and dialing the travel agent.

What kind of deadline pressure were you operating under?

I had absolutely no time whatsoever to do them. I did one right after the other. There's sort of an unwritten rule at the AP that when you go on a hot ticket assignment like that, you try to do a story a day, because there's a lot of money being spent on it. And they gave me the kind of blank check to go in and just get close to it.

Why did you want to talk to killers? Usually stories about massacres are written from the point of view of whatever survivors are still around.

You have wars all the time. Somalias and Gomas, Sudans, Biafras, Bosnias, where there's mass movements of people, and people die. There's something almost primal about it, something almost inevitable.

But this is one of those weird things that happens once in a blue moon—in Cambodia. In World War II Nazi Germany. This wasn't just malicious. This was one group of people in one village systematically killing their neighbors. They killed the "other" people. And it happened so robotically that it just boggled my mind.

You have ethnic conflicts, but this was so systematic, and so sweeping, and so quick. How often in history do you have a half-million people wiped out in six weeks? I mean, just the speed and the efficiency, and everyone was killed individually. You walk into a village where there are thousands of dead people. Everybody has been killed separately. Somebody was killed running away. A family was killed when they were hanging onto each other.

You have to see it through the eyes of some mother who's swinging a club with a big heavy ball on the end at a bunch of little kids herded into a circle. You've got to see it through a guy who macheted a couple of his classmates.

That was the big question. How could they do it?

I started out the day working on the possibility that we'd be able to talk to some killers. Knowing how things worked in Rwanda, up until the words were actually tumbling out of their mouths, there was no guarantee that I would get close to doing that.

Were you surprised how forthcoming the killers were? I can't imagine the guards at Dachau being so honest.

Yeah. These are peasants, you know. The voice from above said, "Do it," and so they did it.

**How long had you been in Rwanda by the time
you did that story?**

Just a few days. What I remember more vividly is
the day before, the two days we were trying to
find the massacre site, the wiped out village.
Karubamba.

We were looking for villages where there were
massacres. A guard who was with us as an escort
said he thought there was one in this part of the
country. And we went—Jean-Marc and I. We
took this long, grueling drive to this one village,
and there was a sector commander there, and we
had to go and check in with him, and he was very
hospitable, and then we went off down this small
road, and it's hot. Blazingly hot. But not completely unpleasant. Rwanda is just beautiful.
There were incredible birds of paradise in that
country, and we're going down this road, and then
you smell that smell. And you could see in the
woods little clumps of bodies, where people had
been either running or they had been lined up.

Then all of a sudden, they're along the sides of
the roads. Body after body. And then you come to
this main parish complex and you just see hundreds, thousands of them. God knows how many.
A large school, a medical complex with the out-
patient clinic and maternity clinic, and you look
in every window in every room.

We wrapped T-shirts around our faces and went
to work. The first thing we did, we walked into
the church, which is where most of the people
were. And it was just a nightmare, just wall to
wall dead.

Everybody had died in action. It had been three
weeks since they'd been killed. There was decay,
and there were flies, and just the smell and the
sounds. The quiet with the occasional warbling
bird and then this roar, this constant, almost baritone buzz of all these flies, so heavy they could
barely fly. It was as if they'd eaten too much. You
would see bushes that were basically sagging with
the weight of the flies.

They went to their deaths like sheep to the slaughter. There was this other spine-chilling scene. We walked into a typical classroom with a blackboard in the front. And there was a guy sprawled there, and he was almost pointing at this chalk map of Africa.

I wandered around, and the thing that was going through my mind was, I'm in this city filled with people. None of them is alive. That was another one of those things where you don't really intellectualize your approach so much. I toyed briefly with a first-person account, and I thought, "I don't belong here. No." You just try to get out of the way of the material and let the city speak.

You came into this village where there's nobody there except dead people, and it's just you and Jean-Marc Bouju and your guide?

Yeah. He's got his cameras. I've got a black Berlin T-shirt around my face. I've got sunglasses. I've got a Detroit Pistons baseball cap on. I've got my notebook and a pen, and that's it.

I was writing down everything. I was trying to write down every characteristic of every building, and everything I saw. I wrote down, "Hundreds of dead people. Thousands of dead people." It sounds callous, I guess, but you're working. And I was thinking I had to find out what happened. I have to get as much detail from this to fill my story, in case I don't find any survivors who can tell me what happened in this specific place. So I was writing a lot of stuff down, because I knew I'd have to write a story.

What time was this?

It was already starting to get to panic time. I'm always going for A.M.s, and I'm always thinking East Coast deadlines—digest time at noon and get that story in by 2 o'clock so they can have it out by 4 and catch those first editions on the East Coast.

Do you have an audience in mind when you're writing?

The American who could care less about Rwanda, or Somalia, or East Germany, and doesn't particularly seek out foreign news in the paper, and can't relate to it.

Why are you writing for that American?

Because maybe I was that kind of American. Maybe because that's most Americans. I think it's more satisfying when you get someone to read a story about the Ivory Coast who has no idea what the Ivory Coast is.

What do you want your stories to do to that American who doesn't care?

Make him care a little bit. Make him interested in it. After that Karubamba story, I got some letters to the editor, which you don't get at the AP on foreign stories. There are too many levels between us and the reader.

Somebody used one of those yellow highlighters and circled paragraphs. And they said, "I didn't know anything about Rwanda. I didn't care. And this story made me think about Rwanda, and made me interested." One was a letter to the editor in a newspaper in Colorado that said, "Why can't you do more stories like this instead of boring NAFTA stories?"

That's what the job's all about. It's to tell people about something important that's happening. When you're overseas, when you don't have a built-in audience, the trick is to create one. And that's all you have. That determines how you get in the newspaper. We have to compete with an ever-proliferating number of supplemental news services.

I was sitting there thinking that everyone's writing about a massacre. But when I came back, they said, "Nobody was writing about massacres like that. Nobody found a massacre."

When I was interviewing my killers, I was thinking, "God. I bet the *Times* interviewed the killers yesterday." That's my motivation. That's why I can't wait for tomorrow to do the story, because I figure the *Times* has got the same story. So I've got to get it out.

And then you check in, and they say, "Wow, nobody had that." And you say, "That's great." Because there is a competitive element to that, too.

We tried to find a massacre, and we found it. And then you try to portray it the way you saw it as much as possible, and make the reader see it too, as vividly as you saw it.

You take four paragraphs to describe this city with all this horror. And then in one sentence, you put it in context: "...one breathtakingly awful example of the mayhem that has made beautiful little Rwanda the world's most ghastly killing ground."

Then you background the reader: "Karubamba, 30 miles northeast of Kigali, the capital, died April 11, six days after Rwanda President Juvenal Habyarimana, a member of the Hutu tribe, was killed in a plane crash whose cause is still undetermined.

"The paranoia and suspicion surrounding the crash blew the lid off decades of complex ethnic, social and political hatreds. It ignited a murderous spree by extremists from the majority Hutus against rival Tutsis and those Hutus who had opposed the government."

You write with such economy. Is this kind of summary difficult to do?

You have to weave the history of the country in there as background. I'm not saying you have to know it all, but you have to know much more than is there to be able to compress it accurately. It's just studying, and trying to understand the country you're studying.

The story, "Death By Design: Planning for the Apocalypse," made sense of the senseless, and it

gave the historical, political, and ethnic causes. When did you get the idea to do this story?

That idea came from Reid Miller, the Nairobi bureau chief. We were running low on provisions, and we drove back to Kampala for a few days of R&R. Reid said we could use something that looks at how this began, and the genesis of it, and there were reports that this thing had been planned, and that these militias had been trained.

When I went back in, I had that in my mind, to try to find people who could speak to that issue. And that was also when I found this book that had a lot of inside history, a lot of detail that you didn't see in the Western history books about Rwanda.

How important is the off-deadline preparation that a reporter like you will do?

It's the difference between a good story and a bad story. If you know the story inside and out, you find the history and the background just surfacing.

It doesn't sound like your job—certainly in the field, but maybe never—is this 9-to-5 thing. When do you do this kind of background reading?

There are people who study much more than I. But when you get an assignment like that, you try to be prepared. You just do a lot of cramming, and you take a lot of stuff with you. I run off stories that have a lot of background, and I take things I can refer to. I have a big sheaf of notes and papers and photocopies and things that I carried with me in my bag.

I was really struck by the power of the prose, the brute force of the language. What do you think makes you such a good writer on deadline?

It helps to be inspired by the material.

I write badly on the first draft. But you find a

way to skip the first draft, to write the first draft in your head. The evolutionary process that usually takes place in front of a screen or a typewriter largely takes place in your mind. Some people are better at it than others, but I think everybody, if they do it enough, can write a story on deadline that's pretty close to as good as they can do.

Details seem to be a very big part of your prose. Like "the chalkboard map of Africa." It's not just a map, it's a chalkboard map.

You do look for precision detail. You're trying to create a picture in the reader's mind, and you don't describe a couch in a room. You describe a forest green couch. A wood floor.

I was constantly looking for precise details. Because everyone died individually. It wasn't like somebody dropped a bomb on the place. Everybody was killed by hand, or by a bullet, one at a time. And it was in an environment that people could relate to—a school, a church, a clinic. What was so haunting about it was these touchstones that are universal, and you had to put that in the story. A maternity clinic. Pregnant women. Families in church. Kids at school. A teacher. A chalkboard. People can relate to that.

Are there rules that guide you as you write?

Don't bury your lead. Get your lead up there with your nut graph.

How would you define your lead?

The hook, the thing that makes the reader interested in reading the story. Hit them with the news, the peg. Why are you writing this story? What's it all about?

And then after the nut graph, what kind of framework do you try to create for a deadline story?

You support your nut graph with statistics and with quotes, something to prove your story.

Are there strategies or tips or techniques that you apply when you're in the field like this?

Learn as much about whatever you're going to cover before you cover it. Take notes, printouts, things you can refer to. It takes a degree of skepticism—a lot of reporters automatically go to the American Embassy and talk to the political officer. I know of no way to get your story more wrong, more quickly, than to do that. You have to find alternative sources.

Don't do what everybody else does because everybody else does it. Try to connect what you're doing and who you're covering with who you're writing for. Try to find those bridges, those little familiar touchstones.

And sometimes it's just as simple as leading with a human being. I try not to do it all the time, but, fundamentally it's the best way to connect your story with somebody who doesn't know anything about the place you're writing about.

What advice would you give to the reporter who has 45 minutes to write the story?

I've been in the exact same position many, many times. And a little trick that seems to help is to put away your notes and try to write the story without consulting them, and sometimes the rudimentary framework will come together and you won't have the technical detail getting in the way of the gist of your story.

Sometimes I've spent more time on the lead than the rest of the story. I'm one of the people who believes that if you get the lead right, if you nail your story in the first couple of graphs—maybe leading with an anecdote and then your nut graph—if you nail that, the rest just flows.

Get your lead—just put away your notes, and try to think about what your story is about and what example you have that most compellingly explains your story.

Talk about the story of the 12 kids trooping down towards the water pump.

It was an off-day story. I'd done something the night before about how the militias came together. It was about 7 o'clock in the morning and I heard these kids singing, and I went outside and just stopped them on the street and interviewed them.

"Dad was drowned in a cattle dip and mom was taken away by a man with a machete..." You use analogy in a way that makes it possible to bridge the gap between American readers and Africans. Everybody's got a dad, whether in Rwanda or Kalamazoo.

I actually said "daddy" and they changed it to dad. And a couple of newspapers changed it to "her father." It sort of sounded like a country and western song. "Daddy was drowned in a cattle dip," and it had a certain rhythm to it. I don't know why. I was punchy, and it was a day when I finished up the story that was grueling and difficult and long and complicated about the Doomsday Machine.

I felt like I needed another story that day, and I was tired, and there was something compelling about these kids. And I had some material from other places in my notebook that fit into this story.

Do you not walk outside without a notebook?

I sleep with it. I carry these little memo pads that fit in your shirt pocket. And I usually just have one in my back pocket.

So you're sleeping in your clothes?

In Rwanda, I sleep in my boots and everything. Sometimes, you gotta go fast.

I grabbed our driver, who translated for me, and

I just interviewed the kids, You know, that old joke about the ugly Western correspondent who stands up and says, "Is there anybody in this room who's been raped and speaks English?" At one point I said, "How many here have lost your parents? Raise your hands." And I felt bad about that, but I also felt that I had to say something. Here's a random sampling of kids who are refugees, who are on the run. Most of them were Tutsi. And I wanted to know how many of them had lost their parents.

Why did you want to know that? Why did that question occur to you?

Kids on the street, they're victims in this thing, and their lives are forever changed.

In this brief story, you tell the massacre through the most vulnerable victims, the children left orphaned and still living in fear from their enemies. It's a really wonderful story. How long did it take you to do it?

Maybe an hour-and-a-half or so. It was that "do a story a day" mentality, and I didn't particularly have anything when I woke up, and I was tired, and we didn't know where we were going to go, and we had no exact plan that day. And the kids were there, and I just said, "This is the story today." But a lot of newspapers used that story.

Does it surprise you still that they used it?

A little bit. It's kind of a soft story.

How do you mean "soft"?

It didn't really break anything. I like to write a story that has something that somebody else doesn't have.

The quotes are just stunning in their simplicity. Were any of these people English speakers?

Some were. Most of the rebel army was raised in Uganda, which is an English-speaking country. But mostly it was through a translator, speaking French, or Rwandan.

You ask the question, the translator asks it, and gets the answer and then tells you?

Sometimes you've got to watch out for the translator being too embarrassed to ask a question, and who will come back and say, "He says he doesn't know."

But you just have to keep plugging away and asking the same question several different ways to make sure you're getting what you're confident is a legitimate answer.

How would you describe your style of interviewing?

I try to have a conversation, but I can be pretty intense about asking specifics. What I tried to do in Rwanda was just have a friendly conversation with someone, not be intimidating by acting like the secret police, so they let their guard down.

How do you know when you have the story? Does it come during an interview?

I think so. That one person who's news to you. Seeing a village full of dead people—you know there's a story here. It's just up to me to do it justice. You find people who are being held because they're murderers, regular people who killed regular people.

There's no rocket science there. It's just a question of stepping out of the way and don't screw it up.

The genesis of the militia was a bit more abstract. I knew I had pretty good stuff, and I just needed to find an interesting and intriguing opening.

Before you start laying on the history of Rwanda, the history of militias and the political material, always assume that the person you're writing for knows absolutely nothing about your topic. Try to write for that reader who has absolutely no reason to look for a story about Rwanda, and capture their attention, and lure them into a story that you think is important, and that they would think was important if it were made interesting for them.

Do you make formal outlines?

Only sometimes in the notebook. I'll say, "Put this here, put this there." Yeah, I guess this is kind of an outline.

When you don't have a lot of time, you've got to write while you're reporting, and assign what you have either to the story or not to the story, and if it's to the story, put it somewhere.

Will you sit down and write it just once, all the way through? How do you do your rewriting?

If I get the lead right, I can inch my way through the story. I can bring it to the end. And sometimes, if I don't have that lead, I'll just start throwing notes up on the screen, stuff I know is going to go in the story, and look at it, and just wait for lightning to strike.

I have a real hard time forcing a lead. I have to do enough reporting that I know what the story is and how it's going to begin. If I have a deficiency putting those notes together from my notebook, I didn't do enough work on the story. If I'm going through my notes and I'm trying to think about how to start the story, or what my nut graph is, then I haven't done enough reporting.

The best way to write a story is to report the hell out of it. Then you know before you write that you have a story, and it's just a short hop to actually beginning it.

Do you give yourself time to go through it one last time when you're trying to hit the button and get it out so it makes the A.M.s? How much revision can you do?

I've never read a story of mine that I've been happy with, frankly. I mean, even days or weeks afterwards, I think, "Why did I do that?" It's always been my philosophy that it's great to be first, but you know, it's better to be right.

What questions do you apply to your stories before you kiss them goodbye and send them off?

Don't use anything you're not confident of. Don't use anything that you're not absolutely certain is solid. There are enough academics out there, particularly in Britain and Belgium, who are combing through this stuff, so if you blow it on a historical passage or a fact, you pretty much hear about it.

How do you take to editing?

I take it pretty badly, because I do have a vision of a story and how it should be written. I'm not always successful at it, but I try to write in a circle, to bring it back to where I began it, and reintroduce my initial point. There's a symmetry to it. I like a story that's like a drum, so tight you could beat on it. The ending is just as important to me as the beginning.

What advice would you give somebody facing a tough deadline story?

There's nothing wrong with preparing some material that you can put in your story. Graphs, boilerplate. I don't think there's anything wrong with thinking in advance.

Talk a bit about the conditions you faced reporting and writing.

We were always short of water. There were checkpoints, particularly in the government-held territory, there was artillery, and there was shooting when we were covering the war end of it, and

the food was bad, and there were insects and parasites where we slept.

**Were there times when you were literally typ-
ing on your knees in the dirt?**

Yeah, I was outside, because I could never keep
my Toshiba charged up. So I'd basically have to
plug it into the generator. That was really just another case of meatball journalism, where the bugs
are out, and you're uncomfortable, you're un-
washed, and your notes are flying around, and
you're trying to write a coherent story...

Is it at all glamorous?

When people ask you about it, and you tell them
about it, you think, "Wow, that sounds kind of
glamorous," but it's hard, and it's uncomfortable.
But it's exciting. I can't get past the fact that it's
exciting. When you're in a strange place, and
you're writing an exciting story and a lot of
people care about it, and you get something at the
end of the day.

**Humanity is such a hallmark of your work. It
must have been painful to report these stories.
What was it like for you, psychologically, to be
in the middle of this?**

That is the question that people ask me the most.

What do they want to know?

How did you deal with it? How did you handle it?
You must be permanently scarred. All I can say is,
how does a cop or a doctor deal with it? I've covered things like this before. I was in Somalia
where everyone was starving to death, and a girl
died while I was hunched over her. And I've been
in a section of Liberia where there were war ca-
sualties and starvation.

I wasn't completely prepared for the horror.
But it's your fear or your sense of horror—on a

personal level; it's not really a debilitating or an overriding thing.

The scariest part of going to Rwanda was not crossing checkpoints staffed by killers, or getting lost on side roads and smelling that smell, or seeing that clump of bodies out in the woods, or driving through an empty village and wondering what's around the next bend. It's getting on the plane on the way there, when you just get the assignment.

Was there ever a moment when it just was too much?

No, it is horrific to see it, and your jaw drops. You're stunned. But not to the point where you're incapacitated.

You're seeing something amazing and horrible, but for me, and I think for most of my colleagues, the instinct is to tell people about it. "Jesus. Did you see what I saw? It was amazing. The whole village was dead."

You talk about it. You have a beer, and then the sun rises, and there's someplace new you have to go.

David Von Drehle

Finalist, Deadline Reporting

David Von Drehle last appeared in *Best Newspaper Writing* in 1990 when he won the deadline writing prize for his vivid first-person account of a night with the "pure fury" of Hurricane Hugo. Since then, he moved from *The Miami Herald* to *The Washington Post,* where he served as a national politics writer and New York bureau chief (a post he also held at the *Herald*). He began his newspaper career writing sports at *The Denver Post.* After graduating from the University of Denver and Oxford University, he went to work as a city desk reporter at *The Miami Herald* in 1985. There, he covered social services, the environment, and general assignments. He is the author of *Among the Lowest of the Dead: The Culture of Death Row,* and his work appears in *Best American Sportswriting 1992.* He is now the *Post*'s arts editor.

Von Drehle filed his story, "Men of Steel Are Melting With Age," his editors recall, about 90 minutes after former President Richard M. Nixon's coffin was lowered into the ground. Rich with insight and penetrating description, his story displays the graceful power of the elegy and the long-term memory of the obituary. The piece stands as a cautionary tale for the powerful, and as a model of elegant writing for the deadline reporter.

Men of steel are melting with age

APRIL 28, 1994

YORBA LINDA, Calif., April 27—When last the nation saw them all together, they were men of steel and bristling crew cuts, titans of their time—which was a time of pragmatism and ice water in the veins.

How boldly they talked. How fearless they seemed. They spoke of fixing their enemies, of running over their own grandmothers if it would give them an edge. Their goals were the goals of giants: Control of a nation, victory in the nuclear age, strategic domination of the globe.

The titans of Nixon's age gathered again today, on an unseasonably cold and gray afternoon, and now they were white-haired or balding, their steel was rusting, their skin had begun to sag, their eyesight was failing. They were invited to contemplate where power leads.

"John Donne once said that there is a democracy about death," the Rev. Billy Graham told the mourners at Richard M. Nixon's funeral. Then, quoting the poet, he continued: "It comes equally to us all and makes us all equal when it comes."

And here, the great evangelist diverged for a moment from his text to make the point perfectly clear. "We too are going to die," Graham intoned, "and we are going to have to face Almighty God."

Coming from Graham, the words were especially poignant. He is the only American who claims the place of honor in our solemn national ceremonies, even above the sitting president. And once he was the vivid, virile lion of God, with a voice like Gabriel's trumpet. Now he is a frail old man who struggles to his feet.

The senior men of the Nixon administration looked quite old: George P. Shultz, the all-purpose Cabinet secretary; the disgraced vice president Spiro T. Agnew, who emerged from his long seclusion clearly stooped; the foreign policy guru Henry A. Kissinger, who seemed small and somehow vulnerable.

And the junior men looked very senior: Nixon chief of staff Alexander M. Haig Jr., resembling a retiree at the yacht club; political legman Lyn Nofziger, still looking like an unmade bed but now your grandfather's unmade bed; muscle man Charles W. Colson, his crew cut replaced by a thinning gray thatch. G. Gordon Liddy, with his bullet head, looked the least changed of all.

"Let not your heart be troubled, neither let it be afraid," Graham said.

They arrived full of the old sangfroid, smiling and glad-handing for as much as an hour before the service began. Nixon's men and many of the other dignitaries worked the crowd like a precinct caucus; surely Nixon, the best pol of his era, would have approved. As a Marine band played Bach's ineffable hymn, "Jesu, Joy of Man's Desiring," Republican National Committee chairman Haley Barbour pumped hands with a broad grin on his face, and nearby David R. Gergen, the perennial presidential adviser, worked a row of mourners like a rope line.

And in the beginning, perhaps, the event reminded them of just another political event. A very small number of people attended, compared to the number who no doubt wished to honor Nixon, but even among the exclusive group, the crowd was separated by various shades of lapel pin. Purple was the best, the regal color—bearers of purple buttons could go right up to the front rows, where generals mixed with corporate titans and international arms dealers mingled with movie stars.

The band had shifted to "God of Our Fathers" when the congressional delegation arrived, and this ignited another flurry of politicking. A number of people had dusted off old Nixon campaign buttons, which they displayed proudly as they milled among old friends. Nixon speech-writer Patrick J. Buchanan caught sight of an old friend and stepped lively to meet him, while nearby White House Chief of Staff Thomas F. "Mack"

McLarty chatted amiably with Colson. (They call McLarty "Mack the Nice." No one every called Colson "nice" when he served Nixon; Colson was the one who offered to run down his grandmother. But that was a long time ago.)

It is possible to pinpoint to the instant when the mood of a political rally evaporated. It was when Kissinger, almost invisible behind the bulky presidential lectern, quoted Shakespeare in speaking of Nixon: "He was a man, take him for all in all, I shall not look upon his like again."

And that great rumbling Kissinger voice— which once spoke of war and nations and nuclear strategy as if all these things were mere entertainments, mere exercise to tone his Atlas-like muscles—cracked into a sob.

The sky darkened just then. The sun gave up its hours-long struggle to penetrate the clouds. The day turned cold, and after the shock of hearing Kissinger cry, moments later Senate Minority Leader Robert J. Dole (R-Kan.) was crying too.

It was appropriate, perhaps, that the funeral of the first U.S. president from California should be held on a parking lot, across the street from a strip mall. The Nixon Library and Birthplace stands on the spot where Nixon's parents raised a mail-order house nearly a century ago.

This was the frontier then; now it is just another cookie-cutter suburb. Tough people settled this place—"Chinatown" tough. They diverted vast rivers, crushed powerful unions, and made this remote land of dry winds, hard ground, earthquakes, fires, droughts into the great postwar city. Richard Nixon was one of them, and he went farther than any of them: He remade the country through his unstinting use and abuse of power; some say he remolded the world.

But none of that kept him from the leveling end that awaits even the most vigorous and clever wielders of power. The cannon boomed; the rifles popped; the polished wooden coffin sank into the wet ground. Chilled, the mourners hastened across the green grass to a gathering where canapés were served by uniformed staff.

And though their smiles returned, the end of power lay before them, down the path, beneath the trees, under the ground.

Lessons Learned

BY DAVID VON DREHLE

The day of Richard Nixon's funeral was unseasonably cold. The sky was overcast and the air was damp. I don't know why a wet chill goes right to the bone, but it does. Sitting in the press tent, watching the minutes tick away toward deadline, I lost the feeling in my fingers.

But then, deadline always makes me shiver.

My seat was next to the team from *The New York Times.* Earlier in the day, I watched them arrive with the same sick feeling pitchers experienced watching the '61 Yankees take the field. Maureen Dowd, Johnny Apple, David Margolick—they were so deep in talent they had a Pulitzer Prize winner, William Safire, shagging quotes. So I was cold and I was scared.

At a time like that, you have to fall back on the basics: Sit down and tell a story.

What happened?

What did it look like, sound like, feel like? Who said what? Who did what?

And why does it matter?

What's the point? Why is this story being told? What does it say about life, about the world, about the times we live in?

Newspaper writing, especially on deadline, is so hectic and complicated—the fact-gathering, the phrase-finding, the inconvenience, the pressure—that it's easy to forget the basics of storytelling. Namely, what happened, and why does it matter?

I did this story the way I always work on deadline: I wandered and watched and listened and wrote down everything as I waited for the story to emerge. Until I figured out the what and the why, I had no way of knowing what details would prove important.

Then I saw Henry Kissinger, the cerebral Cold Warrior, and Bob Dole, the stoic veteran of World War II, each burst into genuine tears. And I heard Billy Graham speaking of the "democracy of death." It hit me that I was watching one of the oldest and most important stories there is: the leveling effect of death, and the fear, the awe, it inspires. Thomas Gray wrote his famous "Elegy in a Country Churchyard" on just this theme:

The boast of heraldry, the pomp of pow'r,

And all that beauty, all that wealth e'er gave,
Awaits alike th' inevitable hour,
The paths of glory lead but to the grave.

Once I realized what the story was, I targeted my reporting to find details that would drive it home. The signs of time in the faces of the mourners. The ineffable music floating over the babble. The landscape remade in Nixon's lifetime, by once-powerful, now-forgotten, men and women.

I learned long ago: Don't get fancy on deadline. Keep the structure simple; start at the beginning, march through the middle, end at the end. That's what I did here. There are no flashbacks, no digressions, no interwoven storyline. Just beginning, middle, end. Lead, chronology, kicker.

What else? Lots of short sentences. Active verbs. Clear metaphors. Pithy quotes. Vivid details.

That's about it.

And that's the lesson I learned: Fall back on the basics. They'll get you through—even when you feel like you're going to freeze.

New York Newsday
Team Deadline Reporting

In 1992, *New York Newsday* won the Pulitzer Prize for local reporting for coverage of a subway accident that killed five passengers. And when a firebomb exploded on a subway train a few days before Christmas, 1994, injuring dozens of passengers, the news staff again responded with the team approach that readers, competitors, and contest judges have come to expect since the paper was created as a separate edition a decade ago. This time, more than 30 reporters, columnists, and editors hit the streets and pounded phones, wresting order out of the day's chaos to produce a package ASNE judges called "comprehensive, detailed, colorful, and succinct." The stories, columns, and sidebars are remarkable for their breadth of reporting, concise and clear writing, storytelling sense, and perhaps most impressive, the organizational clarity that results when reporters and editors work as collaborators.

On July 16, 1995, the Times-Mirror Co. closed the paper citing unacceptable losses.

Conversations with 10 reporters and editors on the *New York Newsday* team appear following the stories they reported, wrote, or supervised.

Some of the *New York Newsday* reporters who won the 1995 Jesse Laventhol Prize for Deadline Reporting by a Team are pictured with some of the staff who also worked on the winning story. Front row: Gale Scott, Anthony M. DeStefano, Patricia Hurtado, Julio Laboy, Bob Liff, Joseph Queen, and Tom Collins. Second row: Jessie Mangaliman, assistant managing editor Richard Galant, Paul Moses, Susan Forrest, Joseph Gambardello, William K. Rashbaum, day city editor John Mancini, Juan Forero, night city editor Chapin Wright, and reporter Molly Gordy. Rear row: Wendell Jamieson, deputy metro editor Deirdre Murphy, David Kocieniewski, William Bunch, Kevin McCoy, deputy metro editor Steve Gunn, Alfred Lubrano, Russell Ben-Ali, and Otto Strong. Team writers not pictured are Maurice Carroll, Mitch Gelman, Nicholas Goldberg, Louis Hansen, Ellis Henican, Wendy Lin, Michael Moss, DeQuendre Neeley, Susan Price, Karen Rothmyer, and Dwight Worley.

Blast on No. 4 train causes holiday panic; 41 injured

DECEMBER 22, 1994

By Kevin McCoy, Mitch Gelman,
and Wendell Jamieson

A crude firebomb possibly carried by a New Jersey man turned a crowded subway car into a raging inferno at a lower Manhattan IRT station yesterday, injuring at least 41 people, including four critically.

A severely burned Scotch Plains resident identified by police investigators as Edward Leary, 49, was awaiting questioning by police detectives last night at the New York Hospital-Cornell Medical Center.

The 1:34 p.m. blast aboard the Brooklyn-bound No. 4 train at the Fulton Street stop shattered an otherwise calm pre-Christmas afternoon, sending scores of gasping passengers fleeing to the streets near the financial district, prompting a heroic rescue effort by an off-duty transit cop and disrupting afternoon subway service for thousands.

"There was a loud boom, and then absolute chaos," said passenger Bennett Fischthal of Brooklyn, describing the pandemonium as passengers managed to flee because the doors were open at the time of the blast.

"People were running and trampling over each other," Fischthal said. "It was very scary."

At a City Hall news conference, Mayor Rudolph Giuliani called for calm and said the disaster appeared to be an isolated though tragic event. He said the injuries could have been far worse if not for a "close to miraculous" response by city rescuers, including off-duty Transit Officer Denfield Otto.

Otto, a 25-year-veteran and one of an estimated 50 passengers in the fifth car, where the device exploded, said he heard several popping noises "like firecrackers," followed by a roar and searing flames.

"The inside of the car burst into fire. That's when the panic really began. When I looked over, I saw two men lying on the platform, totally on fire," Otto said.

As city police, fire and medical service personnel speeded to the scene through the narrow and crowded streets south of City Hall, Otto and other passengers tried to extinguish the flames that enveloped several fellow straphangers.

"We pulled up and it was like a swarm of people with burns. Their skin was blackened, there was blood, the burns were so deep they were bleeding from them," said city Emergency Medical Service technician Alina Badia, one of the first rescuers there.

"Their clothes were stuck to their bodies," added Badia. "Their gloves were sticking to their hands. One man, when we cut his gloves off, his skin came with it."

In all, 41 people were wounded by the blast or treated for injuries or shock suffered during rescue efforts or afterward. Four of the injured remained in critical condition at Manhattan hospitals last night.

Two law enforcement sources said a woman passenger questioned by detectives after the rescues said she saw a suspicious-looking male straphanger on the train before the blast. The woman told detectives the man carried a paper bag that she could see contained glass jars that smelled of chemicals or gasoline, the sources said. The woman moved elsewhere in the train moments before the explosion, the sources said.

City Police Commissioner William Bratton said transit police internal affairs officers found a seriously burned man about one mile from the explosion scene at the Clark Street IRT No. 2 station in Brooklyn shortly after the blast. EMS technicians transported him to the hospital.

Bratton pointedly declined to classify the man as a suspect, saying only that detectives were "anxiously awaiting" a chance to question him.

Other police investigators, however, identified the man as Leary, and confirmed that the New Jersey man was indeed under suspicion in the blast last night as doctors treated him at the hospital.

Leary's pants were shredded from the knees down and his face was burned when transit police found him, the investigators said, speaking on condition of anonymity. One quoted Leary as telling transit cops that he was injured at Wall Street, six blocks south of the explosion site.

"I was on my way to see my wife, who is a nurse," the sources quoted Leary as telling the police.

Investigators theorized that Leary may have fled on foot from the Fulton Street station, making his way through the long passageway that links the No. 4 Lexington Avenue line with platforms for the No. 2 trains. From there, investigators believe the injured man rode a No. 2 train two stops to the Clark Street station, the first stop in Brooklyn.

Police in New York and New Jersey said Leary was an unemployed computer operator with no known criminal record. He and his wife, Marguerite Shaller, lived in Brooklyn before moving to New Jersey about eight months ago, former neighbors said.

In Scotch Plains last night, city police waited outside Leary's home for the arrival of a search warrant that would authorize them to look inside for evidence.

Hours after the blast, investigators continued to search the charred subway car for evidence. Police found a coat near the scene of the fire that they believe Leary stripped off after fleeing the subway car. They said that witnesses identified the coat—apparently a dark, cloth coat—as the type the man on the train was wearing. In addition to having frayed pants, Leary's shoes were also melted, police said, apparently from the fire.

Bratton described the explosive device as a glass container about the size of a mayonnaise jar. It was crudely rigged with an external detonator, Bratton said, and contained an unidentified flammable liquid that sprayed fire upon explosion. One investigator said glass shards found at the explosion scene suggested the device may have been rigged to explode from the heat of a light bulb hooked to a battery.

Police officials said they were uncertain whether the device exploded accidentally or intentionally.

Recalling deadline with Kevin McCoy

I'd been working on a long project. I had gone out to get a bagel and Steve Gunn, one of the editors on the city desk said, "I need you." At that point, we already had reporters on the way downtown, and obviously the police shack reporters were working the story. The police headquarters is just north of where this firebombing happened.

Steve wanted me to start database searching so we could get background on people involved and to take feeds from reporters as they came in and write the main story.

We got the name from police about (suspect Edward) Leary fairly early on. We had a break in that one of our photographers had taken a picture of him in Brooklyn, which is where Leary turned up on a stretcher being taken away by EMS.

I started working with our library here, trying to figure out where he lived, trying to locate his wife. Once we got the name, we used a Department of Motor Vehicles database for New York. New Jersey isn't on line but we called up the New Jersey Department of Motor Vehicles, and sometimes they'll help us out by giving the information from their computers, and in this case, they did. So we were able to get an address for this guy.

The librarians here are just terrific. They're very well-trained and know all kinds of online sources out there, how to access them and the best way to do it, both in terms of time and in terms of cost-effectiveness. I worked with Christine Baird, one of the assistant librarians. As I got the information, I'd say to her, "Here's what the guy's name is, and here's what I would like. Can we run this? Can we run that?" to see where else he had lived. One database has postal forwardings in it, and that's very important; you find out other addresses that this person has lived at. And in the case of Leary, he had a couple of co-ops in Brooklyn that he was trying to sell. We would not have known that quite as quickly through other reporting routes, and by finding it out through this particular database, we were able to send reporters out there and find out a little bit about the properties themselves, and find people out there who knew a little bit about him. It gives you a head start on the story.

Deadline Tip:

No detail is unimportant. It may not make it into the story, but we need to get everything to make that evaluation. So try to cast the net as far and as wide as possible and get it all in.

Kevin McCoy is an investigative reporter for New York Newsday.

Disaster below jolts the city's spinal cord

DECEMBER 22, 1994

By Jimmy Breslin

Sirens pierced the Christmas music on the chilly streets of downtown Manhattan. Renee Harris, 39, standing on a traffic island on Broadway was talking quickly, because of the nerves.

"I was going to get on the Number Four."

"For where?"

"Two twenty-seven Schermerhorn. I work at the food stamps."

"Did you get on the train?"

"I got to the stairwell, going to the train, then boom! I lean up against the wall. Then this young Hispanic boy comes running up the stairs. He says, 'The train blew up. I saw a man missing his arm.' He was real upset. He kind of leaned on me. Then there was all this black smoke coming up the stairs. I walk off."

She stopped for breath. "I'm hyperventilating."

Whoever did it, whatever the reason, whether by accident or a deranged act, the subway firebombing yesterday put the smell of burned flesh into the Christmas air and gave us the scene of people in flames running through a subway car.

She had short dark hair and a round expressive face. She wore a button with the picture of a smiling young boy. "That's my Eric. My five-year-old son," she said proudly.

Then she said, "People were burning. The man ran out of the token booth and he covered them with foam."

Somebody asked her where she lived and she said "South Jamaica Houses."

"The Forty Houses" somebody said.

"That's right. I live there 15 years."

"Then you've been around explosions," somebody said.

Right away, she snapped, "Yes. When the cops ran and was shooting at people while we was sitting outside."

She looked around at the metal river of police cars and fire trucks. "Makes me nervous to think of it," she said.

And over in Brooklyn Heights, a man came out of the elevator at the Clark Street stop, trembling, with his face scarlet from fire, his pants legs shredded from flames.

Transit police officers stopped him.

White guy with an Irish name. Edward Leary. Age 49.

They asked him why he was here. He said that he had been burned in the subway explosion over in Manhattan. When they asked him why he had come to Brooklyn, he said it was because his wife was a nurse and she knew how to take care of him.

The transit officers decided that the burn unit at New York Hospital-Cornell was better for treatment and also for keeping Leary in sight.

When Leary was brought uptown, detectives began talking to him. One of their bosses said last night that Leary told them that he had been out looking for a job and that he had been carrying these résumés with him. Then one of the résumés fell and went right into this bag that was sitting there on the floor of the subway car. So, needing the résumé, he bent down and pulled the résumé out of the bag. The bag now exploded, he said. He raced away from the flames.

"Why did you go to Brooklyn?" he was asked again.

"So my wife could take care of me. She's a nurse. She knows what to do for me."

When Leary left the No. 4 train after the explosion yesterday, he had to run through a tunnel and onto another platform to the train to Brooklyn. Detectives felt this showed a greater concern with getting out of the area than it did caring for his burned legs.

Leary said he had been depressed and was on the drug Prozac. He said he owned a home in Scotch Plains, N.J., that was valued at $280,000.

He and his wife, Marge, and son lived for 15 years in one of two co-ops he owned at 10 Plaza St. in Park Slope in Brooklyn. It was 12A.

Last night, his former neighbors said that Leary was a quiet man. People don't remember what he did for a living. "Something with computers in the financial area," one thought. The wife worked in the medical field, although nobody knew her specific job.

Leary and his wife and son moved to Scotch Plains eight months ago. Both co-ops have been up for sale for eight months. Neighbors say each could sell for $120,000, but the market is poor.

A neighbor named Rob was a friend of Leary's wife and he accompanied her to the hospital yesterday. He called his house and left a message for his wife, who said that it was: "I'm here with Marge. She needs me to be here." When Rob returned last night to the co-op, he was accompanied by detectives.

Leary's present marriage sounded all right on tape when a call was put into the Scotch Plains number late yesterday. "Hello. You have reached the home of Edward, Marge and William. Please leave a message."

Now police were on the phone to get somebody to take a look at Leary's house in Scotch Plains, N.J.

And they still were all over the narrow streets of downtown Manhattan in the late afternoon because there is no crime or catastrophe bigger in this city than something that happens on our subways. For they are the iron spinal cord of the city.

Hate in a jar

DECEMBER 22, 1994

By William K. Rashbaum and Bob Liff

In layman's terms, it was like a glass mayonnaise jar filled with gasoline—a firebomb. But to police explosives experts, it was an improvised incendiary device that erupted yesterday sending flames and terror shooting through car No. 1391 of a No. 4 train in the Fulton Street station.

Speaking at a City Hall news conference, Police Commissioner William Bratton drew a distinction between yesterday's device and an improvised explosive device or bomb.

"The damage to the train as you would expect is from a flame—seared, charred, no blown out windows or twisted metal," Bratton said.

An explosive device releases a huge burst of energy creating a shock wave and concussion, while an incendiary device such as the one that injured 37 people yesterday releases heat and flames.

Bratton said the device was a glass jar filled with flammable liquid and investigators believe the liquid was gasoline.

The firebomb differed from the traditional Molotov cocktail in that it had what he called "an external igniter" to create a spark or detonate the fluid rather a rag or wick stuffed in the top, Bratton said.

A flash in a packed car, then flames and terror

DECEMBER 22, 1994

By William Bunch, Bob Liff,
and Joseph A. Gambardello

It was lunchtime, and the fifth car of the south-bound No. 4 express train was crowded—so crowded that Bennett Fischthal had to walk back and board the car right behind it when he transferred from the local train at 14th Street.

Fischthal, a 27-year-old Brooklyn Law School grad who had been studying for his bar exam, put on his Sony Walkman and was listening to Peter Gabriel's "Biko." His fellow passengers—an off-duty transit police officer among them—were a typical melting pot of New Yorkers.

At 1:34 p.m., their routine was shattered by a wall of flame.

It happened with the train in the Fulton Street station. The doors were apparently open—although one witness said they'd just closed. The off-duty transit cop, Denfield Otto, said he heard a small explosion, followed about 15 seconds later by a larger one.

No one came forward to say they saw the bomber—just the fiery aftermath.

"I saw two men laying in the ground ablaze," said Otto, 54, a 25-year veteran of the transit force. "There were passengers who were heroes, they were using their coats" to put out the flames. Meanwhile, Otto had grabbed a fire extinguisher.

In the car behind, Fischthal said he heard "just a huge noise, a loud noise, an explosion. It was followed by a ball of flame. It was coming towards my car. The people on my car panicked and all of them started running. And they ran to the exits, which had opened, luckily."

Then, he said, there was a second noise and another blast of orange flame. "We could feel the heat," he said. "People were definitely running over people, stomping on people."

Both witnesses and fire officials said the bomb sprayed its victims with intense, liquid fire. One woman, Fischthal said, "was in flames. Her hair was on fire, her jacket was on fire, her pants were on fire."

He and another man knocked her to the ground. "She was rolling over and over when eventually she was either unconscious or gave up. We finally got all the flames out. Her hair was completely burned. Her pants were gone."

Many passengers on the crowded train were confused. Althea Taite, a copy editing trainee for *Newsday,* was in the train's second car, headed home to Brooklyn from Christmas shopping, and didn't hear the blast.

"People were rushing to the front of the train, yelling, 'Get off,'" she said. "I was afraid of being trampled—I'm not that big of a person."

Renee Harris had just attended a training session run by the city Human Resources Administration and was entering the station at Broadway and Fulton when the device went off.

"I had just got to the entrance in the stairwell," she said. "I heard a big boom and the ground started moving. I had to grab the railing and a Puerto Rican kid came up the stairs crying, 'The train blew up. A guy's arm got blown off.' Then this black smoke came up and we had to run away."

Within minutes, police and emergency medical workers began to arrive on the smoky, chaotic scene. Witnesses said there was a lot of yelling. The inside of the subway car was charred, and smoky residue lingered on the platform.

"I couldn't see the train in front of me for all the smoke," said Thomas Monahan, a specialist with the city's Emergency Medical Service. He and another rescue worker started working on one of the most seriously injured men, who was on the ground unconscious.

The man came to and looked up at Monahan. He said: "There was an explosion, and then I woke up and you were here."

Above ground, the scene on lower Broadway's "Canyon of Heroes," where heroes from Charles Lindbergh to Nelson Mandela have been showered with ticker tape, was a nightmare of billowing smoke and screaming victims.

Harry Patel, owner of B and H Discount Deli on Dey Street, just off Broadway, was behind the counter when the commotion started.

"I saw people running out and they were screaming that there was a big explosion, and yelling, 'Don't go inside! Don't go inside!'" he said.

People started running into Patel's delicatessen, shaken by the blast. Some of them had soot on their hands and their coats. "An old lady came in here; she said she had to call 911," he said. "She said her heart was going too fast. I gave her a glass of water."

Many, such as Nerlande Estimphil, 25, of Brooklyn, saw scenes of pure horror. She said one girl emerged from the station with her back and hair burned, while another woman still aflame was rolled onto the sidewalk by passers-by trying to put out the fire.

She told the Associated Press one victim sat on the ground chanting, "Thank you, Jesus. Thank you, Jesus."

Recalling deadline with Joseph A. Gambardello

I work in the Brooklyn office. A call came in from police headquarters.We turned on the television, and (Bennett) Fischthal (a passenger on the train) was being quoted. So I looked him up in the phone book, spoke to him briefly, and said, "I'll come over." His apartment was in walking distance.

It was strange because the old 15 minutes of fame syndrome seemed to have grabbed Bennett Fischthal by the throat. He was acting as his own flack. He was waiting for CNN to put him on live. And he had called ABC and CBS and *Nightline,* and he was on top of the world in the midst of this tragedy. It's almost as if you can get on television, your existence is somehow validated.

My goal was to basically find out everything he had seen, something to point you in the direction of what actually happened. He didn't help much in that regard, because he was in another car. He hadn't been injured. He did show me what looked like a little burn mark on his raincoat. But he was able to provide a lot of detail of the chaos that was going on down there.

I wanted to find out what he was doing when all of this happened. I was just trying to get that one detail to show this one person at this one time. He could have been reading the paper. He could have been reading the ads on the subway. You just ask. "What were you doing?" "I was listening to the Walkman." "What were you listening to?" "Peter Gabriel." "What song?" "Biko." It's the sort of compelling detail that people hold onto, especially when you're making such a jump between the day-to-day routine of a subway ride home to a disaster.

I was at his place for 45 minutes, using a tape recorder and taking notes. I never trust the recorder.

I came back to the office and wrote it up in about 15 minutes and I sent it up to the main office. One of the great things about a breaking story is that the series of events are so compelling that you don't have time to ponder it; they tend to write themselves. If the story is so compelling that an editor sends out small armies, it had better. But it's not going to write itself unless the reporters come up with the details that make the story.

I love breaking news. I did 10 years at UPI. It's the most thrilling aspect of this business. On a day-to-day basis, you tend to forget that you're all part of a team that is putting out a product. And there's nothing like a story like this, where people from diverse beats and backgrounds are thrown into the mix, because that's what news is. That's when it becomes the most demanding, when it's happening right in front of you.

Deadline Tip:

Try to find the detail that is that punctuation between normalcy and abnormalcy, from the routine to the disaster, the thing that shows people are just leading their day-to-day lives when something like this explodes all around.

Joseph A. Gambardello is a special writer in the Brooklyn office of New York Newsday.

Recalling deadline with Juan Forero

I was at lunch with my sister, one of the rare times that I go out. I usually eat at my desk. I got paged, and I rushed down to the subway station. I managed to get there fairly quickly. Just by the urgency and how we were all rushing around, I knew that it was a huge story. I had to get down there and get comments, quotes, color, judge for myself what had happened. Check my theories with officials, check with as many people as possible. Interview witnesses. It was pretty clear cut. Whenever a big story like this occurs, it's always a team effort.

The entrance to the subway station is right on the corner. Shopkeepers, people who have newsstands got involved, helping these people who had come out of the station, some of them on fire. So I went around and canvassed all these places. There were hundreds of reporters down there. Everyone is trying to get something that somebody else doesn't have.

Deadline Tip:

In a mob scene like the subway bombing story, try to recreate what happened. Get a timetable: what time the incident occurred, what time the authorities arrived. Get color. It's just hustle. It's getting there as fast as you can, and talking to as many people as you can.

Juan Forero is a general assignment reporter for New York Newsday.

Recalling deadline with
William Bunch

It was a slow afternoon. Word came over the scanner there had been some sort of explosion in the subway. When something like that happens, basically, the world stops. They asked me to do the "tick-tock," or the reconstruction of how this unfolded. ("A Flash in a Packed Car, Then Flames and Terror") That's one of the things that we specialize in. Obviously, you have a main story that presents the facts in traditional inverted pyramid style. You want to answer the basic questions. Did they catch who did it? How many people were injured? Was anybody killed? But in a story like this, you want a sense of the narrative. Not just the facts, but the drama.

I spent the afternoon on the phone trying to get the best anecdotes, a sense of what was it actually like for somebody on that subway car. What were people doing in the routine seconds before it happened? What was the explosion like? How did people react afterwards? The people in the field did such a good job of getting people right away, I had all the quotes laid out by 5 o'clock. It was just a question of trying to string them together as a story

I did it pretty quickly. I have two very small children. Most nights, getting home is the most important thing to me. In this case, because it was such a big story, getting home to see the kids wasn't the prime issue. But I think the skills that force me to do that on most nights helped.

Deadline Tip:

Try to develop characters. Go into detail on a few people rather than single quotes from a lot. I can't say we went into incredible depth, but it's nice to be able to say this guy's a law student, he was listening to his Walkman. He's a character now. And don't forget, this is a tick-tock. The element that sets the story apart is time. In a story like this, the clock is the driving force.

William Bunch covers the environment and city planning for New York Newsday.

Charred walls mark the eye of the storm

DECEMBER 22, 1994

By Wendell Jamieson

The light fixtures had melted. The paper ads were charred and dangling. Black soot covered the walls in the back corner of the car.

But no windows were broken, no part of the car was twisted or mangled.

Whatever ignited in the back of a southbound No. 4 train burned, but did not explode.

Just moments after the firebomb went off at 1:34 p.m. yesterday, heavy gray smoke poured from the entrances to the Broadway-Nassau subway stop on Broadway at Fulton and Dey Streets.

Down on the platform, next to the blackened car with its doors open, the three most seriously injured passengers lay on stretchers.

The car itself was eerily silent just 15 minutes after the fire. Passengers' packages and several briefcases stood exactly where they were left next to benches in the car. Pieces of clothing were scattered throughout the car. Black soot covered the floor, but most of the damage appeared to be on the walls and the ceiling.

Recalling deadline with
Wendell Jamieson

I was at police headquarters. The scanner started going crazy, talking about an explosion on a train, and I talked to my editors up town, and we determined that it was in a subway stop about six blocks from my office, close to the World Trade Center, which had exploded about two years before that. I'd also covered that story.

I tried to make a couple of quick calls to the fire department and the police, and Debbie [Henley, city editor] called me back about 30 seconds later and asked me if I'd heard anything. By that point, I still hadn't been able to nail anything down, and she and I agreed that I should get over there as quickly as possible. I grabbed my cell phone and my press card, and I ran over there. I had this incredible sense of *deja vu*; there was an unbelievable convergence of emergency vehicles, and sirens, it was just very reminiscent of the day when the bomb went off at the World Trade Center. And I ran over to the subway station before they had cordoned it off, or before anyone knew what was going on, and I ran down the steps and on to the platform, and into the train where the bomb had gone off. And I saw everything that was happening down there.

The chaos really helped me. I had my scarf over my face, because there was smoke. I was trying not to be too conspicuous with my notebook. I didn't ask anyone any questions. I just tried to see all that I could. As soon as I started asking questions, I knew I'd get thrown out. I eventually did get thrown out of the subway station.

I showed them my police headquarters press pass, which has a little police department badge on it. But it didn't work. One cop told me to leave, but then he turned around and went back to what he was doing. I walked about 20 feet, and then I doubled back. Then he saw me again, and he got really pissed off. He threw me out, and that was it.

From the subway stairs, I called Debbie on the cell phone, and one guy was on his radio saying, "It was a device. It was a device." And I was able to tell Debbie, "Looks like it was a bomb." That gave us the extra added jump, I think, that this was a big story. And then I stuck around for the rest of the day, for eight or nine hours, on the street, talking to survivors, talking to cops, and then they told me, "Get back. You have to do a first person account" ("Charred Walls Mark the Eye of the Storm").

I thought about it as I came back to the office, and I had to write it as fast as I could in about 10-15 minutes.

Deadline Tip:

Writing on deadline allows you to focus completely. You don't have the luxury of sitting around and worrying to death about every single word. You just write as fast as you can. You have no choice.

Wendell Jamieson is a police reporter for New York Newsday.

Blast shatters holiday cheer

DECEMBER 22, 1994

By DeQuendre Neeley and Susan Price

Alma Foster was just returning from a frustrating day of Christmas shopping, searching for Power Rangers for her 3-year-old foster child.

As she sat reading her Bible aboard the Brooklyn-bound No. 4 train, a bag exploded and sent her and the 50 or so passengers on that car hurtling toward the exits.

"People started screaming and hollering and running," said Foster. "I didn't think I was going to make it."

John Parks, 35, an off-duty special police officer who was also Christmas shopping, stood on the platform.

"It sounded like two gunshots when the door opened. One went off then another went off." Parks, who was in stable condition at New York Downtown Hospital last night, responded in writing to questions from reporters.

The explosion knocked Parks into a stanchion on the platform. When he got up, he and 10 others tried to extinguish the fire. "It was real but it looked unreal...There were people on fire.

"All I could see was a man's face burning."

"Practically everyone in that train was blazing," Foster said. "The two women next me were nothing but fire."

Foster, 65, of Brooklyn, was knocked down in the rush to escape and the back of her coat caught fire. She had second-degree burns on her right ankle and both ankles were bruised, said Richard Westphal, associate director of emergency medicine at St. Vincent's Hospital and Medical Center.

"I was shaken, and I prayed and prayed," said Foster, who added that she left everything, including her Bible, on the train. "It was the scariest thing I've ever seen."

Two other victims who were kept overnight at St. Vincent's Hospital were Joseph Schendelman, 51, from New Jersey, and Marie Lexidor, 44, hometown unknown. Schendelman suffered third-degree burns over 20 percent of his body. He was listed in stable condition. Lexidor suffered from smoke inhalation and a possible seizure after being trampled in the stampede.

Louis Hansen contributed to this story.

Easy-going Jersey man's life seemed to unravel

DECEMBER 22, 1994

By Wendy Lin, Julio Laboy, and Susan Forrest

To hear some neighbors talk, one would assume Edward J. Leary is an average Joe.

Leary, the former president of his Brooklyn co-op board and a suburbanite who decorated his Scotch Plains, N.J., home with Christmas lights earlier this month, seemed a man able to fit in and get along.

But there apparently was a darker side to the 49-year-old man being questioned in connection with yesterday's firebombing.

A computer expert, he had recently lost his job and—according to city hospital sources—was suffering from depression and taking medication for it, including the controversial antidepressant Prozac.

And about two months ago in Scotch Plains, according to several neighbors, there was a fire at the home of a neighbor, and the home owner blamed Leary for it, though he was never charged. Five years ago, a suspicious fire blew out a door of an apartment in the Park Slope, Brooklyn, building where Leary and his wife owned two apartments, according to neighbors there. Leary was not charged in connection with that incident.

Leary, his wife, Marguerite Shaller, and their young son William moved to the affluent New Jersey suburb, living in a $280,000 two-story home on a ¾-acre lot they bought in June of 1993, according to real estate records. But it is not clear exactly when they left Brooklyn for New Jersey—some say two years, some say eight months ago.

Shaller, who is known as Marge, is a primary care nurse at the Plainfield Health Center in nearby Plainfield. According to center spokeswoman Althea Johnson, Shaller has worked there for a year.

But as Shaller was visiting a patient yesterday, she received a call from New York Hospital-Cornell Medical Center and was told her husband had second- and third-degree burns, but not that he was a possible suspect.

"She was hysterical when she got the call," Johnson said. "She's an extremely nice person. All the patients like her." Johnson said Shaller was still getting over the death of her father at Christmas last year.

In the couple's upper middle-class neighborhood, where their yellow colonial house was festooned with Christmas lights and an American flag, neighbors were startled last night at the notion that Leary could have instigated the subway explosion.

"They say he's not a suspect and I want to give him the benefit of the doubt," said his neighbor Barbara Doyle. "I saw them decorating the tree two weeks ago and they seemed like an average family."

But other neighbors said the family had had a run of bad luck, beginning with the death of Shaller's father. Leary had apparently lost his job, although neighbors interviewed were not sure exactly where he had worked.

"I know he's unemployed because we've seen him a lot at home in the past couple of months," said one woman who declined to be named. "He's always outside, always coming in and out."

Joseph Doyle said that although he didn't know Leary well, he knew that Leary took the train from the Summit station each morning. "I spoke to him in the driveway yesterday or the day before yesterday," Doyle said. "He's an everyday neighbor. My reaction is one of total surprise."

Leary and Shaller still own two apartments in the Brooklyn building—a one-bedroom apartment on the eighth floor and a two-bedroom apartment on the 12th floor—according to neighbors.

"I don't know that he had a grudge against anything or anybody," said his next-door neighbor, Victor Banescu. "I find it very unlikely. He's not that type to get involved in something like that."

Another neighbor who refused to be named, described Shaller as a "country person," who is "open, healthy, with basic values." Leary, she said, was more quiet.

Recalling deadline with Susan Forrest

They sent me to Scotch Plains, New Jersey, to cover
the neighborhood where Leary (the suspect) lived.
Within two hours (of the firebombing), I was with
a photographer in nightmare traffic, hyperventilating. He screamed at me at one point, "What do you
want me to do? Fly over these cars?" I wanted him
to drive on the grass—'cause I do that. I'm already
planning to go from neighbor to neighbor. I knew it
was going to be a media circus. An editor once told
me, "There are two kinds of reporters. Reporters
who come back with the story, and reporters who
come back with the excuse." My only thought was,
"I got to file something about Ed Leary."

I separated from the photographer, because he
was shooting scenes of the FBI and the police preparing to enter Leary's home with warrants, and
there were neighbors everywhere. When you have
a media circus situation one reporter runs right, all
the other reporters chase that reporter. If everybody
goes right, I like to go left. I literally walked four
blocks on all sides, even knocking on people's
doors after the sun had gone down. But that was
good, too, because I was freezing, and I didn't have
a coat on, and every house I went to, they gave me
coffee. A lot of them initially shut me out, and in
two of the cases, they said, "No comment, no comment," because they were scared. They had this alleged lunatic living in their neighborhood, and they
didn't know anything.

On two occasions when they shut the door on
me, I stood outside the door and I begged. A lot of
times it works for me. It's not an act, it's just the
way I am. I don't lie. I don't make things up. I
begged, "Please, open the door. Please. Please." I
said, "Listen to me. I am freezing out here. I left
my coat in Manhattan because they sent me up
here. I was in traffic. If nothing else, do you have
two Advil?"

This guy came out with two Advil. And then ultimately, the sympathy factor works, and I got so much good information about the guy, stuff that no one else had. Every neighbor I spoke to let me use their phone and I filed from their homes what they said to me, using *Newsday*'s credit card.

You build up a quick relationship. I joke with them. Try to make them feel as comfortable as possible. You never ask their name right away. But you never ask it at the end either. I always shove it in about the second question, as sort of an afterthought. They're really into answering you, and you throw it in. "What's your name again?" and if they say "Smith," I'll say, "Spell that." And when they're in the middle of the interview, usually they just spell it. Then they forget they gave it to you. Then they never say, "Don't use my name."

My editors would rather have names, but if they say "I'm scared. Don't use my name." I say, "Absolutely, your name's out." And I've always abided by it. You never, ever hurt a scared neighbor. You never lie to anybody. And you use the unattributed quote, and if it's controversial, usually it won't get in. But if you've talked to eight, 10 neighbors, they've painted a picture for you. You don't need all 10. You can say "Neighbors say."

Deadline Tip:

Get there and look at it like a set of dominoes. Start with the next door neighbors, and go to as many people as quickly as you can. If they're not letting you in, try everything in your power to change their mind. Use everything from, "We want your side of the story" to "Please help me out."

Susan Forrest is a police reporter for New York Newsday.

Heroes: They just show up

DECEMBER 22, 1994

By Ellis Henican

Showing up.

It's the first rule for being a hero. You have to show up. And yesterday, as a tornado of liquid fire went ripping through car 1391, Transit Police Officer Denfield Otto didn't have far to go.

He was right there, in the car.

"The inside of the car burst into fire," Otto said, after he had finished saving people and gone upstairs for a breath of fresh air. "That's when the panic really began.

"When I looked over, I saw two men lying on the platform, totally on fire. Another passenger, a girl, had flames coming out of her hair. Two men were throwing their coats over her head to put the fire out."

Otto was supposed to be on vacation yesterday. Instead, he had walked to the subway near his home in Harlem for a ride to downtown Brooklyn. He was on his way to practice for the annual Christmas concert with the Transit Police Department Choir. Otto's been a cop in the subway for 20 years now, a baritone for longer than that.

When the bomb went off yesterday, his pitch was perfect.

"The first explosion wasn't that loud," he said. "It was more like a firecracker. Honestly, the first thing that went through my mind was 'gunshot.'"

Otto leaped out of his seat. Instinctively, he surveyed the car with his eyes. He looked inside, then outside the train.

Then, a second blast went off. "That's the one that caused all the fire," he said. "That's when the real panic began. The train was in the station. The doors had already opened up. You had people getting off the train, other people getting on. Then, like crazy, everybody was trying to get out of there."

Otto ran straight for the token booth, where he knew a fire extinguisher would be waiting. He banged on the door. He grabbed the extinguisher. He raced back to the train. And he foamed the fire out.

Then, he started on the victims. One by one, he began helping people off the train. Skin was scorched. Hair was singed. Clothing was drenched by the burning liquid from the home-made bomb, then left in tatters.

"There were at least 100 people in the car, lots and lots of people burned," he said. As Otto pressed ahead, two uniformed transit cops spun into action, as well. They too, followed the first rule of heroism. They were promptly on the scene.

James Rudolph and Joseph Stabach were as-signed to the Fulton Street station yesterday. They were working regular patrol.

"We were standing on the A-platform," Ru-dolph said. "We were just going back to the dis-trict's headquarters on Canal Street.

"We heard this pop," he went on. "We stood there and listened for a second. Then the radio started to crackle: '85, 85.' That's an officer needs assistance. 'Fulton Street on the 4.'"

The two started running toward the No. 4's platform.

Up a stairway. Down a corridor. "The first thing we hit was a big wall of smoke and all these panicked people running off the train."

"The people were burned all over," said Stabach, his partner. "They were down on the platform, inside the car, everywhere."

"There was one guy," Rudolph recalled. "He was down on the platform, crying. His pants were totally burned off his legs. His skin was pretty bad, too. He was sitting there in his underwear, with this horrible look on his face."

Other people were stretched out on the seats and on the floor of the car.

"There was a horrible chemical smell in there," Rudolph said—Otto's fire-extinguisher foam. "It overpowered everything else. You didn't really smell any powder. You didn't really smell the flesh. It was just all these bodies, and that stinking foam."

But the smell was nothing, compared to the sights and the sounds.

"The whole place was chaos," Stabach said. "A lot of smoke. A lot of screaming. A lot of people in pain. All you could do was get the people out of there."

Yesterday, as they went about the business of doing just that, Otto, Rudolph and Stabach did their work like pros.

They lifted the people. They calmed the cries. They did what they were trained to do.

There was a bad explosion in the subway. They started the way heroes always start.

By showing up.

Recalling deadline with Ellis Henican

I was actually going to take the day off. My little brother was in town from New Orleans. We had gone and done tourist stuff in the morning, and had just finished lunch on West Broadway down in SoHo, and my beeper went off. It was one of the editors saying, "Do you know about this subway thing?"

One of the lessons I've learned is that the subway in New York is usually the quickest way to get somewhere, except when something bad happens in the subway. And that is the time to get into a taxicab. The traffic was bad, but we got there within a couple of minutes. I wasn't the first person on the scene, but I was among the first.

It was one of these overwhelming New York disaster scenes. Huge numbers of cops and firefighters and EMS workers. They were bringing injured people out. The initial fear was that there were more bombs on the train.

As a columnist, I'm not trying to get the basic facts of what happened. *Newsday,* in these kinds of stories, throws a lot of resources at it. We outswarm 'em. My job is to find something that's different from the straight news story that has a lot of human drama in it, and grip onto that.

The paper has a longstanding and very deep commitment to covering the subway. We have for the past 10 years had a three-day-a-week column called "In the Subways," an opinionated, personal report about life in the subways and I was actually the third person to write that column. My two predecessors, Jim Dwyer and Dennis Duggan, also were involved in the coverage.

When you spend a huge amount of time in the subway, you do get to know people who, when something really horrendous happens, remember you. So when the subway explodes, this paper is uniquely positioned to deal with it. It's been a smart investment by this newspaper.

A cop I know came over to me and said, "Come here." By this point, they had already set up police barricades and crime scene lines. He took me behind the lines where Denfield Otto was standing by himself and said, "Do you see that guy over there? He's somebody you ought to talk to." I'd never met Otto before. We were the first people to get to him, or at least to get to him in any detail.

It was a basic cop interview. You know, "Hello, officer. What happened?" I got interrupted two or three times by other investigators who wanted to talk to him. But he was a real gentleman. He kept coming back until he had told his story.

Otto turned out to be this kind of New York folk hero. He was scared, too. And I thought he was just very real. Off-duty transit cop, older black guy. Once you hear, "I was on my way to choir practice," you know you got something here.

We go around trying to find little human details that make people feel like they're there. So you got all these facts. Then you've got to impose some theme on it. The first thing you try to do is figure out what you're trying to say. A story like this, it is especially important to give the reader something beyond what they're going to get in the news stories. What takes time is making it look easy. Making it look very conversational, and very natural, and very real. You want it to look like you did it in 15 minutes. But of course—I can't do it in 15 minutes.

Sometimes it's totally clear what you're going to do. And I know immediately, and I can start with the lead and write to the end.

But frequently I figure out what I'm going to say as part of the writing process. I sit down with the notebook, and in the process of going through the notebook, and going through my memory, I figure out what I had.

I'll do the people first. I'll do the quotes. I often write the lead late. I don't know what the lead is until I figure out what I'm saying. If you don't suck 'em in with the lead, there is no ending.

I wrote the strongest paragraphs of description that I had in my mind and in my notebook. And it became clear that's what the story was here. It was ordinary people showing up at this extraordinary event and performing heroically.

I do spend a lot of time with the writing. I mean, I care about it, and I enjoy it, And so I'm just writing and rewriting and rereading and just pushing it until there's an absolute gun at my head, and then turning it over to the guy who edits me here.

I think the truth is that these things are works in progress until they're done. We really are figuring out how the house looks while we're laying the floors, and putting in the doors, and carving out the windows.

Deadline Tip:

The only lesson that I have is do the same thing that heroes in the fire did. Go there. Show up. It all works better in person than over the phone. The columnists who get burned out and bored are the ones who never go out. And the ones who stay good over the decades are the ones who go out every day.

Ellis Henican is a columnist for New York Newsday.

Bloody drama hits hospitals

DECEMBER 22, 1994

By Mitch Gelman, Gale Scott,
and Jessie Mangaliman

The worst of the wounded were sent to the burn center at New York Hospital-Cornell Medical Center, beginning to arrive shortly after the fireball exploded on the southbound No. 4 train.

It was around 2 p.m. when Dr. Roger Yurt, head of the unit, saw the gurneys come out of the ambulances outside. Paramedics carried the victims—hair singed, faces blackened and winter coats melted to their skin. The victims, ages 16 to 60, went first to the emergency room and then to the hospital's burn center.

"The most dramatic part of the day was seeing so many severely injured patients all at once," Yurt said during a break yesterday afternoon.

One woman, whose face was burned, said she was in a lot of pain and she didn't know what happened. "I'm scared," she told the doctor, who observed that burns covered 20 percent of her body. "What is going to happen to me? Am I going to be all right?"

As with all yesterday's burn patients, Yurt said the doctors checked the woman's lungs to see if she had suffered any inhalation injuries. She appeared to be all right. But two of the 13 patients who came to the hospital from the explosion did have injuries to their lungs. They went right on respirators, Yurt said. Nine others also critically burned were being monitored to make sure that their throats didn't swell and block their air.

The 13 patients who went to the burn center were among 39 patients brought to four area hospitals yesterday afternoon, including New York Downtown Hospital, St. Vincent's Hospital and Medical Center and Bellevue Hospital Center, according to Emergency Medical Service officials.

At the burn center, seven burn specialists were aided by five doctors from the trauma unit, who helped clean patients' wounds.

No one had died from the explosion as of last night, Emergency Medical Service officials said.

Victims brought to the burn center included Brenda Dowdell, a 40-year-old mother from Manhattan, who sustained second-degree burns to 35 percent of her body.

"Just before the explosion, I saw a man bending over and smelled gasoline," Dowdell told paramedics on the way to the hospital. "And then I heard a Pop! Pop! Pop! and saw the fire."

The victims also included a 16-year-old Midwood High School student, Charlene Wiggins, who was on her way home from a dentist's appointment. Her mother, Monica Wiggins, got a call at home that her daughter was in the subway fire, and she rushed to the hospital.

"I was hysterical," said Monica Wiggins, a day-care worker who was wandering the streets outside the hospital, waiting for word on her daughter's condition. "It was a relief to find out she was alive, but I am so worried."

One of the patients, a man from Brooklyn later identified as Edward Leary, 49, was followed by transit and city police detectives and federal agents, who are questioning him in connection with the explosion. While detectives spoke with him, doctors worked to salve the burns on his legs and face.

New York City Emergency Medical Service workers Raymond Healy and Alina Badia were the first unit on the scene, arriving at 1:41 p.m.

It was extremely smoky, and the nature of the station, with ramps that go up and down and crisscross, made it difficult to evacuate patients, but the operation went smoothly, officials said. They were met by a stream of burned, bleeding, hysterical subway riders.

"We pulled up and it was like a swarm of people with burns. Their skin was blackened, there was blood, the burns were so deep they were bleeding from them," Badia said.

"Their clothes were stuck to their bodies. Their gloves were sticking to their hands. One man, when we cut his gloves off, his skin came with it."

Healy said he poured sterile water on patients' hands and faces on the way to New York Hospital-Cornell Medical Center's burn center. "They all wanted cooling down," he said.

EMS spokesman David Bookstaver said both emergency medical technicians were debriefed for their "critical stress" afterward. Badia was particularly shaken, he said, because she was among the first emergency workers to arrive at the scene of the World Trade Center explosion last year. "She thought it was happening again," he said.

"The burn team and emergency department were incredible, magnificent," said Dr. John Daley, chief of surgery at New York Hospital-Cornell Medical Center. The hospital's emergency teams were just finishing up a major crisis, he said, in which an amputation team had been dispatched to treat a man whose arm was caught in elevator machinery.

The burn patients had singed hair—even their nasal hairs—burned clothing and facial burns, Dr. Alexander Kuehl, director of the hospital's emergency department, said. For a while, Kuehl considered closing the emergency room to deal with the burn victims, but they were able to absorb them without shutting down. Some of the patients were unconscious. Others were given massive amounts of fluid intravenously to replace the fluids they lose because their skin is gone.

Past tragedies echoed in rush of ER patients

DECEMBER 22, 1994

By Dennis Duggan

Memories of the World Trade Center bombing swept through the already crowded emergency room at St. Vincent's Hospital yesterday when the subway explosion call came in.

"I was thinking terrorist," admitted Dr. Richard Westfal, "because the first reports we had were similar to the ones we got when the 1993 bomb exploded at the World Trade Center. We heard about an explosion, fire, possible fatalities, and another bomb that didn't go off."

But there wasn't time to dwell on the underlying New York fear—that terrorists now have the city in their sights. Room had to be made for the people who were injured in the subway explosion.

"Every stretcher was filled, so we called upstairs and asked them to make space for at least a dozen of the patients in ER. And in less than 20 minutes, those who could be safely moved were," said Dr. Westfal, 47, who was born and raised in Queens.

Dr. Westfal and his staff then braced for the worst as the injured began to arrive in the emergency-room bay at Seventh Avenue and 11th Street.

By the end of the day, the hospital had admitted 13 people into the emergency room, including a transit cop and three city cops, all suffering from smoke inhalation.

But the rumors kept coming in with the patients and the ambulance drivers. "We didn't know how many more people we'd have to care for," said Dr. Westfal. "Would it be 30 or 40, or would it be just like the Trade Center, when we had 207 people here?"

Of those 13, only one was sent upstairs to the surgical intensive-care unit. That was a man who needed further treatment of second- and third-degree burns over 10 to 15 percent of his body. Third-degree burns are the worst, and are so named because the burn goes through three layers of skin and tissue.

"I think he's going to be OK," Dr. Westfal said late yesterday of the man in intensive care. "Right now I am going to go out and tell eight of the patients they can go home. And that will be a great relief for them and for their relatives."

The others were still being closely monitored by machines for the level of oxygen in their bloodstream and for minor injuries they suffered—either when the train was jolted or during the rush to escape the subway cars.

It was an awful story in a city where even the awful is almost commonplace. "You can't go anywhere and expect to be safe," said Betty Bangs, who has been a crossing guard at the ER's intersection for the last 10 years. "Have a nice Christmas," she told me.

Tragedy has been a regular visitor to this emergency room, where yesterday sirens wailed and police put flares and orange traffic cones in front of the hospital to make room for incoming ambulances.

"The worst was the World Trade Center," said Dr. Westfal, surveying the chaotic street scene. "But a few years ago, a woman crashed into a bunch of NYU students in Washington Square Park, and we had a dozen people here with critical injuries.

"And it was in 1991 that a subway crashed into a barrier in Union Square. I will never forget that night and the early-morning scene there as the St. Vincent's emergency room was transformed into something resembling a M*A*S*H unit."

Burn victims face mental scars too

DECEMBER 22, 1994

By Alfred Lubrano

The victims of the subway fire-bombing may be facing agonies most people could not comprehend, burn experts say.

The physical and psychic wounding is so intense, many burn victims often ask their doctors, "Why did you save me?"

Treatment is never anything but painful, said Dr. Roger Simpson, chief of Nassau County Burn Center.

"An incendiary device often spews hot liquid, igniting clothing," Simpson said. The victim could also face lung-related injury if he or she breathed noxious fumes from other burning materials.

In the worst possible case—a third-degree burn—the skin is destroyed down to fat and muscle.

Simpson said doctors typically will coat the burn with silvadene, which penetrates the dead, burned skin and controls the growth of bacteria.

The skin is scrubbed to be cleaned and wrapped in bandages. The pain, said Simpson, "is horrible." Often, morphine is used.

Sometimes, patients are placed in Clinatron beds, which have mattresses made of silicone beads pumped full of air, Simpson said, adding that such beds remove pressure on burned areas.

Some hospitals place patients in hyperbaric chambers, which drive additional oxygen into the skin.

Doctors continually pump in fluids. "After a burn, the patient's engine is churning at a high rate to maintain the body," and must be replenished, Simpson said.

Within three days, doctors usually will begin grafting non-burned skin onto burned areas.

Typically, a patient who suffered third-degree burns over half his or her body will be in the hospital for six to eight weeks. It can take two to three years of plastic surgery for a patient's face to be reconstructed.

And then there are the psychological scars. Harry Gaynor, founder of the National Burn Victims Foundation, said burn victims experience a sense of hopelessness. "They feel like freaks in a beauty-oriented society," Gaynor said from his Orange, N.J., home.

"Spouses can't stand the sight of burned spouses and leave," said Gaynor. Divorce and alcoholism are common. "The scars last a lifetime," he added.

Recalling deadline with Alfred Lubrano

I had been out on another story. So when I came back at about 4 o'clock I was really behind the curve. They asked if I could help out by doing this sidebar. One of the editors, Dee Murphy, said, "See if you can find out about what burn victims have to face."

The first thing I did was check the clips for mentions of burns units. The problem was all the experts were involved in the emergency. It was impossible to talk to any burn doctor in New York City. Fortunately, Nassau County had the head of the burn unit around that day, but he couldn't answer the phone at that moment. They beeped him for me. Time is running out. I had to give them something by 6-6:30 So I spent the time waiting for him learning about burns. I just called the places that have earlier time zones.

One of the things that I tell myself when I'm doing stuff like this is it's like a football player. You won't go down if you keep your legs moving. So that's what I did. Because sometimes there's a tendency to just sit back and wait for the phone call. But I didn't want to do that, because you never know if it's ever going to come. As long as I'm on the phone, then I still have a chance.

I do a wide variety of stories. I try to write down every number that I come across. I had some numbers for some doctors out in California. And these doctors were able to tell me who's got the better burn units. I called some Army bases, because I was just trying to figure out what kind of folks get burned with any kind of regularity. I wound up calling the Brooke Army Medical Center. I was asking some pretty elemental questions: I had even forgotten which is worse, third-degree or first-degree. I wanted to know about the medication, the treatments, all the tools they use.

At that point, I'm asking for the public affairs folks. This was easier than trying to fight your way through the bureaucracy. Reporters are always bitching about flacks and public relations people, but, you know, we do need them. And this is one of the cases, because you got to get a doctor who's probably off-duty, or going off-duty, somewhere in a hospital 70 miles away, or however far it is. And you need him 10 minutes ago.

I probably made 15 to 20 calls. I interviewed eight or nine people. You just keep trying different things. If A doesn't work, try B. If B doesn't work, try C. As long as you keep doing that, then you're not going to get stuck, because you're still waiting for the phone call from the doctor. And in my head, he's going to be my salvation. He's going to be the one to answer all my questions. I finally got Dr. Simpson from the Nassau Burn Unit and he put everything into place. When he said, "The scars last a lifetime," I knew that was the kicker.

Always in the writing, I wanted to keep in mind that this is happening to a human. I was struck with the unfairness of what had happened to them. Every one of us who lives in New York has ridden on the subway, and so this random act could have easily hurt any one of us. So when he said, "The scars last a lifetime," it did two things for me. It summed up the horror that happened to them, but it also predicted a lifetime of misery. It would sum up my story, but it would also springboard me into the future.

A lot of what we have to do in newspapers is difficult. It's like playing baseball in an elevator. You have to tell the whole story, but you've got to do it in such a small, cramped space. So when somebody gives you a quote like that, it's a real gem, because it can help convey a lot of the things that you want to talk about. It can help give you those elements of storytelling just in those small words.

You are writing when you are reporting, because in your head, you're organizing: "Oh, this will go here and this will go there," and "This is important to keep up top." And also, you will ask questions with your story in mind, with your structure in mind, to elicit the kinds of answers that will help you realize that structure.

I think I wrote it in about a half-hour before I had to hand it in. I jotted down very quickly on a sheet of paper the name of the source and some of the important quotes. That's as close as I get to an outline. There's no revision in this. There was no time. I wrote it on the screen, and then I read it once before I sent it, just to make sure that I spelled the words right. I just have a horror of misspelling someone's name. I printed it out before I sent it. So while they were reading it, I was reading it too. That's a good way to check yourself. "Wait a minute. I didn't mean 36. I meant six."

I think the front line reporters are doing the tough job, because they're out there trying to figure out what happened. But at the same time, there are press conferences and police, fire people, victims, and you can talk to them, and get their reaction. When you're trying to do a sidebar like this, you're inventing it as you go along. And so you're making your own form, your own structure. And there's no definitive path to take. There's no road to go down, other than what you do instinctively, and whatever you do, you have to do it very quickly.

A sidebar augments the main story. Something unusual, or touching, or dramatic that resonates on its own. The moon has no light; it's lit by the sun. But I don't think that a sidebar should get its total energy from the main story. Even though it is a satellite around the bigger story, the sidebar should have its own light.

Deadline Tip:

The only way to get a story right, especially a technical story, is to ask the most basic questions so that you understand it. There's a great line in the movie *Philadelphia* where the lawyer, played by Denzel Washington, says, "Explain it to me like I'm a 4-year-old." The worst feeling in the world is hanging up from an interview and you look at your notes and you see that you just don't get it. There's a difference between being stupid and being ignorant of a particular area. You get past that sheepishness of not knowing, because the only thing worse than asking a stupid question is not being able to answer your editor's questions when he asks you, rather pointedly, why didn't you clear this up? Because you can't have any ambiguities, and there's no time to go back.

Alfred Lubrano is an enterprise and feature writer for New York Newsday.

Recalling deadline with Deborah Henley

Getting the news over the scanner, we very quickly realized the seriousness of the story and what it was going to become. In those first few minutes, two or three editors on the desk—Dee Murphy and Steve Gunn, started to think, "Where do we have reporters? Who's closest to the scene?"

That's how it all starts. From there, we start to involve all the editors on the desk in the effort. Editors who deal with specialty areas, like medical reporters. Those people are clearly going to be needed at some point, when we understand the extent of injuries. We start to brainstorm, after that initial 30 minutes of getting everybody immediately on the street. What are the components of this story? What are the logical questions that readers are going to have of us, and let's start thinking ahead to reporting out those lines.

Very early on, we sit down with a map and we speculate which hospitals victims will be going to. All the editors sit down, from the top down. Don Forst, who's the editor, rolls up his sleeves. Rich Galant is involved, and the editors on the desk. Throwing out ideas about where—what are possibilities, where the story might take us, what we need to be prepared for and have background on, involving the library and our databases. How they can help us, give us tips and leads to go on and follow.

Out of that process comes a skeleton of a budget, which looks very messy.

It has an awful lot of ideas to begin with, but it's important to just get them down and to attach reporters' names and editors' names to them. And put it in a place that everyone has access to so we're not wasting a moment's time redoing work, but moving forward.

We put it in our city queue, and it's available by computer to anyone in the room.

I take charge of that, and continue to update it as the story changes, so that's one way that we communicate. To get out a broad message to everybody about how the story is growing and changing, and who's where. If you have a tip that's useful to somebody out on the story at a particular scene, you could call up this file and see where they are, how to get to them, how to get to their editor.

New Yorkers live on the subway. And we need to be thinking about what questions readers will have tomorrow. How does this affect service? Do they have questions about security?

The other thing is that we are willing to send a lot of people out on the story. We had probably 30 reporters out on the street, and another 10 reporters in here, working the phones, taking feeds, putting together that story on the first and second day.

I remember a joke that afternoon that a reporter from another paper said: "I'm tired of turning around to interview someone and it's a *Newsday* reporter."

I felt really good about that. Strong writing comes from strong reporting, and from having a lot of stories coming in off the street so that we can provide an accurate, full picture of what's going on.

We have people who are strong, street-smart reporters who very quickly see how a story is moving, and move with it. There are strong beat reporters, and your beat becomes crucial to getting the sources who will help you move quickly and give you the tips of how the story is changing, and help you put together what's going on with the story. And they have an eye for the small things that tell the big stories: burns that bleed because they were so deep. Clothing that was melted onto parts of people's bodies. They also have a great appreciation for the art of storytelling.

What the editors were able to contribute is that, as these stories began to shape themselves in the course of the day, we talked a good deal about what goes in which story, and who's contributing to what story, and how do we make sure that this story has the lead it needs to accomplish what we're trying to accomplish with this story, and that it doesn't mimic what we're doing in the main story, and that they're divided in a logical way. That the reader gets something new, something important as they go along to each paragraph of each story. And that's the goal by the end of the day. Then we immediately started drawing up a budget for the next day. We went ahead and called reporters who were on their way home, or had just arrived home, weren't yet asleep, to say, "We're going to need you to do this first thing in the morning."

And you're starting to think, "Well, the weekend is coming up. What sort of Sunday package do readers want on this?"

There is no knob that you could turn on that would give you the completeness that the newspaper was able to give you about all the different things that happened to different people, and the different emotions at work that day. And the power of the still photo, and the power of the written word is just incredible. When you go back and read this, it still jumps out at you.

Deadline Tips:

Think quickly about how best to use the people you have at the moment. Use them in a smart way, and move them quickly. Because the story is changing every second that ticks by.

You can't have strong writing without strong reporting. Small things tell the big story. When you talk to people out in the field, make sure that they see the color, that they're looking for the detail that's going to immediately make a connection with your reader and put them side by side with the reporters who are out there, seeing the story develop.

The best thing an editor can do in a story like this is to give clear communication and direction back to the reporter.

Talk to the editors who are helping you to coordinate the effort, so that reporting that's being done is cross-checked, is challenged, turns into new story ideas, makes its way straight to the top, and to the next day's paper.

Talk constantly and openly on the desk about what you're learning, what you're thinking, what your ideas are. Because we all build on each other's ideas.

Deborah Henley is metropolitan editor and assistant managing editor of New York Newsday.

Recalling deadline with Richard Galant

When something like this happens—it's so ingrained in the culture that people just go, and
people drop whatever they're doing, and give
their extra effort. This thing happened at 1:34 in
the afternoon, and essentially we had to have the
entire paper locked up before 11 o'clock that
night. The vast bulk of the reporting and the writing got done by 9 p.m.

The most important element in a situation like
this is teamwork, because you have to be able to
divide up the reporting, and divide up the writing
in such a way that every angle gets covered, and
given that time is so critical, that you don't have
duplication of effort.

The desk, under Debbie Henley, has set up a
good division of labor, so that one editor was responsible for the victims, one editor was responsible for the investigation, one editor gets the
responsibility of figuring out who the suspect is.

My job was to raise questions and make sure
that we covered every angle, that we were putting
together a package that was intelligent and that
could give the appropriate play to every story so
that we didn't have key parts of the story getting
shortchanged, or getting overplayed.

In a disaster situation like this, in which there's
no safety net, you have a very limited window to
get the key information that you need. The editors
tend to get more immediately involved in oversee-
ing the reporting.

We have to give people a compelling enough
package that we can continue to convince people
it's worth reading a newspaper rather than getting
their news in five minutes from television.

I think that the audience for newspapers is an
audience that wants more than the surface. They
want to have a feel for what happens. They want
to know more than just that there was a fire
bombing in a subway. They want to know what it

was like to be in the car. There's basic human emotion, or basic human desire, to know as much as possible.

The writing challenge is to make it as concrete as possible, as colorful as possible. To make it easy to follow for the reader, to avoid duplication so that each story is fresh and works on its own.

In this case, you had three columnists who are storytellers. But also, you had one story on what it was like to be inside the car, and you had one story on Leary's background and what his neighbors thought of him. And they were constructed with anecdotal leads—or, at least, not with straight news leads. In many cases, that's the way to hook readers, and make the story much more inviting. Our feeling was we needed a hard news lead on the main story.

The work of our photographers is a vital element. We're not as much of a visual medium as television, but I think without strong photos, it's very hard to carry off a package like this. And in this case, I think one of the things that made it work was the terrific picture on the cover by Richie Lee. When I saw it, I knew that this had to be our Page One, it almost looks like victims of violence in Bosnia. You would never imagine this kind of scene in a New York City subway.

Deadline Tips:

Somebody needs to have the authority to assign people, and make sure that the right resources are put on to something like this, and that they're headed in the right direction. It's important to put one person clearly in charge of the effort. And for that person to divide up areas of responsibility to promote the view that the paper's coverage is stronger if everybody is working together, and on the same team.

The other thing is to be very rigorous and very clear in directing people to just absorb all the facts that they can possibly get, to steep themselves in as much detail as they possibly can, because there's no amount of fancy writing that can cover up for a lack of good reporting.

Richard Galant is managing editor of New York Newsday.

Writers' Workshop

Talking Points

1) For the main news story of this multi-story package ("Blast on No. 4 Train Causes Holiday Panic; 41 Injured"), *New York Newsday* relied on the inverted pyramid, the form that Roy Peter Clark calls "the workhorse of American newspaper writing" for more than a century. Study how closely this story about the subway firebombing follows the form, which presents information in descending levels of importance. Discuss the values and drawbacks of utilizing this structure.

2) Verbs are the pistons that drive the engine of narrative. Note how vivid, active verbs propel the reader from the first paragraph, creating the "steady advance" described by writing coach Don Fry: "A crude firebomb possibly carried by a New Jersey man turned a crowded subway car into a raging inferno at a lower Manhattan IRT station yesterday, injuring at least 41 people, including four critically." Track the movement of this story, using verbs as mileposts.

3) "The right-branching sentence is the staple of effective journalism in the modern era," Clark says in his 1994 essay, "The American Conversation and the Language of Journalism." The structure is simple: A sentence begins with a subject and verb, followed by other subordinate elements. Paragraph three is a prime example. Find other examples and consider why Clark says such sentences "make meaning early."

4) In the newsroom of *New York Newsday,* the story titled "A Flash in a Packed Car, Then Flames and Terror" is known as a "tick-tock," a narrative reconstruction that uses time as its organizing device. At what time does this story begin and end? How much time does it cover in all?

5) Sense of place is critical in a narrative reconstruction. Notice how the writer endeavors to locate the "tick-tock" in its historical and geographical settings. "Above ground, the scene on lower Broadway's 'Canyon of Heroes,' where heroes from Charles Lindbergh to Nelson Mandela have been showered with ticker tape, was a nightmare of billowing

smoke and screaming victims." In the very next paragraph, a single phrase, "just off Broadway," helps the reader locate the scene precisely. What is the value of such details?

6) The writer of this piece said he likes to begin a "tick-tock" at the moment just before the ordinary becomes the extraordinary. Study how he does that in the first three paragraphs.

7) Another story in this book, "Surgical Team Rescues Trooper from Death's Door," by Gerald Carbone of the *Providence Journal-Bulletin,* relies on the narrative reconstruction. What are the major differences between this story and the *New York Newsday* tick-tock, apart from length? What are the similarities?

8) Sidebars, related stories with their own headlines, are satellites of larger news stories. "A sidebar helps the main story by making it easier to read and helps the whole package by providing another entry point, another headline that may draw readers into the page," says Jane T. Harrigan in *The Editorial Eye,* (St. Martin's Press 1993). The *New York Newsday* package presents several examples of this form: the time line or chronology, the scene setter, the fact box, the profile. They are tightly focused, usually brief and provide multiple entry points to a story. Study the sidebars in the package and discuss why they were published separately.

9) Even a sidebar can bear all the hallmarks of good storytelling. Study "Burn Victims Face Mental Scars Too," by Alfred Lubrano. Notice how he structures the piece to mirror the process of injury, treatment, and painful recovery the subway firebombing victims will experience. The ending is especially effective; at the story's conclusion, the reader is projected into the future.

10) Reporter Wendell Jamieson was one of the first reporters on the scene at the subway firebombing. He wrote the sidebar "Charred Walls Mark the Eye of the Storm." In six paragraphs, he puts the reader in the subway car where minutes before a bomb had exploded. He relies on his sense of sight to vividly describe the scene. Notice how he refers to the absence of sound: "The car itself was eerily quiet." What other senses could have added to this scene-setter?

11) Compare the work of the *New York Newsday* columnists with the news reporters. How does the columnist's job differ? What license does the columnist enjoy? What re-

strictions does each labor under? Debate who has the better job on a story like the subway firebombing.

12) The use of specific detail is an important element in good newswriting. In "Disaster Below Jolts the City's Spinal Cord," columnist Jimmy Breslin describes suspect Edward Leary's living arrangement in great detail. He tells us the value of a home he owned in Scotch Plains, N.J. He tells us that Leary and his family lived in a Brooklyn co-op. He gives us the address. And in a final short sentence tells us, "It was 12A." Speculate on the effects of such detail on the reader. And why that detail in such a short sentence?

13) Although an effective piece of writing contains one dominant message, news writers often are guilty of dumping all the contents of their notebook into their stories. "Heroes: They Just Show Up," by Ellis Henican, is a study in relentless focus. What is his message? How many variations on that theme does Henican employ? In what ways does he buttress that theme?

14) Hero stories are standard fare when journalists write about disasters. Discuss this story in terms of similar hero stories you've read in the newspaper. What elements seem the same and which ones seem different? What value does such a story have to the people reading about this disaster?

15) Good writers try to use active verbs. Henican uses strong verbs throughout to describe the dramatic action of this terrible event. The transit cops "lifted the people. They calmed the cries." But in one key paragraph describing the victims, the writer prefers the passive: "Skin was scorched. Hair was singed. Clothing was drenched by the burning liquid...." Discuss the value of passive verbs in such a context.

Assignment Desk

1) In 1984, Roy Clark gave the name "hourglass" to an alternative to the inverted pyramid that had become increasingly popular. It has three parts: 1) the top, which tells the news quickly to the reader, usually in three or four paragraphs; 2) the turn, a nimble transition; and 3) the narrative, a chronological retelling of events. Rewrite this story in an hourglass form.

2) The main story drew on the reporting of more than two dozen reporters. See how many different sources you can identify.

3) Role play the job of editor supervising this coverage. Where do you deploy your reporters? Map the reporting plan for this story.

4) Are you writing right-branching sentences that allow you, as Clark puts it, to "create sentences of infinite length that are equally clear"? Rewrite them if you're not.

5) Report and write a tick-tock. Reconstruct an event based on extensive interviews. Mine your sources for details that will make the event come alive in the reader's mind.

6) As you plan your story, look for that decisive moment just before the ordinary becomes the extraordinary.

7) Rewrite the top of the tick-tock so that the explosion occurs in the first paragraph. Does it make the story seem melodramatic?

8) Draw up a sidebar budget for the *New York Newsday* package. Use the existing pieces and devise new ones. Write a headline and one-line description for each.

9) Cut the sidebar "Hate in a Jar" in half. What elements can't be left out?

10) In the sidebar on burn victims, Alfred Lubrano drew on a variety of sources in his reporting. Identify as many sources as you can. Give yourself 15 minutes to devise your own reporting plan—experts to interview, library resources —for the story. Identify several electronic resources— World Wide Web sites, databases, bulletin boards—where you could find information.

11) Re-read the headlines of both of these sidebars. Then read the endings of both stories. It appears as if the headline writer decided, in each case, to use the "kicker" as part of the headline. Discuss the implications of this technique. What are its strengths and weaknesses? What are the benefits to the reader? Write alternative headlines that do not steal important elements from the story.

12) Take one of your news stories and write it as a column. If you have to, write a first draft in the first person and then delete those references. What is the most difficult part of the process?

13) The first and last sentences of "Heroes: They Just Show Up" are not even complete sentences. They might be called "intentional sentence fragments." Describe the effects of this technique for each individual sentence, and the effect of repeating it at the beginning and the end. Examine the story throughout for variation of sentence length. Read it aloud to test the relationship between sentence length and the pace and rhythm of the story.

KNIGHT RIDDER

Knight-Ridder Washington Bureau

Finalist, Team Deadline Reporting

The Knight-Ridder team assembles near the site of the plane crash on the White House lawn under the magnolia tree planted by President Andrew Jackson. Team members (l. to r.): Steve Goldstein, Frank Greve, Angie Cannon, James R. Carroll, Aaron Epstein, Ricardo Alonzo Zaldivar.

The Washington Bureau of Knight-Ridder Newspapers covers the nation's capital for 28 daily newspapers and hundreds of news service subscribers around the globe. In a city teeming with journalists, the bureau's work stands out for coverage that is as compelling as it is clear and complete. After a private plane crashed against a wall of the White House on a suicide mission last September, a team of Knight-Ridder reporters assembled a package of stories that ASNE judges praised for "clarity, readability, and seamless integration of the story's various elements." Within hours, Aaron Epstein, Steve Goldstein, Angie Cannon, and Ricardo Alonzo Zaldivar traced the final flight of Frank Corder, and produced a story that unfolded the troubles that apparently led the Maryland trucker to kill himself in an incident that drew worldwide attention and led to historic new security measures around the president's home on 1600 Pennsylvannia Avenue. Meanwhile, Frank Greve and James R. Carroll drew on terrorist and security experts to report the disturbing conclusion that the White House couldn't be protected from air attack. The result was a package that took readers beyond the headlines with a vivid blend of informed journalism and lively storytelling.

Aaron Epstein, Frank Greve, Ricardo Alonzo Zaldivar, and Angie Cannon are national correspondents for Knight-Ridder Newspapers. James R. Carrroll covers the capital for the *Long Beach* (Calif.) *Press-Telegram,* while Steve Goldstein is a Washington correspondent for *The Philadelphia Inquirer.*

A troubled life ends with crash at White House

SEPTEMBER 13, 1994

By Aaron Epstein and Steve Goldstein

WASHINGTON—It was after midnight. Frank Corder knew the aircraft he wanted.

He walked down the line of 15 planes parked on the grass at a tiny, unguarded airfield north of Baltimore and climbed into a two-seat, single-engine Cessna with "1405Q" printed on its tail— the plane he learned to fly in.

Less than an hour later, he would guide the little plane low over downtown Washington, bank left at the Washington Monument and smash it into a magnificent magnolia tree that Andrew Jackson is said to have planted on the South Lawn of the White House about 160 years ago.

The Cessna would wind up in a crumpled heap against a White House wall, its wheels in the air, its tail broken away, jagged pieces of metal and wire strewn around the lawn.

Corder would wind up in a body bag, his head severed, his bizarre flight early yesterday morning the subject of yet another investigation into what had gone wrong with the President's security— and what had gone wrong in the dead man's mind.

Corder, a stocky 38-year-old truck driver from Maryland, was wearing a plaid flannel shirt and bluejeans when he fired up the plane and taxied out to the Harford County Airpark runway. The Cessna's wheels barely left tracks on the dry grass. In moments, he was aloft, flying south over farm country toward Washington, 70 miles away.

He had never been more alone, nor in deeper personal trouble.

His father, Bill, an aircraft mechanic for the Aberdeen Flying Club, had died a year ago last April. His prize possession was his father's guitar. Ironically, his father had worked on the very

Cessna in which Frank Corder spent the last hour of his life.

Frank Corder's 10-year marriage to his wife, Lydia, a licensed practical nurse at the Veterans Administration Medical Center at nearby Perry Point, had broken up three weeks ago. They had lived in a two-story wooden frame house, painted off-white, with azaleas and yellow marigolds in front. They had no children together, and neighbors said they kept to themselves.

Corder had longtime drug and alcohol problems. He delivered goods by truck out of Baltimore-Washington International Airport but lost his commercial driver's license for 90 days last year after being convicted of drunken driving. It was his second alcohol-related offense.

The state allowed him to drive only to work and school. Last month, according to state records, he went through a stop sign.

Corder's cousin Dee George, 45, a psychiatric nursing assistant at the Perry Point hospital where Corder was once hospitalized for detoxification, said yesterday: "I think he just wanted to kill himself. He had nobody. Nobody and nowhere to go.

"When Frank was down on drugs and alcohol, he told me many times he wished he had a gun and could end it. He was probably in that situation again and just wanted to end it."

No one really knows what made Corder steal the plane and take that last flight, but it seems apparent that he kept the Cessna at a low enough altitude that it eluded radar detection for its entire flight.

His likeliest route was straight south along Interstate 95, passing above Baltimore and into the nation's capital. Flying conditions were superb. The temperature was in the mid-50s, the winds came out of the northwest at only 5 mph, and the visibility was 20 miles.

What could have been in Corder's mind as he reached the Washington Beltway and spotted the Washington Monument, standing like an incandescent toothpick in the distance?

Was he thinking of Mathias Rust, the 19-year-old German who penetrated the security of the Kremlin in Moscow by landing a single-engine Cessna in Red Square in 1987?

As far as his relatives know, Corder liked Bill Clinton. Dee George remembered her cousin Frank saying a few months back, "You know, President Clinton is the best thing we have."

"There's no political nature that I'm aware of," said Corder's brother, John. "It was just out of the blue."

After a preliminary inquiry, the Secret Service, too, discounted any political motive. The bizarre flight of Frank Corder "does not appear to be directed toward the President," Secret Service official Carl Meyer said.

Flying at treetop level, Corder pointed the Cessna down 17th Street, then made what pilots call a left "J" turn as he approached the glowing monument and arced easily over the black iron fence that hems the South Lawn of the White House.

"It had lights on both wings, it turned left and lined up with the White House," said an eyewitness, Adolphus Roberts. "I heard a large boom sound. There was no fire, no nothing."

The Cessna tore into the grass of the South Lawn about 50 feet from the mansion, gouging out deep tracks, smashing into Andy Jackson's ancient magnolia, cutting a patch out of a holly hedge, and tossing debris on wrought-iron furniture on the White House patio.

It was "as if it had been hit head-on and rear-ended," a Secret Service agent would say later.

The damage to the nation's most famous mansion was minimal: a cracked window of the White House doctor's office, a few exterior scrapes and gashes.

"Fourteen seconds and it was over. That baby was against the wall, and he was dead," a Secret Service official said.

Security guards at the White House didn't spot the plane until "it was coming in," Secret Service official Meyer said.

No shots were fired. Meyer said the agents on duty barely had time to seek cover after they spotted the Cessna.

The President and Hillary Rodham Clinton were asleep at Blair House across Pennsylvania Avenue, where they have been staying while workers renovate the White House heating and air-conditioning systems.

Awakened by a call from White House chief of staff Leon E. Panetta and informed of the crash, "the President asked a few questions and then went back to bed," deputy press secretary Arthur Jones said.

Yesterday, Clinton took public note of the crash in an afternoon satellite broadcast to mark the beginning of AmeriCorps, a national service program for young volunteers.

"We take this incident seriously because the White House is the people's house," he said. "And it is the job of every president who lives here to keep it safe and secure.... So let me assure all Americans, the people's house will be kept safe, it will be kept open, and the people's business will go on."

Washington has a building-height restriction in the downtown area that may have made it easier for Corder's plane to fly undetected. The restriction, which bars tall buildings that would obscure the city's landmarks, also eliminates hazards for low-flying aircraft.

Corder's cousin, Dee George, said Corder told her last week that he was planning a truck trip to Georgia and asked whether she wanted some peaches.

"I made some peach cobbler last night and took it to work, and everybody wanted some more," she recalled. "So I called him this morning to tell him I wanted peaches.

"And the Secret Service answered."

Other intruders have penetrated the grounds

SEPTEMBER 13, 1994

By Aaron Epstein

WASHINGTON—Several intruders have tried to penetrate the White House compound in recent decades. A few succeeded.

In 1974, an Army private stole a helicopter and landed it on the South Lawn of the White House. Guards armed with shotguns wounded him and led him away for a psychiatric examination.

That same year, a man crashed his car into a gate on the Pennsylvania Avenue side of the White House. After emerging from the car and appearing to be wired with explosives, he held Secret Service officers at bay for four hours before being captured. The man said he wanted to deliver a religious text to the President.

Two years later, a 30-year-old Washington man carrying a 3-foot-long metal pipe climbed over the White House's 19th-century wrought-iron fence. Officers ordered him to halt. When he didn't, they shot and killed him on the North Lawn.

Later, new steel gates were built to protect the President and his family.

In late 1983, concrete barriers were installed at White House entrances to thwart terrorists from penetrating the White House with vehicles loaded with explosives.

Reports circulated that surface-to-air missiles had been placed on or near the White House grounds to defend against possible terrorist attacks.

The next year, a man was captured after climbing over the fence, and a 25-year-old Pennsylvania man was shot outside the Executive Mansion when he allegedly pointed a sawed-off shotgun at Secret Service officers.

Lessons Learned

BY AARON EPSTEIN

As I remember that morning, our objective was clear from the beginning: Forget the pyramid-style rules of formulaic journalism and write this as a real story, not a traditional who-what-when-where-why article to wrap flounder in.

We already had the bizarre event—a plane crackup at the doorstep of the White House itself, for God's sake—so all we needed was to learn everything about the pilot and why he did it, get pungent quotes, strive for a sense of time and place, and provide as much revealing detail as possible without lapsing into fiction.

Oh, and by the way, the story was due in seven hours.

What I relearned from the experience was that, given an energetic and resourceful bunch of reporters in the field, it can be done despite the difficulty of the assignment and the tyranny of the deadline.

As the anchor, my job was to track developments on the wires, talk to our reporters by phone, skim the cream of their notes, tell them what gaps remained, and discuss ways to fill them.

Amazingly, our expert field hands pinned down the details that helped lift the story out of the ordinary: the path of the plane, the look of the pilot, his troubled past, his father's guitar, his cousin's peach cobbler, his fatal collision with Andy Jackson's magnolia.

All I had to do was plan the path the story would take, make a few calls, write a lead that might stop the reader's eye, find the right words to sustain the drama, put them in an intelligible order, and press the send button.

Afterward, I felt good, really good. And that's another lesson: In this individualistic, turf-jealous business I've chosen, the greatest joy can come from being on a team that somehow does the seemingly impossible.

There's little chance to stop aerial intruders, experts say

SEPTEMBER 13, 1994

By Frank Greve and James R. Carroll

WASHINGTON—It is illegal to fly over the heart of the nation's capital—much less into the side of the White House—but there's little chance of intercepting someone intent on doing it.

"Frankly, anybody can strike at the President if they're willing to lose their lives doing it," said retired Army Lt. Gen. Richard G. Trefry, head of the White House Military Office in the Bush administration.

And a small plane like the one that despondent Maryland trucker Frank Corder crashed into the White House lawn early yesterday presents a particular dilemma.

It can fly low enough to avoid the ground-based radar units that monitor the restricted capital airspace from across the Potomac.

And it's hard to know when to open fire—the White House is said to be equipped with heat-seeking Stinger missiles—on a small civilian plane that could be lost or in trouble.

If one of the shoulder-launched missiles was fired before the plane crossed the cast-iron White House fence, the plane could crash in flames into downtown Washington. But hesitation could send the flaming plane into the White House itself.

"What are you going to do if you *do* spot 'em?" asked P. Hamilton Brown, executive secretary of the Former Agents Association, a Secret Service retirees group. "Fire off a heat-seeking missile into an area where, most of the time, you're in the midst of heavy air traffic?"

There's another problem if the target is a small propeller-driven aircraft like Corder's Cessna.

"There's not enough heat [from the engine] for a heat-seeking missile to find it," said Thomas Amlie, a veteran government missile designer.

Top government security experts have known for years that the White House was vulnerable to assault from the air, but concluded the problem was insoluble.

"The White House has been vulnerable to that kind of attack for as long as I can remember," said Robert H. Kupperman, a counter-terrorism specialist who directed the Federal Emergency Management Agency in the 1970s. Among the agency's duties was ensuring that American leaders survived disaster, nuclear war, or terrorist attack.

According to Secret Service spokesman Carl Meyer, uniformed agents protecting the White House had no warning that Corder's single-engine Cessna was coming until they spotted the aircraft "visually" moments before it crashed into the side of the mansion about 50 yards from the Oval Office.

The insoluble problem, according to Kupperman and others, has always been spotting a suspicious airplane like Corder's in time to do something about it.

All flights are prohibited over a narrow racetrack-shaped zone of downtown Washington that includes the White House and the Capitol. Parts of the zone are less than a mile wide, however, which gives spotters and the Secret Service as little as 15 seconds to detect and respond to suspicious aircraft likely to be flying at 100 mph or more.

For their warning, Secret Service agents at the White House depend on air traffic controllers at the Federal Aviation Administration tower at National Airport, former White House security agents said.

The airport is on the Virginia shore of the Potomac River about three miles south of the White House, and its radars are about five feet above ground level.

At 1:45 a.m. or so, as Corder flew by the White House, "only a couple of people would normally be on duty" at National Airport's air traffic control tower, said an FAA radar specialist who asked not to be identified.

"All the flights they're expecting have filed flight plans," the FAA official said. "They know their arrival times, they have transponders on so they can be identified."

The business is so routine, he said, "that if somebody is not obeying those rules, you're just not going to find them."

Two administration investigations began yesterday: one into how Corder made it through the White House defenses and a second into what security improvements might be made.

Prohibition of private flights into National—the airport virtually just across the river from the White House—would be fought by the many corporate fliers who use it. Widening the protective zone around the White House—and the vice president's mansion three miles northwest—also would be hard to do without interfering with National's operations.

Improved radars would help, and House sources said the Secret Service apparently requested money for some kind of tactical radar system for the White House in the late 1980s. But the Secret Service's parent agency, the Treasury Department, never forwarded the request to Congress in its budgets.

Rooftop-high chain link protective fences around the White House and the adjacent Old Executive Office Building were proposed in the 1970s, according to Kupperman.

"The idea was rejected out of hand because it projected the image of a nation under siege," Kupperman said.

Lessons Learned

BY FRANK GREVE

God is sometimes kind to insecure deadline writers and lets things happen before dawn. In the case of Frank Corder's flight into a magnolia tree on the White House lawn last September, God gave Jim Carroll and me a lifetime .200 hitter on deadline, a full day to answer an urgent, complicated question: Is there any way to protect the White House?

In hindsight, that's the obvious sidebar question. But it wasn't clearly so on the morning of the crash, when an editor might logically have scrambled all hands, sent them scrounging, and had an anchor make order late in the day of the tidbits they harvested. There's a problem with that approach that we happily avoided: High-profile accident stories with multiple reporters tend to have messy reporting jurisdictions that make everybody inefficient.

You don't notice the inefficiency when an entire city room is emptied in response to an earthquake. But Knight-Ridder's Washington Bureau had only six reporters to put on the crash, only four for the full day. (*The Washington Post* bylined nine.)

News editor Gary Blonston, who framed the sidebar question for Jim and me, assured us that we weren't to scrounge for crash details, just to determine whether the White House could be protected. This conferred on all of us the singular advantage of clear assignments and assured that we would be coming at the story from distinct points of view that converged only productively. If we did our jobs right, just one reporter would be calling the National Airport tower to ask whether there was too much ground clutter for air traffic controllers to spot off-course, low-altitude blips. In fact, Jim and I crossed paths with Knight-Ridder colleagues only once, late in the day, to trade information.

Our sidebar's quality depended almost entirely on the authority of the sources replying to the question of whether the White House could be protected. The Secret Service and FBI wouldn't respond, so the sources had to be outside the government. The first was a well-known *bona fide* expert whom I reached at home before he got to work, Washington being one of those cities where newsmakers are often easier to get to between 8 and 9 a.m. than during their business day. Reaching him early had a second advantage: He was still excited and easily engaged. By noon, multiple interviews had reduced him to soundbite patter.

In almost every story, and nearly every interview, the question arises for the reporter: How hard will you push? It came up in this story when Lt. Gen. Trefry's wife said I'd just missed him, he was heading for the airport. She knew his ultimate destination was London and that it entailed a connecting flight, but no more. What to do? Partly because I was teamed with Steve Goldstein, an admirably hard pusher, I pressed Mrs. Trefry to call her husband and get his itinerary in something like the national interest. She did, and Gen. Trefry, from the American Airlines check-in counter, delivered the sidebar's best quote seconds before he remembered that he didn't talk to reporters.

No one could read this account without noting luck's large role. It was luck that Gen. Trefry had left an itinerary and had a cooperative wife, luck that the predawn crash gave us a full day to report and write, luck that sources were, with remarkable frequency, sitting by their phones. Finally, to speak the unspeakable thought that crosses my mind whenever reporters win recognition for covering a disaster well: We were also, like Heimlich maneuver trainees in a restaurant at just the wrong moment, lucky to get the chance to show our stuff.

Gerald M. Carbone
Non-Deadline Writing

Gerald M. Carbone is a staff writer for *The Providence Journal-Bulletin* in Westerly, R.I. He joined the paper in 1988 from the Biddeford, Maine, *Journal Tribune* where he was sports editor. He has also reported for papers in his native Massachusetts and New Hampshire and was, very briefly, the publisher and sole editorial staff of *The Old Orchard Sun,* a weekly in Old Orchard Beach, Maine. After studying fiction at Bradford College, Carbone switched to journalism at the University of New Hampshire, where he graduated in 1982. Juggling responsibilities for routine community coverage with occasional forays into feature writing, Carbone reports and writes with ferocious concentration, quickly turning out lengthy narrative reconstructions that have long been a hallmark of the *Journal-Bulletin.* (The paper counts two other ASNE non-deadline winners: Carol McCabe and G. Wayne Miller.) To his

stories about the harrowing surgery on a wounded
state trooper, a treacherous mountain rescue, and
the disappearance of an eccentric millionaire,
Carbone brings a novelist's eye for detail and the
storyteller's knack for creating suspense. Weaving
richly-detailed scenes that inform as well as entertain, he has created narratives that are irresistible to readers.

Disaster shatters dreams
of college hiking pals

JANUARY 23, 1994

The meteorologists stationed atop Mount Washington had just sat down to a Saturday night treat: a turkey dinner with all the fixings.

Outside the temperature was 32 degrees below zero and plummeting. The winds howled, then shrieked, with 84-mph gusts that rattled the weather station's bulletproof windows, thick glass designed to deflect the blows of rime ice falling from the tower.

Thirteen people sat down in the warm glow of the observatory's dining hall, a much bigger crowd than the usual staff of four; howling wind and the occasional thump of falling ice served as background noise for the dinner conversation.

The meteorologists were joined by two mountain climbers who had banged on their door for refuge, and by a group of journalists and scientists enrolled in a "cold weather school" to learn about the climate atop Mount Washington, one of the coldest spots on Earth. It was a good time—good food, good conversation—until Ken Rancourt shot up from his seat, stood ramrod straight, and announced: "Something isn't right."

Conversation stopped. Rancourt was the chief meteorologist atop Mount Washington on the night of Jan. 15, and if he wasn't happy, no one could be happy.

Rancourt heard something strange, something besides the screeching winds and thumping rime. There were a dozen other pairs of ears present, and no one else heard anything odd. But Rancourt had spent parts of 13 winters atop this mountain, the highest in New England, and he trusted his instincts.

He turned to Ralph Patterson, one of the staff meteorologists, and told him to grab his gear: They were going out.

Rancourt and Patterson climbed up one level to the observatory roof. Rancourt peered out into the floodlit night, wondering: Could that rhythmic thump he was hearing be a loose antennae on the weather station's 40-foot tower? Unlikely.

The knock sounded again, and Rancourt bellowed into the wind: "Hello-oooo."

A human voice answered.

"Oh my God," thought Rancourt. "How could there be somebody out there?"

Rancourt and Patterson stepped back inside, leaving the door open behind them. They clanged down the metal, spiral staircase to ground level and stepped out into wind so cold that it would "flash freeze" exposed skin, turning a flexible finger into a stiff piece of ice within 30 seconds.

It took them 10 minutes to walk the 400-foot perimeter of the observatory. They found nothing out there but wind and ice, so they scrambled back in through the door they'd left ajar.

Rancourt said he would search the observation tower's upper levels while Patterson went down, just in case the person had slipped inside while they were walking around the building. Patterson clanged down the staircase and there in a corner stood a man with a frostbitten face.

Rancourt came down to the unheated stairwell and began interrogating the man: "Where did you come from?" he asked, his breath steaming in the air. "Are you alone?"

The man was lethargic, obviously suffering from hypothermia. A lot of his answers didn't make sense, but the answers that Rancourt could understand were disturbing:

"I left my partner on the trail," the man said, and Rancourt knew there was bigger trouble. The man repeatedly mumbled directions about where to find his friend, as if he had been rehearsing them while climbing the summit through inhuman conditions:

"Five cairns up the Jefferson Loop Trail," he said. "Five cairns up."

A cairn is a slender pile of boulders stacked every 50 feet to mark trails above the treeline, where there is no place to hang a marker. If Rancourt correctly understood, this lethargic, frostbitten young man had left his partner five cairns up Jefferson Loop, just below the summit of Mount Jefferson more than 4 miles away—an impossible distance to cover now, at night, in some of the coldest weather that had ever been recorded in one of the coldest spots on Earth.

Rancourt managed to get the man's name: Jeremy Haas, age 20; his partner was Derek Tinkham, also 20. Rancourt telephoned down to the Appalachian Mountain Club's rescue headquarters in Pinkham Notch at the base of the mountain. Word spread through the network of telephone lines stretched over the mountains and through the valleys: Get your gear together. We're going on a rescue in the worst conditions that you have ever seen.

'WORST...ON EARTH'

Friends say that Derek Tinkham of Narragansett and Jeremy Haas of Ithaca, N.Y., had been planning this trek since October. They wanted to complete a winter traverse of the Presidential Range, always a difficult hike. Weather usually turns back even the most experienced hikers.

In his book *The Worst Weather on Earth,* William Lowell Putnam wrote: "There may be worse weather, from time to time, at some forbidden place on Planet Earth, but it has yet to be reliably recorded."

As far as mountain ranges go, New England's White Mountains don't look like much. The tallest peak, Mount Washington, stands 6,288 feet, a dwarf compared with Everest at 29,028, or North America's largest, Denali (Mount McKinley) at 20,320.

But climbers who scale those bigger peaks often train on the Presidential Range of the White Mountains because the Presidentials consistently kick up weather as bad as anything they may face anywhere. The highest wind gust ever recorded on Earth, 231 mph, whipped across Mount Washington on Aug. 12, 1934.

The wind speed soars because mountains take up space between the ground and the upper atmosphere, so winds that blow over free space above the ocean or the plains run out of room when they hit mountains. The same volume of air must squeeze through a smaller space, and it does this by blowing through faster, much as a gentle spray from a garden hose becomes a stinging stream when the hose is constricted.

More often than not, one of three weather systems is trying to squeeze across the White Mountains no matter what the season. And the higher you go, the colder the air mass gets—about 5.5 degrees colder for each 1,000 feet.

So on a 90-degree day in Providence, the temperature atop Mount Washington is likely to be about 60 degrees, with fog and high winds. New Englanders often find it difficult to grasp that even a sunny day promising perfect hiking can be deadly atop the mountain. These mountains claimed 110 lives between 1849 and the day Haas and Tinkham set out on their trek.

Haas and Tinkham fit the average profile of people who have died in the White Mountains: males, younger than 25, hiking in bad weather. But they differed from the statistics in this: Most victims of the White Mountains died in summer.

PREPARING FOR THE RESCUE

The phone rang at Paul Cormier's house in the tiny town of Twin Mountain; before he even picked it up, he knew.

Mike Pelchat, president of the Androscoggin Valley Search and Rescue outlined the scenario: A man had come into the observatory on his hands and knees and there was still one person out there on the mountain.

As he packed his gear, Cormier, a veteran climber, held out some hope for the stranded climber's survival. He knew that the climber's partner had wrapped him in a sleeping bag and a bivouac sack, and there was a slim chance he might make it.

Cormier met Pelchat at snow-covered Jefferson Notch Road at 6 a.m. last Sunday, where Fish & Game workers on snowmobiles ferried the pair to the head of Caps Ridge Trail.

Cormier knew that it was foolhardy to climb Caps Ridge Trail. The temperature had plummeted to 41.9 degrees below zero after midnight, a record for the date, with winds gusting above 100 mph. Sunrise added just 3 more degrees and did nothing to slow the wind. But Cormier pressed on, recalling a mission two years ago, when rescuers found two lost hikers in Great Gulf ravine, holed up and healthy in a snow cave.

He joked to Pelchat: "Boy, it would be just like us to meet this guy coming down the trail."

Cormier arrived at the trailhead wearing some of his gear: two pairs of socks, one polypropylene and one wool; long underpants; wool pants; polypropylene undershirt; turtleneck wool sweater; wool shirt; a one-piece expedition suit (like a snowmobile suit); a thin pair of polypropylene gloves; and a wool hat.

In his pack he carried wool mittens with leather liners; down mittens; a big down jacket; a facemask; and overboots to cover the double insulated plastic mountaineering boots he was wearing.

He also carried chocolate; granola bars; gorp; a space blanket; a first-aid kit; matches; food; fire starter; a whistle; pencil and paper; a map; duct tape; a headlamp; a compass; and a canteen.

Lashed to his pack were crampons to give his boots the power to grip ice; an ice ax; a wide shovel; and snowshoes.

Cormier carried enough equipment it seems, to survive in outer space, but it was barely enough for that mountain this day.

Cormier is an accomplished mountain climber who can handle himself, yet when he speaks of the mountains and their power, he speaks softly.

"When you're hiking in very cold temperatures, it's a lot of work to stay alive," he explained. "You have to move slowly, because you don't want to sweat. If you sweat, you're signing your own warrant.

"You have to move slowly, but you can't stop. You're always wiggling your toes and wiggling your fingers (so blood will circulate). You have to pay attention."

Step by step, Cormier and Pelchat climbed the Caps Ridge Trail.

"The caps" are three false summits, or ridges, on the trail. The last cap ends just below the timberline—the spot where the weather turns so harsh that trees will not grow, and so there is nothing to buffer the wind.

Cormier heard the wind howling above the caps as he approached the timberline and he knew that he was about to step into the worst conditions he had ever seen.

Cormier and Pelchat stopped for a snack behind the second cap. Cormier unzipped a vent in his expedition suit and wiggled his gloved fingers through layers of clothing until he reached his undershirt, where he'd stashed a bar of chocolate. The chocolate was frozen hard as brick, so he smashed it to bite-sized pieces with his ice ax.

He pulled his insulated canteen from deep in his pack, where it had nested inside his down coat, but the canteen was useless; his water was ice.

Crampons—spikes strapped to boots—replaced snowshoes as Cormier and Pelchat crested the treeline. The wind hit with the roar of freight trains, punctuated by howls. The only other sound was the deep gasp of their own breathing.

It was so cold that vapor clouds of breath froze instantly, building icicles on Cormier's facemask. Communication was only possible through muffled shouts from inches away. Slowly, but steadily, Cormier and Pelchat stepped their way toward the ridge where Jeremy Haas said he had left Derek Tinkham at sunset the day before.

THE TREATMENT

While Cormier and Pelchat struggled up the Caps Ridge Trail toward the cairn where Tinkham lay, Jeremy Haas ate an enormous breakfast of blueberry pancakes and sausage inside the observation tower.

Patterson, the meteorologist keeping night-watch when Haas stumbled into the observatory on Saturday, checked Haas throughout the night. He slowly warmed Haas, first by wrapping him in blankets, then giving him mugs of hot chocolate, and hot orange Jell-O.

Dr. Jim Beattie, a pathologist, and his wife, Lyn, a registered nurse, volunteer their services to the nonprofit society that operates the Mount Washington observatory. They just happened to be on hand when Haas came knocking.

Beattie telephoned down to Littleton Hospital to get some tips from Dr. Harry McDade, a recognized authority on the treatment of frostbite. Cold destroys tissue by constricting the small blood vessels until blood can't flow through them. The tissue, robbed of nutrients and warm blood, stiffens.

When he pulled Haas's gloves off, Beattie saw fingers that were swollen, white and waxy. He followed McDade's orders and heated water to 105 degrees; he bathed Haas's hands in warm water and wrapped them in sterile gauze.

The job of bringing Haas back from hypothermia was trickier. Bill Aughton, the search coordinator, who lectures on hypothermia, said that cold kills people by sucking away heat faster than they can produce it.

First, the brain shuts down circulation to the feet and toes because it doesn't want to pump warm blood down there and have it come back cold. Circulation to the legs and arms slows as the brain tells the heart to direct precious warmth to the core organs.

Walking becomes difficult; simple tasks, such as pulling a zipper, are impossible. After a while, muscles don't even have the energy to shiver anymore. Blood pools, becoming acidic.

As the heartbeat slows, even the brain isn't getting all the blood it requires, and clear thinking is impossible. A person becomes lethargic, apathetic, indifferent to his plight.

When Haas came knocking on the observatory door he was showing signs of confusion and lethargy. As Beattie and Patterson warmed him, they took care not to warm him too quickly, as a sudden rush of cold, acidic blood could have shocked his heart.

"It took him a good while to come around," recalled Patterson. "He started shivering really bad, which was a good sign because he had the energy to shiver. It took a good hour to warm him up."

At daybreak, Haas feasted on pancakes as clouds cleared from the summit revealing the peak of Mount Jefferson, where Derek Tinkham lay.

The summit of Jefferson "looked like it was so close you could spit on it," recalled Royal Ford, a *Boston Globe* reporter who was on Mount Washington to write about the cold weather school.

Bad weather kept the group pinned in atop Mount Washington until Tuesday morning. During the next 48 hours, Ford, meteorologists, and the two stranded hikers learned enough of Haas's trek to piece together an account of what went wrong.

ESCAPE TO THE MOUNTAINS

Derek Tinkham dreamed of becoming a surgeon, and those who knew him say that he was gifted with the intelligence, dexterity and drive to realize the dream. He was an honors student at Narragansett High School, a champion wrestler and a member of Narragansett's elite surf-rescue team.

As part of his dream, Tinkham enrolled in the University of New Hampshire's pre-med program, in which he studied biology. He blossomed in college, bulking up from the 145 pounds he weighed in high school to nearly 200 pounds while maintaining an athlete's build.

Tinkham joined UNH's Sigma Nu fraternity, where a lot of the members were into mountain climbing. "When he came here, he was into his bike-racing phase," recalled Adam Doyle, who was Sigma Nu's "rush chairman" when Tinkham joined. "He was a great bike racer."

Tinkham turned his energy toward mountain climbing, and joined Sigma Nu members in building a climbing gym in a fraternity garage last fall. Tinkham helped hammer handholds into the garage's walls, and laid down wrestling mats so he'd have a safe place to land if he fell while climbing the walls.

Tinkham and Doyle escaped to the White Mountains whenever time and money allowed. They didn't own snowshoes but that didn't stop them from taking a winter hike in the mountains last year—they brought a big dog to break trail.

It was almost inevitable that Tinkham and Haas would find each other on the UNH campus, where both were juniors. When they met this fall, they discovered a shared passion for hiking.

In his freshman year, Haas was a member of the UNH Outing Club for a while. But in February 1992 he quit the Outing Club, after its leaders placed him on probation for being too demanding on members during a hike.

A month after he quit, he and fellow UNH student Chris Rose launched a winter climb to Mount Washington's summit. Rose lost all his toes to frostbite.

"Jeremy is definitely a prepared hiker, but he's definitely gung-ho," Outing Club President Susan Adams told the Associated Press. "He's very much into himself and into achieving his goal. Unfortunately, that attitude gets people hurt."

In October Haas and Tinkham told friends of their plans for a winter traverse of the Presidential Range.

Haas, who has declined interviews since he came down from the mountain, told Ford of *The Boston Globe* that he had warned Tinkham: "This is going to be the most difficult, the most painful thing you've ever experienced.

"I told Derek before we left that this is a life-or-death situation, that being up here in this kind of weather is such an individual effort that this is essentially a solo," Haas told the *Globe*. "Derek said this is something he very much wanted to experience."

'I WAS CONCERNED'

On Friday, Jan. 14, Tinkham's girlfriend, Jennifer Taylor, drove Tinkham and Haas from Durham to the Appalachian Mountain Club's lodge at Pinkham Notch, where the two hikers signed the log book before beginning their trek.

Under the heading "Trip Itinerary" Tinkham wrote: "Presidential Traverse, North South." For "Group Leader" he signed "Jen Tinkham," giving his girlfriend his last name, as if they were married.

When Tinkham signed the log, the temperature on Mount Washington was a balmy 13 degrees above zero, with winds at a mild 11 mph. But forecasters had been watching a polar air mass sweeping down from Alberta for the past week, and they were issuing severe forecasts for the next 48 hours—temperatures of 30 below, winds gusting to 80.

Chad Lewis, a 24-year-old worker at the lodge in Pinkham Notch, talked to Haas and Tinkham as they were signing the log. Lewis had planned to traverse the range with the pair. In fact, the initial plan was that Haas and Lewis would guide four less experienced hikers on a traverse of the range through its steepest ravines, using ice screws and ropes to scale frozen cliffs.

But one by one the other hikers dropped out; some couldn't get a ride, or the money, or, in Lewis's case, the time off from work.

"I gave them the forecast, and I emphasized it quite a bit," recalled Lewis. "I've gone hiking with Jeremy (Haas) and I know that when Jeremy sets a plan, he likes to stick with the plan. He told me he wanted to do a four-day bivouac."

A bivouac is tentless camping. Instead of using a tent, hikers wrap their sleeping bags in a bivouac sack and sleep beneath the stars. "It's questionable as to how wise a choice bivouacing was, given their experience," said Aughton, the search coordinator. "Bivouacing is a questionable way to do it. It's not a good way to spend a night for most people. You can't light a fire, you can't change your socks."

When Haas told Lewis his plans, Lewis asked him to leave a written day-by-day itinerary because, he said, "I was concerned."

'DEATH WEATHER'

Below the treeline the White Mountains in winter are a vision of heaven. Deep snow gives them the texture of whipping cream. Boulders become soft pillows. Sounds are muted by the snow. Wind in the frosted pines is a whisper, a caress.

Haas and Tinkham walked into this dreamy world about 3 p.m. Friday, Jan. 14. They walked about 50 yards up the Airline Trail before a yellow sign warned in capital letters that this trail that looked like heaven often led to hell:

TRY THIS TRAIL *ONLY* IF YOU ARE IN TOP PHYSICAL CONDITION, WELL CLOTHED AND CARRYING EXTRA CLOTHING AND FOOD. MANY HAVE DIED ABOVE TIMBERLINE FROM EXPOSURE. TURN BACK AT FIRST SIGN OF BAD WEATHER.

Haas and Tinkham trudged past.

On Friday Haas and Tinkham hiked until sunset, pitching their bags—rated as safe for sleeping at minus 10 degrees—and bivouac sacks just below the timberline along Durand Ridge.

From all accounts they spent a good night, though temperatures fell dramatically as the front from Alberta crashed into the mountains. At midnight the temperature was minus 6 degrees; when they awoke for breakfast six hours later, temperatures had plummeted to minus 18.

Haas and Tinkham fired up a pack stove and ate a hot breakfast before heading along the ridge about 8 a.m.—when the temperature was minus 24 with 40-mph winds, what Aughton describes as "death weather."

Despite the weather, Haas and Tinkham pushed on to the top of Mount Adams, the first mountain in the Presidential Range. They could have taken the Gulf Side Trail around the mountain, but they chose to go up and over it.

As they came down the mountain, they hiked straight into the northwest wind, to a place called Thunderstorm Junction. Four trails intersect at the junction, including Lowe's Path, which slopes 1,000 feet down to Gray Knob, where a winter caretaker keeps a fire burning in his cabin for cold hikers.

Peter Collins, a 29-year-old mountain climber from Quebec, sprained his ankle climbing Mount Washington on that frigid Saturday, and he limped into the observatory for emergency shelter. He was stranded atop the mountain with Haas for three days, and he and Haas spoke in depth.

Haas and Tinkham didn't hike down to the cabin, Collins said, because they didn't feel cold at that point. ("Impossible," said Aughton. "Given the temperatures and the clothes they had on, we know they must have been mildly hypothermic at this point.")

ONWARD

The two hikers decided to press on toward Sphinx Col, where they planned to bivouac for the night. A col is a flat spot between two ridges, and they're notorious for high winds that funnel through them.

About one mile beyond Thunderstorm Junction the trail forked, forcing Tinkham and Haas to make a choice: Go right, down Israel Ridge Path toward the Gray Knob Trail and shelter, or go left along the Gulfside Trail toward Edmands Col. They chose to go to the col. The temperature at noon was minus 24 degrees with 55-mph winds.

"When you step out of Edmands Col you're heading into the death zone," said Aughton. "We know damned well that's one hell of a place to be."

When they came through Edmands Col, Haas stopped to put on his heaviest coat. Tinkham chose not to, Haas told Collins, because Tinkham's coat was down and he feared it would make him sweat.

After Edmands Col the trail forked again: This time they could have stayed on Gulfside Trail, which runs along the lee side of Mount Jefferson, or climbed Mount Jefferson via Jefferson Loop. They chose to climb the mountain. ❨

Haas first recognized trouble near Jefferson's summit. The wind, gusting near 60 mph, frequently knocked Tinkham down. He'd get up, stumble and fall. Get up, stumble and fall. Haas told Tinkham to slip into his down coat, but he mumbled one-word answers to questions and refused to put on the coat.

When they reached the summit, Tinkham told Haas he thought he'd do better now, going down the mountain. But he didn't.

Five cairns from the south side of the Jefferson Loop Trail, Tinkham leaned close to Haas's ear and spoke a complete sentence above the roar of the wind: "I want to get into my bag," he said.

Haas nodded. He led Tinkham to a flat spot on the lee side of a boulder. Then he slipped off his outer pair of gloves to help an unresponsive Tinkham slide into his bag. He struggled with Tinkham and his bag until sunset, when the temperature hit minus 26 and the wind hit 86 mph. Then Haas shed all of his gear—his pack, sleeping bag, bivouac sack—and began a desperate nighttime climb for the summit of Mount Washington.

STUMBLING FOR HELP

Haas couldn't put his outer gloves back on because his hands were so stiff from trying to cover Tinkham. He crossed his arms over his chest and cradled his hands in his armpits.

Blowing snow and the onset of night cut Haas's visibility to 50 feet, just enough so he could see one cairn from the other. For three and a half hours, he focused on getting to the next cairn.

As he struck out from one cairn to the next, the wind frequently knocked him down. He'd stand, with his arms still wrapped around his chest, and stumble to the next cairn. He could only look up for brief snatches, for fear blowing snow would freeze his eyelids shut. He'd snatch a glance, stumble and fall. In this way, Jeremy Haas passed 400 cairns, remembering that he'd left his partner five cairns up the Jefferson Loop Trail.

Haas lost the Gulfside Trail near the summit, but he wandered onto the snow-covered tracks of the Cog Railway and followed them to the observatory. He circled the building pounding on doors and windows with his frozen hands. When he peered through a window he saw Jasper, the observatory cat, curled up snug on a bed while the winds shrieked in his ears.

REVERENCE

Nine rescuers from the Mountain Rescue Service caught up to Cormier and Pelchat about 11 a.m. Sunday, as they crested timberline on Caps Ridge Trail. The MRS climbers had planned to climb Mount Washington and retrace Haas's hike toward the Jefferson summit, but they abandoned that plan as suicidal.

The 11 rescuers gathered at the base of the Jefferson Loop Trail before heading up the trail side by side, where they hoped to find Derek Tinkham alive. As they climbed, a 90-mph gust knocked Pelchat off his feet and, in Cormier's words, "rolled him like a tumbleweed."

About 300 feet from the Jefferson summit, rescuers spotted a corner of Tinkham's red-and-black bivouac sack snapping in the wind. When they reached him, rescuers found Tinkham lying on his stomach with the sleeping bag covering just his legs. It was obvious that he'd been dead awhile.

"I think after Jeremy left him he just rolled over and never moved again, which is a blessing because I don't think he suffered," Aughton said.

When they knew he was dead, some members of the rescue team shouted that they should bail out, leave the body there and get back safely. But someone else yelled: "We're up here, we have the manpower, so let's go for it and see what happens."

In the end, Cormier said, it was "a reverence for the dead" that drove the rescue team to carry Tinkham's body down Caps Ridge Trail into the teeth of a freezing wind. Blowing snow packed onto the eyelids of rescuer Andy Orsini and built up there like rime frost, freezing his eyelids shut. Team members led a blinded Orsini down to the timberline while hauling Tinkham's body on a sled.

When the team reached the shelter of the second cap they gathered for chocolate and a hot drink. MRS volunteer Joe Lentini, who has climbed Mount McKinley, looked at the assembled group and said, "Be truthful, anybody been in worse conditions?" Not one hand went up.

Writers' Workshop

Talking Points

1) Carbone's stories are studded with vivid sensory impressions. Here is a particularly poetic example: "Below the treeline the White Mountains in winter are a vision of heaven. Deep snow gives them the texture of whipping cream. Boulders become soft pillows. Sounds are muted by the snow. Wind in the frosted pines is a whisper, a caress." Break down this paragraph and identify the various literary devices Carbone employs.

2) Organization is central to the success of a narrative. Carbone's editors noted how his Mount Washington story "is really several stories interwoven like a climber's rope." Notice how Carbone shifts between the climb Jeremy Haas makes to seek help for his companion and the rescue attempt.

3) Details ensure that we don't just read the story of the rescue on Mount Washington, we live through it. Witness how Carbone reveals just how cold it is: "Cormier unzipped a vent in his expedition suit and wiggled his gloved fingers through layers of clothing until he reached his undershirt, where he'd stashed a bar of chocolate. The chocolate was frozen hard as brick, so he smashed it to bite-sized pieces with his ice ax." Find other examples of resonant details and analyze their impact.

4) Carbone's details are not just lyrical and rich in specifics; they are purposeful and serve the news writer's need to inform as well as to entertain. There are several passages in the story that amount to a mountaineering primer, equipping the reader with the technical knowledge needed to go along on this suspenseful rescue. Study them.

Assignment Desk

1) Scenes are the bricks that storytellers use to build their powerful narratives. Isolate the scenes in Carbone's stories. On your next assignment, report and write a scene that incorporates sense of place, sense of people, sense of time, and sense of drama.

2) This story and Carbone's account of the surgery on a wounded state trooper focus on dramatic moments when life and death hang in the balance, revealing people at their most vulnerable and heroic. As you organize your stories, look, as Carbone does, for pivotal moments that make story beginnings dramatic and irresistible:

When things change.

When things will never be the same.

When things begin to fall apart.

When the ordinary becomes extraordinary.

3) One of the chief ways Carbone is able to lead the reader through this braided, technical narrative without interest flagging is by anticipating the reader's questions. For example, after the surviving hiker tells rescuers that he has left his companion "Five cairns up the Jefferson Loop Trail... Five cairns up," Carbone immediately explains that a "cairn is a slender pile of boulders stacked every 50 feet to mark trails above the treeline, where there is no place to hang a marker." Find similar examples in your own stories or incorporate this question-answer approach in your next ones.

4) Carbone is a writer fascinated with process, whether it is how hypothermia shuts down the body or what a mountain climber packs for a harrowing journey up a frozen mountain. Using Carbone's description of hypothermia as a guide, concisely describe a process: a Breathalyzer test, how search dogs find victims in a bombed building.

5) The search ends with the discovery of the hiker, frozen to death, but Carbone prolongs the narrative. Rewrite the ending by stopping at a different point. Discuss the merits of your and Carbone's choices.

6) Carbone says he writes "Sight," "Sound," "Smell" in his notebook and jots down his sensory impressions, often in prose that he places directly into his story, such as the description of the White Mountains in winter. Try that on your next reporting foray. Collect as many sensory impressions as possible.

Surgical team rescues trooper from death's door

Dr. Allen Leadbetter was sewing the final stitches in an emergency gall bladder operation when a nurse stepped into the operating room at Westerly Hospital with a terse message: E.R. called; there's an ambulance bringing in a state trooper. A trooper's been shot.

Leadbetter felt his heart kick up a notch. "How far away are they?" he asked.

"About five minutes."

"I'm going to go down there," Leadbetter told Russell Lenihan, his physician's assistant. "Get this patient over to the recovery room."

Leadbetter, dressed in the short sleeves and baggy pants of his surgeon's "greens," walked down the flight of stairs toward the emergency room. His mind raced but he didn't have much information to analyze. He recalled thinking: "God, I hope he's just grazed or something."

Leadbetter's hopes were in vain.

* * *

When he felt the bullet slam deep into his midsection, State Trooper John Lemont would later tell Leadbetter, it felt "like getting hit with a sledgehammer right in the gut, swung by Hulk Hogan with all his might."

Lemont staggered, was able to run back to his cruiser and—crouched behind an open door—squeezed almost a dozen shots into the fleeing red pickup truck he had stopped on Route 95 because its license plate looked stolen.

"Shots fired, shots fired!" the wounded trooper's voice crackled over the radio, shattering the calm of the autumn afternoon on Oct. 15 in Richmond. "Officer in need of medical assistance."

The urgency in Lemont's voice snapped Judy Sposato to attention in a tiny room of her Ashaway home, where she runs a dispatch center, directing volunteer firefighters and ambulance workers to local dramas great and small.

Sposato leaned toward the microphone in her console: "Hope Valley Ambulance, what's your location?" she said. "Start heading toward Exit 4 on 95, I don't know the exact location at this time. I'll update you when I have some more information."

Sposato logged the time of her call: 16:20, or 4:20 p.m.

For the 28-year-old Lemont the seconds had begun to drain away in what doctors call "the Golden Hour"—the crucial 60 minutes after a trauma which often mean the difference between life and death.

* * *

In his 25 years as a surgeon, Leadbetter has done his share of trauma surgery, but he doesn't enjoy it. The unknown, the unexpected that come with trauma—he doesn't like that at all. He knows doctors who left the business because they couldn't handle that kind of pressure.

Leadbetter stepped into Westerly Hospital's main trauma room, T1, and noted that all the monitoring equipment was in place and an empty litter was waiting for the trooper. More often than not, he assured himself, you get a call like this and it's something exaggerated and overblown; people get excited.

An oddity about hospital emergency rooms is that workers there never hear a siren. And this case was no different. The ambulance silenced its siren when it drew within the hospital's quiet zone, so its arrival wasn't announced until the doors slid open with a buzz and the attendants burst in.

With one glance at Lemont, Leadbetter knew his hopes for an exaggeration were dashed. Lemont was in agony.

* * *

Westerly Hospital was not Hope Valley Ambulance's first choice for trauma treatment. The small community hospital holds a Class 3 emergency room, which means that the only personnel who must be at the hospital 24 hours a day are an emergency room doctor and a nursing staff. Additional doctors are not mandatory, which often means a delay in assembling a surgical team.

But Rhode Island Hospital's big-city trauma center almost 30 miles away was out of the question: Lemont was southbound when he was shot, so the ambulance would have had to drive south to Exit 3 then turn around and head north, passing through a section where construction crews had pinched the highway to just one lane.

And thanks to a stroke of luck, Leadbetter, the surgeon on call, was already in the hospital.

Lemont's gurney came bursting through the door at 4:52 p.m., 32 minutes after he'd been hit, and a team of doctors, E.R. nurses, and respiratory therapists was already assembled, hovering over him. The torn, blood-soaked remnants of Lemont's uniform—gray with red piping—were heaped at his feet on the gurney.

The first doctor at Lemont's side was Russell Bingham, an emergency room doctor who—unlike Leadbetter—loves emergency medicine, saying he thrives on being a "whirligig doctor."

* * *

As Lemont writhed in pain, a series of questions immediately popped into Bingham's mind, and like a pilot preparing for takeoff, he ran through them:

How many bullet wounds are there? (One.) Did the bullet go all the way through the body? (It did.) Where's the entrance wound? The exit wound? Is there bone fragmentation? Bullet fragments? Blood in the urine?

Bingham called for nurses to sink two more intravenous needles, adding to the two that ambulance workers started; soon four bags of clear Ringer's lactate solution were leaking into Lemont's veins, replacing fluids that he may have been losing through bleeding deep in his gut.

A nurse stuck a tube into Lemont's nose, asking: "Can you swallow for me, John?" He swallowed, forcing the tube into his stomach so the doctors could decompress it for surgery.

Bingham believed that it was just as important to reassure Lemont as it was to ask questions about his condition. As a trooper, Lemont was used to being the one in charge of a crisis—but here he was on his back looking into bright lights as eight faces hovered above him, prodding him with needles and catheters as his life ebbed.

"You're in good hands," Bingham said. "You're in the hospital. Everything should be find. Dr. Leadbetter, the surgeon you're going to have, is great. He's going to take good care of you."

Bingham watched Lemont closely as he spoke to him, buoyed by what he saw: The trooper was in extraordinary shape—large chest, flat belly— good skin color. As important, his attitude was good.

"I could see that the pain was unbearable," Bingham said. "But it was clear that he wanted to make it. I got that feeling right off the bat. This guy wanted to walk away from this, it was obvious from the word go."

Madeline Martin, a respiratory therapist, placed an oxygen mask over Lemont's mouth and nose and cradled his head in her hands: "John, just take it easy, we're going to help you; hold on."

Lemont twisted his head from beneath the mask and vomited blood on the yellow walls and white tiles of the trauma room floor. For Bingham that set off alarm bells, signaling that something was terribly wrong.

* * *

Leadbetter looked at the entry wound—about 2 inches below the breastbone—the most vulnerable part of the body.

That's a bad spot, Leadbetter thought. Two previous patients he had with gunshot wounds there both died. It's bad because of what's underneath it: colon, liver, stomach, pancreas, duodenum, spleen, kidney, spine, spinal cord, aorta, vena cava—a lot of things that are extremely difficult to take care of.

There was no blood in the wound itself; blood doesn't squirt out when someone is shot. The visible wound was a neat pink hole the size of a penny.

Through the choreographed confusion of the E.R., Leadbetter ordered a catheter and two sets of X-rays: of the chest and the "KUB"—kidneys, ureter, bladder.

"Contrast," he barked. "Gotta have contrast."

E.R. technicians poured a thick, viscous compound into Lemont's veins through an IV tube. If his kidneys were working properly, they would process the iodinized compound within minutes and an outline of the kidneys would appear on X-ray film.

Lenihan, Leadbetter's assistant, had arrived from the gall bladder surgery and run the catheter to drain urine from Lemont's bladder into a clear plastic bag.

Leadbetter was anxious to see Lemont's urine. He was hoping it would be clear, a sign that the bullet had not injured the trooper's kidneys.

Don't let there be blood in there, he was thinking. No blood in the urine please, no blood in the urine.

But when the bag filled, it was purplish red. Okay, boys, Leadbetter thought, we're going to be in for it today.

Technicians developed the X-rays within minutes and posted them on a lighted background, first the lungs then the KUB. Leadbetter looked at the lungs—no problem there. (He would have been surprised if there were lung trouble, but you never can tell with a bullet wound. He once had a patient who was shot in the neck, and a piece of the spinal column had splintered, lodging way down in the aorta.)

Next he analyzed the KUB, which also showed Lemont's ribs, spinal column, and patterns outlining the liver, spleen, and intestines. There was no indication that the bullet had struck bone and no fragments of bone or bullet.

Leadbetter saw a clear image only of Lemont's right kidney. "I don't see the left one, take another picture," he ordered. For the third time, nurses lifted Lemont onto the inch-high cassette holding X-ray film; each time they moved him it was agony.

Again the film showed no left kidney. But Leadbetter did see a good right kidney, and that was a relief. A man can live a normal life with one kidney.

Lemont felt cold and clammy to the touch—a sign of shock—but all of his vital signs were good: the pulse was around 90, a little high but not bad given the circumstances. Blood pressure was strong, 110 over 70. Lemont was stable, ready for nurses to roll him through the corridors, onto the elevator, and up to the operating room at 5:18 p.m.

Thanks to a combination of good luck and practiced skill, Trooper John Lemont was on the operating room table 58 minutes into the Golden Hour.

* * *

Leadbetter scrubbed for surgery, breaking open a pack of "scrubbies"—a combination sponge and brush soaked in antiseptic fluid. He scrubbed all the way up to his elbows, taking care to wash between each finger, then repeating the washing once more for good measure.

He walked into the operating room, his hands held up so water dripped down the elbows and not toward his hands. Operating room technician Mary Siegel handed him a sterile towel, folded once the way he likes it, so he has four sterile sides instead of two.

Siegel has worked in Westerly Hospital's operating rooms for 21 years, so she's aware of Leadbetter's idiosyncracies. She laid out his gloves— one pair of size 7½'s and a pair of size 7's— Leadbetter likes to wear two pairs, but two size 7s pinch his hands and two 7½'s are too floppy.

Besides Leadbetter and Bingham, the doctor team included anesthesiologist Ching B. Huang and urologist Tobias Goodman.

Leadbetter, who has operated with these men hundreds of times, refers to Huang as "Huangy" and Goodman as "Toby." His assistant, Russell Lenihan, is "Rusty."

As Leadbetter pulled on his gloves, he was hoping that Lemont hadn't lost much blood. Then he glanced across the O.R. at the digital readout of the patient's blood pressure flashing on the wall and was stunned: Lemont's formerly healthy systolic blood pressure of 110 had dropped to 70 —a fatally low level.

"He's bleeding out, he's bleeding out!" Leadbetter yelled. "Get him down quickly! Prep him quickly, let's go!"

* * *

Lenihan swings into action, buzzing the hair off Lemont's stomach, then slathering him with a reddish-yellow surgical scrub. He piles sterilized sheets around Lemont's stomach to create a "sterile field"—a space above the patient in which only sterilized instruments may pass. Once a surgeon puts his hands in the sterile field he may not drop them below his waist, or put them behind his back, or turn his back to the field.

When Leadbetter steps to Lemont's side, he is immediately annoyed because Lenihan hasn't shaved Lemont's chest as well as his abdomen. He grabs the electric clippers and buzzes the hair off Lemont's chest right up over his nipples.

Lemont, falling under the spell of Dr. Huang's anesthetics, coughs, and for the first time, blood spills from his bullet wound.

"Knife!" Leadbetter orders. Siegel presses Leadbetter's scalpel into his hand. He begins with a standard incision, slicing the skin just below Lemont's breastbone, down around the bellybutton, and slashing over to the pubic bone.

As he cuts, he thinks about strategy: He's got to find the source of the bleeding and either tie it off or clamp it to restore the trooper's blood pressure.

Leadbetter doesn't even have to ask for his next tool, the bovie, it's on the table next to him. The bovie looks like a pencil that emits a beam that cuts through the fat layer beneath the skin.

With the skin and fat cut away, Leadbetter again asks for his scalpel: "Knife."

He cuts into the fascia, the layer of glistening tissue that holds Lemont's organs in place. As he cuts, blood gushes out—a lot of blood.

Leadbetter suctions it away, amazed at how much there is. All he can do now is react to what he sees.

Beneath the glare of the operating room lights, Leadbetter peers into Lemont's abdomen for a quick inventory: His liver is bleeding; his stomach is extended, completely filled with blood because of two holes piercing it; his pancreas is bruised from the shock of the bullet passing by; there is blood where the bullet ripped Lemont's duodenum; and blood is spouting from the hole where the bullet drilled through the muscles in his back.

It's obvious that Leadbetter's not going to be able to clamp all the torn blood vessels before Lemont bleeds to death. He must stem the blood flow at its source—he has to clamp the aorta, an artery from the heart that is thick as a garden hose.

"Toby, I'm going to clamp the aorta, I've got to get the aorta," he says.

Leadbetter can't see Lemont's aorta; he has to feel for it. He sticks his gloved hands behind Lemont's liver then turns up into his chest. He can feel the tube draining Lemont's stomach, but without any blood pressure the aorta is soft and flat and hard to find.

After half a dozen tries, Leadbetter feels a pulse—a little buzz—above the clamp but not below it, and he knows that he's clamped the aorta. But that brings no sense of relief; all Leadbetter has done is bought a little time. Lemont's blood supply is clamped off below the chest, so none of his organs is getting blood. A kidney can stand that for only 20 minutes before dying; then the spleen goes and other organs follow.

Leadbetter is standing there with his hands in a patient who has no blood pressure and multiple holes in his organs.

And time is running.

"I don't know if this kid's gonna make it," he tells Lenihan.

* * *

Lenihan, not a religious man, says a silent prayer: God, just let us find the bleeding and let John live.

A 1987 graduate of Yale University's rigorous physician's assistant program, Lenihan has never prayed in an operating room before—always satisfied with solving problems through analysis and technique. But he finds this case profoundly disturbing; he feels it merits divine intervention.

"You're working with a guy who doesn't deserve to be there (on the operating table)," Lenihan recalls. "You're dealing with a young, healthy guy who was working for his family and community—that could happen to me, or it could happen to anybody. It's just more likely to happen to a police officer."

* * *

Leadbetter peers in at the liver and sees that the bullet just nicked it, tearing an edge.

"Give me a two-oh chromic on an SH needle, and we're gonna figure-eight this," he says. Siegal hands him a pre-set stitch that he uses to repair the tear, careful not to tie it too tight lest he sever the liver.

The injury that scares Leadbetter the most is the torn duodenum, because if it leaks, Lemont is in big trouble. The duodenum is the mixing chamber between the stomach and large intestine—it takes in partially digested food from the stomach and mixes it with caustic digestive enzymes from the liver and pancreas.

It is these acidic enzymes that make it possible for people to eat fat and digest muscle; but these enzymes do not discriminate between food and human tissue, and if they leak into Lemont's surrounding organs, he will literally digest himself.

If Lemont lives, Leadbetter thinks, the duodenal injury has the most potential for causing long-term problems. But in the short-term, the duodenum is the least of Leadbetter's worries; that wound's not bleeding much and Leadbetter's priority is to stem the blood.

Leadbetter rolls Lemont's intestines back to inspect the damaged kidney. The little nook where the kidney bends round the renal hylum—a pouch with a vessel to drain urine—is a bloody mess. The bullet scored a direct hit on the renal hylum.

"Toby, this kidney's got to go, right? It's got to go," Leadbetter reasons, because how were they going to fix it with all the other problems: the hole in the duodenum, the holes in the stomach, the awful blood loss and the clamped aorta. "The kidney's gotta go."

But Goodman, the urologist, wants to mull this over. After a moment's pause, Goodman agrees that there are too many problems to stop and fix this.

The kidney has to go.

Leadbetter reaches his right hand behind the kidney and sweeps it loose to cut it out.

Lemont's blood pressure builds to a healthy level, and Leadbetter reaches back up into his chest to unclamp the aorta. Next he goes to work on the stomach, which is completely extended with blood. He pumps out a quart, quart-and-a-half. Then he staples off the two holes—piece of cake.

Again, Lemont's blood pressure plummets until the digital readout is flashing 70, mortally low.

"Get more into him Huangy, more blood, let's go!" Leadbetter barks. It would be a constant refrain for the next six or seven hours—more blood, more blood.

* * *

Before the operation is over, Huang, the anesthesiologist, will pour into Lemont's veins 27 bags of red blood cells to carry oxygen; 40 bags of platelets and 12 bags of plasma for coagulation; and 19 liters of salt solution.

Basically, all of the blood in Lemont's 185-pound body was replaced three times. When asked whether he had ever seen so much blood poured into one man in his 25 years of surgery Leadbetter responded: "In a patient who lived? No."

Leadbetter knew early on that he would exhaust Westerly Hospital's blood supply, so he placed an order with the Providence blood bank. After seeing all the blood in Lemont's stomach, he ordered more.

The problem was, no one had told the first driver that this delivery was urgent, so he was taking his time. Bingham made a remark, something about how he was surprised the State Police couldn't ship blood down faster than that for one of their own. And the troopers took it to heart.

Two troopers intercepted the second driver in Providence; one placed his cruiser behind the white blood car, and the first blared an escort from the front. They blew past the first driver on Route 95, completing the 40-mile run from Providence to Westerly in 19 minutes.

"When that driver came in," Bingham said with a smile in his voice, "I thought he was having an acute heart attack. He was perspiring heavily, breathing deeply—that man was a nervous wreck."

But the fact was, the blood arrived with little time to spare.

* * *

A crowd gathered in the corridor outside the operating room—about 40 troopers and local police, many in their uniforms, all awaiting word. Lemont's wife, Stephanie, 22, and his parents and father-in-law sat in the intensive care unit's waiting room, flanked by Governor Sundlun and State Police Col. Edmond S. Culhane Jr.

Lemont's mother, Meredith, showed nurse Abbot the photograph of her grandson, Sam, that she keeps on her keychain; Marjorie Sundlun, herself a trauma survivor, held Stephanie's wrists telling her that she's got to have faith in God.

"Mrs. Sundlun was very comforting to John's wife," Culhane said. "And the governor amazed me—he's not a young man you know, and he stood there that entire night."

A couple of hours into Lemont's surgery, circulating nurse Maureen MacDonald—the O.R. team's link to the outside world—strode into the

surgical theater and announced that Governor
Sundlun and his wife were in the lobby, along
with Culhane and dozens of police officers.

"That's when he (Lemont) became more than
just the organs," Leadbetter recalls. "You know
the governor and his wife are out in the lobby.
The trooper's wife and father and father-in-law,
50 troopers. The colonel. That was a bitch. How
are you going to tell these people he didn't make
it? You can't just keep pouring blood into him
forever—the bleeding has to stop or he's going to
die."

* * *

But with the kidney out and clamped, the stomach holes stapled, and the liver tied off, the bleeding still will not stop.

Every time that Leadbetter gets involved with
something—packing the hole in the back
muscles, stapling the stomach, reaching (for a
third time) to clamp the aorta, blood wells up
around Lemont's spleen.

Leadbetter suctions off the blood, looks away,
and there it is again pooling around the spleen.
The spleen is a delicate organ, a little bigger than
a baseball, reddish brown like the liver, but
rounder. It's an important organ in that it filters
impurities from the vast net of lymph nodes that
transports fluids throughout the body, and it helps
fight certain kinds of organisms, especially a bacterial pneumonia.

As far as Leadbetter knows, the bullet did not
damage the spleen, but a blood puddle keeps forming there—a pint every 15 minutes. Perhaps, Leadbetter suggests, it is an "iatrogenic injury" to the
spleen—that is, an injury caused by the surgeon.
He has, by necessity, been pretty rough on the organs, flopping over the intestines to get at the kidney, poking his fingers up into Lemont's chest.

There is only one way to rule out the spleen as
the cause of all this bleeding—take it out. So
Leadbetter takes a half-hour to cut out the spleen;
and still the hemorrhaging continues.

Leadbetter spots blood trickling down the outside of Lemont's aorta and he thinks maybe that's

it—perhaps he nicked the aorta while he was working around up there.

So Leadbetter makes a decision he will later regret—he decides to crack open Lemont's chest to have a better look at that aorta. He does not make this decision lightly because, in his own words, it requires an incision that is "horrendous" and painful. But if he does not stem this bleeding soon, Lemont will die.

Leadbetter cuts through Lemont's diaphragm, a thick muscle that encircles the body and basically powers the lungs. Then he saws through the chest, cracks it open, and discovers why the aorta appears to be bleeding. While clamping it he had poked a small space beside the aorta; each time Lemont breathes he inhales blood from his gut and it spatters through the hole before trickling down the aorta. Leadbetter realizes that this is not the source of the bleeding; the small hole will quickly repair itself.

Leadbetter has now ruled out the stomach, kidney, spleen, and aorta as the source of Lemont's bleeding. There's only one thing it can be—the hole in the thick muscle of the back. Initially this was the least likely source of the bleeding—soft tissue doesn't usually bleed like that, but through a process of elimination this must be the source.

Lenihan, the physician's assistant, packs a half-dozen large sponges into the hole, but they're quickly saturated. Trash bags full of blood-soaked sponges litter the floor. More dry sponges go in and more saturated sponges come out.

Lenihan has a reputation among his friends as being a tinkerer, someone who likes to jerry-rig things; the back of his motorcycle is held together with duct tape and bungee cord. And all of a sudden he has a thought—what if he slid a Foley catheter into the wound, then inflated the catheter's balloon? That could provide enough internal pressure to stem the bleeding.

Lenihan is aware of Leadbetter's quick temper; but he also knows that the surgeon is open to sensible solutions. Leadbetter is quick to anger only when you suggest something that indicates you're putting your own convenience before the patient's best interest, and this suggestion doesn't seem to fit that category.

So Lenihan floats his catheter idea. Leadbetter is cool to it, shrugging it off with a maybe. Lenihan does not mention it again. But after five more minutes of packing the wound in vain, Goodman says of the catheter idea: "Let's try it."

Leadbetter relents. Lenihan threads the catheter tube into the wound, then depresses the plunger on his syringe, until the tiny balloon is two-thirds full with saline solution, inflating it enough to pressure the wound. The bleeding stops. It is about 1 a.m.—8½ hours after the bullet tore through Lemont, 7½ hours after surgery began.

But Leadbetter is not through yet—he still has to repair the duodenum and put Lemont's chest back together. Leadbetter sews the duodenum shut with two rows of "Gambe" stitches—a fancy stitch that draws the two sides of the wound together so they meet in the middle, with neither flap pulled down below the other.

Leadbetter finishes the job, but it doesn't look right; it looks too tight, like the stitches are pinching the duodenum. He fears this will cause a blockage and subsequent leaks "upstream" toward the stomach, so he takes the extra time to unstitch the wound and do the job again.

Now Leadbetter begins stitching the diaphragm together, then the chest. "All the time I'm doing it I'm bitching about it," Leadbetter said later. "I wished I hadn't opened it."

In retrospect, Leadbetter said, there are a couple of things he wishes he hadn't done: removing Lemont's spleen; and opening the trooper's chest.

But given the context in which he made those decisions—a young man bleeding to death, time running out—he believes those were the right moves with the information available. Leadbetter feels comfortable enough with his decisions to talk about them publicly. And the bottom line is: He brought Lemont through alive.

* * *

Leadbetter sews his final stitch at 3 a.m., takes a hot shower, then steps into the waiting room to speak with the trooper's family:

"The bleeding is stopped—there was a tremendous amount of bleeding. And there were serious organ injuries as well. But," he says, "as long as the bleeding stays stopped I think he has a pretty good chance."

Lenihan wheels Lemont over to the intensive care unit, helping nurses hook the trooper to gauges that monitor blood pressure, heart rhythm, blood gases.

Lemont is in rough shape to be sure: He has a tube stuck through his chest; a feeding tube and a drainage tube; a tube in his bladder; and the catheter tube sealing the hole in his back. He is also hooked to two IV tubes and a respirator, breathing for him with a loud, rhythmic hiss.

Jan Salsich, the morning ICU nurse, squeezes Lemont's hand after sunrise. "You were hurt," she says. "You're in Westerly Hospital. Your family's all here."

She tries to think of positive things to tell him, to lift him out of his fog. "You've been through a lot of surgery and you're coming around and you're doing better now."

Lemont nods that he understands. Salsich and Lemont had small communications like that throughout the morning, but as the day wears on, it is obvious that Lemont is itching to pass on a more complicated message. But he cannot speak through the respirator.

Salsich invites Lemont's father, Paul—who is East Providence's city manager—into the surreal world of the ICU. She hands the trooper a pencil and a piece of paper so he could write what he wants to say.

The handwriting is firm as the trooper poses the question uppermost in his mind.

"Did I get him?"

Writers' Workshop

Talking Points

1) The narrative spine of this story is "what doctors call 'the Golden Hour'—the crucial 60 minutes after a trauma which often mean the difference between life and death." Study how Carbone brackets the hour. Debate whether the story could have begun and ended at different points.

2) A key element of this story revolves around the term "iatrogenic." What is the etymology of the word? Can you relate it to other occupations, including journalism?

3) "Paying attention," Carbone says, is a key element of his reporting. Consider what might have been lost from this story had Carbone not stopped Dr. Leadbetter to ask what he meant by "iatrogenic" injuries that occurred during the operation to save Trooper Lemont.

4) Keep in mind that Carbone was not present during the operation. Identify the elements in this story that make the reader feel like an eyewitness.

5) In a subtle way, Carbone gives away the ending of this story in paragraph seven. What's the giveaway? Does it affect the suspense of the story? Why or why not?

6) Screenwriters try to enter scenes as near the end as possible and leave at the moment of greatest suspense. Notice how Carbone breaks away from scenes in the middle of the action, and discuss how that heightens reader interest.

7) Midway through the story, Carbone shifts abruptly to present tense. Identify that point, how it affects the pace of the story, and provide a justification for the change.

8) Media critic Jon Katz observed, "Newspapers might begin to think about reversing their long-standing priorities, recognizing that everyone with electricity has access to more breaking news than they provide, faster than they provide it. They should, at last, accept that there is little of significance they get to tell us for the first time. They should stop hiding that fact and begin taking advantage of it. What they can do is explain news, analyze it, dig into the details

and opinions, capture people and stories in vivid writing—all in greater depth than other media. They should get about the business of doing so."

Discuss how Carbone's stories are in just that business and how they serve today's consumers of news.

9) Storytellers prepare the reader, doling out background at just the right moments. For example, notice how and when Carbone tells the reader the nicknames Leadbetter uses with the others in the operating room. Identify other examples from Carbone's stories.

Assignment Desk

1) Read Jon Katz's *Wired* magazine article, "Online or Not, Newspapers Suck" (Sept. 1994). Follow his path and conduct your own survey of electronic newspapers on America Online, Prodigy, CompuServe, or the World Wide Web. Stage a debate that pits Katz's observations against an opposing viewpoint.

2) The *Providence Journal-Bulletin* has a long and rich history of publishing narrative reconstructions. The paper has won ASNE awards for non-deadline writing twice before (Carol McCabe in 1980 and G. Wayne Miller in 1992). Read their winning entries and compare them with Carbone's stories. What elements—organization, diction, characterization—stand out?

3) Read *Doing Ethics in Journalism: A Handbook with Case Studies,* by Bob Steele, Jay Black, and Ralph Barney with an eye out for "iatrogenic injuries" caused by journalists.

4) Resolve to stop during your next interview when you hear a term you don't understand, no matter how stupid it feels, to ask for an explanation.

5) Rewrite sections of the story (or, if you are ambitious, the entire story) in present tense. What is the impact?

6) Remove the references to "iatrogenic" injuries and assess the impact on the story.

Is missing millionaire and dog fancier alive?

DECEMBER 27, 1994

HOPKINTON—She was born female, but she wore men's clothing and cultivated a mustache.

Nearly six feet tall, Camilla Lyman—she later changed her first name to the more masculine Cam—was a millionaire recluse with dual obsessions: entering her 58 show spaniels in dog competitions, and becoming a man.

Acquaintances have described her as being so insecure that even when she went to the store to buy milk, she carried at least $10,000 with her.

It was her wish that after she died, her ashes be scattered from an airplane over Madison Square Garden during the annual dog show of the Westminster Kennel Club.

But that wish remains unfulfilled, even though Lyman may indeed be dead—perhaps murdered.

In the summer of 1987, Lyman, then 54, vanished from her 40-acre country estate on Collins Road, so mysteriously that finding her has stymied a private detective agency that says it has never failed to locate a missing person in 8,000 attempts during its 47-year history.

Now, eccentric Cam Lyman has become the missing protagonist in a bizarre tale whose latest twist involves her trust funds, worth a reported $2.1 million. Her relatives—who are not mentioned in her will—have petitioned the town's Probate Court to declare her dead so they can inherit her holdings.

In the years since Lyman's disappearance, private investigators have combed records in all 50 states and Canada, and have probed "the cliquish and somewhat protective" subculture of European transvestites, only to come up empty-handed.

Private investigator Charles John Allen, president of Management Consultants, of Lexington, Mass., testified in Probate Court last Tuesday that "this has become somewhat of a crusade for us, because it's the first case in the history of this company that we haven't been successful with."

The Probate Court became involved because Lyman's sisters—Mary Margaret Goodale of Brooklin, Maine, and Edith F. Kuhn of California—want Judge Linda Urso to declare their sibling dead.

If the judge so rules, she'll then have to determine who inherits Lyman's multimillion-dollar estate—the two sisters and their nephews, or a North Kingstown man whom Lyman named as the sole beneficiary of her bizarre will.

Rhode Island law allows a judge to declare a person dead if he "has been absent from his usual place of residence and his whereabouts have been unknown" for more than four years. No one has heard from Lyman since a phone conversation she was having on July 18, 1987, was abruptly interrupted.

In her will, drafted Oct. 31, 1984, Lyman left all her money and land to George T. O'Neil, a tax accountant and show dog enthusiast who owns the Wicksfords kennel in North Kingstown. Lyman and O'Neil met on the dog show circuit.

In exchange for the $2.1 million in trusts plus land in Nova Scotia and the Hopkinton estate—Lyman required O'Neil to perform these tasks:

- Care for her 58 show dogs, mostly spaniels.
- Make a "suitable" donation to the Dog Museum of America in the name of Ricefields Jon, Lyman's champion show dog of the 1950s.
- Rent an airplane to spread her ashes over Madison Square Garden during the Westminster Kennel Club's annual dog show.

Stephen J. Reid Jr., a Providence lawyer representing Lyman's sisters, contended before Judge Urso Tuesday that Lyman died shortly after her disappearance and was most likely murdered.

But Urso postponed her decision until she can read reports that lawyers will submit to her next month, and review transcripts of Probate Court testimony given earlier this month by O'Neil and Lyman's sister, Mary Goodale.

The earlier testimony by O'Neil painted a portrait of Lyman as a "vulnerable" recluse who disregarded his warnings about the hazards of carrying around large sums of money.

Lyman lived in her hometown of Westwood, Mass., until 1984, when she moved to Hopkinton.

Her parents, Arthur T. Lyman and Margaret Rice Lyman, both came from wealthy New England families; each was a beneficiary of trusts that they passed onto their son, Arthur Jr., who recently died, and their three surviving daughters.

According to Mary Goodale's testimony, Lyman was "obsessed" with showing dogs from the time she was a teen.

She was especially close to her father, Goodale said, and she took it hard when he died in 1968. A few years after her father's death, Lyman began dressing like a man, privately at first. Later, she felt comfortable enough with the habit to wear a shirt and tie, and a man's suitcoat—size 42— while showing her dogs.

O'Neil testified that he and his wife met Lyman at a dog show in the late 1970s. Their friendship began when the O'Neils invited her into their motor home for a cup of tea, later developing to the point where Lyman gave O'Neil power of attorney over her assets.

In his testimony, O'Neil recalled a scene in Springfield, Mass., in the early 1980s, when she handed him an envelope and asked him to take care of it. He slit it open to find it stuffed with stock certificates worth $330,000.

In early 1984, he testified, Lyman called him, screaming over the phone that her home had been burglarized and she wanted to move away.

O'Neil said he arranged for her to buy an 11-room house on 40 acres on Collins Road in Hopkinton. For the next six months, Lyman lived in a mobile home parked in O'Neil's driveway while workers built a 20-run kennel on the Hopkinton land at a cost he puts at $500,000.

Lyman moved into her Hopkinton home in 1984, the same year she granted O'Neil power of attorney to handle all of her finances—checking, savings, bill payments. O'Neil said that Lyman was so obsessed with showing her spaniels that she didn't want to bother with chores like paying bills and making travel arrangements—he did all that for her.

O'Neil said Lyman didn't pay him for his services. He said he helped her "because she was good company," and that, from time to time, she gave him gifts that he declined to describe.

O'Neil said that Lyman was prone to "temper tantrums"—particularly if one of her dogs fared poorly in competition. "She was a poor loser. When she started throwing things around, I'd throw them right back at her. I was the only one who would do that," O'Neil said.

In fact, the last time anyone heard from Lyman, in the summer of 1987, she was in the throes of a tantrum. O'Neil had failed to register Lyman for a dog show in New Brunswick that she badly wanted to attend. It wasn't his fault—there was a mail strike in Canada at the time—but when he called her to break the news, Lyman was incensed.

O'Neil testified that he was trying to explain what happened when suddenly the phone went dead. He called back several times, but got no answer. So the next day—a Sunday, July 19—O'Neil drove to Hopkinton to see her.

When he arrived he found that her phone had been ripped out of the wall, and her attaché case stuffed with jewelry was gone along with the $200,000 in cash that she kept in the house.

Some of her clothes were also missing, but her car and mobile home were still in the driveway. All 58 dogs were there—some in the kennel, some outside, some unfed.

O'Neil said he didn't notify anyone of Lyman's disappearance because "it wasn't out of character." When she lived in Westwood, he said, she once disappeared for six months.

And besides, O'Neil said, for months after Lyman's disappearance he received strange phone calls: Someone would call and say nothing; he or his wife, assuming that the caller was Lyman, would talk about how her dogs were doing—which ones were winning on the show circuit—

and the silent caller stayed on the line until he or his wife stopped talking.

So instead of going to the authorities, O'Neil said, he chose to maintain Lyman's home, dogs, and kennel with money from her accounts. Even today, O'Neil pays a Hopkinton couple a stipend to maintain the kennel. O'Neil said he gave most of the show dogs to other New England kennels, with the caveat that the animals be returned if Lyman returns. O'Neil still keeps two of Lyman's retired spaniels at his kennel, and one dog still lives on Lyman's property.

Reid, the lawyer for Lyman's sister, told Judge Urso Tuesday that violence had occurred at Lyman's estate on July 18, 1987:

"We've got a phone ripped off the wall, dogs in a condition she would never leave them in," Reid said. "The clothes are missing, the money's missing, her jewelry's missing. Wherever she went, she walked or someone took her there. Someone ripped the phone off the wall so she couldn't call for help. Someone who knew she carried large sums of money. Maybe someone victimized her, we don't know. The only person who can tell us is not here."

Lyman's sisters grew concerned around Christmas of 1987, because several people close to her said she hadn't sent her yearly Christmas card. The sisters contacted trust administrators, who then began to ask questions about her whereabouts. Allen, the private investigator, said that a trust administrator hired him to find Lyman in August 1988, beginning a search that brought him to dog shows, to Canada—and to Europe, to check on a tip that Lyman had left the country to have a sex change operation.

Despite 1,500 hours of searching and $33,000 in fees, Allen said he could turn up nothing conclusive.

So, Allen said, he feels that Lyman is dead. "You would really have to be a master spy, someone very high up in the CIA, to disappear without a trace," he said.

Allen's best lead came in 1989, when he learned that hunters in Chester County, Pa., had found a decomposed body in a ditch on Halloween 1987. The corpse was that of a muscular woman, about 6 feet tall, wearing men's clothing—including a size 42 suitcoat.

Allen sought dental records, to compare Lyman's teeth with those of the corpse. But Lyman feared dentists, Allen learned; there were no records. An artist drew a composite sketch of the dead woman's face, but Lyman's siblings were unable to identify the corpse. Pennsylvania authorities buried the body on Christmas Eve 1989, Allen said.

"My opinion is that she is deceased and she's probably been deceased since the time of her disappearance," said Allen. "Because from that time on there has been no information—no information of her existing or living.... She's not leaving any of the trails that a person would leave leading a life."

Writers' Workshop

Talking Points

1) The lead of this story about the missing millionaire contains an example of foreshadowing, a literary device popular with fiction writers that provides both suspense and satisfaction by hinting at what will come later. Study the lead: "She was born female, but she wore men's clothing and cultivated a mustache," and find the two other points in the story where Carbone returns to the detail of Camilla Lyman's affinity for men's clothes.

2) The first four paragraphs of this story furnish an excellent example of what has become a necessary cliché of writing teachers—show, don't tell. Consider the value of Carbone's catalog of bizarre behavior and defend it to the editor who demands a lead that gets to the story quicker.

3) Like the best journalists, Carbone is a gifted synthesizer, weaving related information into richly detailed sentences that draw from several sources. "In the summer of 1987, Lyman, then 54, vanished from her 40-acre country estate on Collins Road, so mysteriously that finding her has stymied a private detective agency that says it has never failed to locate a missing person in 8,000 attempts during its 47-year history." Transform this paragraph into a list and consider where and how Carbone obtained the information.

4) "The flattest story in the world is one that doesn't have enough quotes in it because that's where the breathing comes from and the life comes from," says Donna Britt, columnist for *The Washington Post* and 1994 ASNE winner for commentary. For this story, Carbone sat through a court session on this case and had access to the transcript of a previous hearing. But he was selective in his use of quotes, varying them in length and completeness. Compare their placement with the way you use quotes in your own stories.

Assignment Desk

1) Do what Carbone did to get this story. Visit a public agency or institution in your community that gets little attention from reporters—probate court, paternity court—and

ask the clerks if there are any interesting cases that haven't been reported. Report and write the most interesting one they tell you about.

2) Identify and itemize the sources—people, documents, interviews, and observations—that Carbone drew on to write this story. On average, how many different sources of information contribute to your reporting and writing? How often do you read stories that are based on a single source? Resolve to avoid that in your own stories.

3) There are many ways to tell the same story. Is there another way to tell this story so it doesn't take five paragraphs before the reader learns Camilla Lyman is missing under mysterious circumstances? Write the lead.

4) Carbone concludes the story with the grisly discovery of a body in a size 42 suit that tantalizes the reader with the hope that the missing millionaire has been found at last. But that hope is dashed, leaving the mystery unsolved in chilling fashion. Consider why Carbone gives the last word to the private detective and rewrite the ending without him in a way that still leaves the reader wondering.

5) Rewrite this story as a 200-word brief. Do your best to retain the sense of mystery.

A conversation with
Gerald M. Carbone

CHRISTOPHER SCANLAN: What's your job at the *Providence Journal-Bulletin*?

GERALD M. CARBONE: I have a title, bureau manager, but I'm the only reporter in a one-person bureau, so I kind of manage myself.

Where is your bureau?

Westerly, Rhode Island. It's a nice town to look at; the downtown is on the National Register of Historic Places, and I've got a wide river right out the back of my window. It's a small town newspaper office, really, even though it's part of a big metropolitan daily.

What do you do as bureau manager?

Basically, I write stories of the Westerly-Chariho area. Chariho stands for Charlestown, Richmond, and Hopkinton.

How do you see your responsibilities?

I've given up the idea of being the paper of record in every town, like we used to try to be. Our responsibilities now are to get the bigger stories— preferably first—but if not, the best, the most in depth.

I try to get in at least a couple of times a week to read the police log in Westerly, make daily cop checks. We don't attend all the meetings in town the way we used to, but we try to keep a handle on what's coming out of those meetings by monitoring the papers that do go all the time. So, you basically look for daily coverage of this area, but occasionally I'll get a week to do something fun.

Is that what these three stories represent?

Every one of them was done in five days. Five days to report and write.

Did you feel you were writing on a deadline?

Absolutely on two of them. I mean I was told, "We need to have a look Friday afternoon. You have to get us something." So even though it wasn't deadline writing in the sense of it all being done in one day, I really felt like there wasn't a lot of time to stretch things out. It was pretty compressed. In fact, all of them were done within the same week, except for the one on Trooper Lemont. I actually got to begin that one on a Friday.

To tell you the truth I wasn't too thrilled with the idea, because I thought the State of Rhode Island had seen enough of Trooper Lemont and his guts. I didn't really think there was going to be that much more interest. But my editor, Phil Kukielski, was convinced that there was. So I figured I'd try to get out of it by calling the Westerly Hospital and saying, "Look, I've got this idea for a story, but you've got to give me access like you're not used to giving people or we can't do it." And I thought they would say, "Oh, no, we can't give you that kind of access to the doctor and what goes on in the operating room." But they said sure.

So then my interest in the story perked up. I was thinking, well, maybe it *can* work. I really feared that what I was going to get was some pablum from medical professionals who couldn't reveal certain things, in which case you really couldn't write the story.

What have you found useful in meeting deadlines and doing it with such quality?

Interviewing is key. My first interview was on a Friday with Dr. Leadbetter, who as it turns out, is a great person to interview because he had the smarts to pick up on the fact that there was no detail that was too small. He would say, "Well, I scrubbed up," and I'd say, "What do you use?"

and he'd say, "Well, a scrubby," and I'd say, "What's a scrubby look like?" He volunteered the detail about using two gloves. I would have thought that they all came in one size, kind of like a condom or something, but he volunteered that: "Oh, I use two sizes of gloves." It's rare that you get a person that is so good at being interviewed.

Why is no detail too insignificant to you?

In a story like that, it's basically narrative reconstruction, and you want to reconstruct it as if you were there or ideally, as if the reader is there. In order to do that, you've got to be able to look around that room or that mountain or wherever you happen to be and see what was there. You try to piece together those details to make a larger picture.

My initial goal with Leadbetter was to do a two-hour interview, then break, and then come back and do it again. When we got through with the two hours, he said, "No, let's continue." We talked, I think, three and a half hours, and when I was done, I could begin to feel the fission in that notebook. I was thinking, "Yeah, I've got something here."

The *Journal* was giving me two weeks to do this story. This was a Friday. I was going to have the following week and the week after that. So I was pretty happy, I thought I had some time and some material.

Monday I called up Westerly Hospital. I said, "OK, great, who can I talk to next?" And then the PR person said, "Oh, time out. The hospital's CEO really hasn't signed off on this yet." My theory is that Dr. Leadbetter was so candid that they got a little bit squirrelly about their exposure. She says, "I can't get you any more interviews today; talk to me tomorrow." And then Providence called and said, "We want the story for this Sunday. You don't have two weeks, you've got one." So I'm starting to get squeezed on both ends. Tuesday comes, I called the hospital again and they said, "No."

It wasn't until Wednesday that things resumed
and I had to give them a story by Friday lunchtime.

So you did no interviews on Monday?

I was kind of nervous, so I went out into the community and started talking to the police dispatcher
that handled the call and the ambulance drivers
and stuff like that. And I wrote this rather lengthy
scene about Lemont getting shot and the trip to
the hospital, and I became kind of wedded to that
scene. It wasn't very good, but it wasn't horrible.

I included that scene in my first draft of the final story. It began with him getting shot and the
ride to the hospital. And the first editor, Gerry
Goldstein, tightened it up, made it a little better.
And then every editor that looked at it down the
line said, "Gee, the story's a little slow getting
started," and they took a stab at making that scene
better.

I thought that I had a big mess on my hands on
Saturday morning.

So I called up Sue Areson, the Sunday editor,
and I was ready to freak out. And Sue was very
strong willed. It was kind of like, "Stop acting
like a baby. If you've got a problem, let's address
it." That's not what she said, but that was her general tone, which is what I needed. So I took a stab
at the first scene.

After about an hour and a half, the first scene
was still in there and then I worked on the rest of
the story, tightening it up. I sent Sue the story at
about 6 p.m., maybe a little after, and this is for
the next day's newspaper.

I left the office and I was sticking my car key
into the door and it was just starting to drizzle,
and all of a sudden, it was like a light bulb. I said,
"I like the story when we get to the hospital." As
a reader, that's when I began to like the story.

So I called up Sue and said, "If I had this story
to do over again, I would just take out that whole
scene about him getting shot and getting him to
the hospital. It begins to get good in the hospital."

And I thought she was going to say, "Ged, shut up and go home. It's 6:30. I have a Sunday newspaper to get out here." But much to my surprise, she said, "Well, what critical information would you lose if you did that?" And there were some things—just the fact that someone had been shot. And so we assessed that, and then I went through and hit the Delete key for 12 inches and just started it off in the hospital.

When did you begin writing the story?

I really started writing it on Wednesday evening and I wrote pretty much all day Thursday. What's nice about being in a small office like this— there's me and an office assistant—is I can come in and she will deal with a lot of the traffic while I just drink up the coffee and start whittling and writing.

What lesson do you draw from that experience of putting the key in your car door and saying, "Hey, wait a minute"? Is there a lesson for writers in what happened that night?

Yeah, I think so, and it's basically not to let the pride of authorship force you into including something that doesn't belong, that isn't necessary. Don't get wedded to your stuff just because you wrote it.

Is there a lesson in terms of where a writer should begin a story?

Read your story as a reader. I love to read. I think that's why I like to write, because maybe if I do something good, it gives me something good to read. As a reader, I could tell that my interest didn't pick up until I got to the hospital and that just seemed like the natural place for that story to begin. This was a story about what happened at Westerly Hospital; it wasn't a story about what happened on a road out in Richmond.

It sounds like you needed to go through this whole process before you made that discovery.

Normally, that isn't so because I will have done all my reporting before I sit down to write, and I think you're more likely to find the natural place to begin carving your information when you've got a big block of it.

Let me ask you about this block business.

I'm talking symbolically. Let's call it a big cube of information. You might look at it as a block of marble. And you step back and you eye up that information and look for the natural fault lines and cleavage planes and try to use them to shape the telling of the story. And when you don't have all that, you've got to kind of write as you go. And I think when you write as you go, there is the danger of false pride in the scenes that you should let go of.

Are you talking about something that's in a notebook or something in your head?

Mental, but drawn from what's in your notebook.

You had some roadblocks thrown in your way by the hospital. What did you tell the desk back in Providence?

"Keep it on the budget for Sunday because you want it and I think I can get it."

And how were you feeling?

Oh, definitely nervous. I don't get the chance to do a Page One Sunday breakout all that often. It isn't like in baseball—you come to the plate and you're one for three and everybody's happy. When you get a chance to do a good story, you'd better be batting about a thousand if you want to get the next one.

Do you like that pressure?

Yeah, I do. There's a part of me that still thinks that newspaper writing isn't real writing, that the real literati are fiction writers and poets, and that we're sort of second-class writers. The fact that I still get a thrill out of going to a fire—there's a snobbish part of me that looks down on that—but I do—I still do get a thrill out of sucking down coffee and eating Doritos and just banging things out.

When I asked Dr. Leadbetter early in our interview, "Do you like trauma surgery?" I thought his answer was going to be, "Well, of course." And he said, "No, I hate it," which really surprised me. After I talked to the man for a while, I realized a surgeon would have to be insane to like trauma surgery, that's not the ideal way to be going about helping someone's health, to be under the gun and making decisions without all the information you'd like to have.

But deadline writing isn't trauma surgery. If I don't do it exact, nobody dies. And so even though I could feel the weight of tons of newsprint vibrating on the roll, getting ready to go on Sunday, and I've got to get my stuff on board there, it isn't the same kind of pressure that Dr. Leadbetter feels on doing trauma surgery.

So I can allow myself to enjoy this kind of almost self-imposed pressure a little bit and get a thrill out of the rush of it, whereas he can't and doesn't.

I decided to take a perverse pride in delivering a miracle. It's almost like fighting someone much bigger than you. If you lose, you don't look like an idiot.

Let me ask you about the conversation with the dispatcher you quote early on. Where did you get that dialogue?

I drove out there and sat down with her and she didn't have any tapes. "OK, what did you say, what did you do?" And basically what you see in there is her recollection of what she said.

That brings up the whole question of attribution. Should I have said, " 'Hope Valley Ambulance, what's your location,' Sposato said she said." I can see leaving out that kind of attribution. We have a very good editor, Hillary Horton, who will not let you get away with that. She wants to know, as a reader and editor, where the information is coming from. And I tend to push it a little bit.

Why do you do that?

When you're writing on a word processor, a lot of times there will be little computer codes in the text that you can see on the screen, but when it's printed, you don't see it, because you don't want that computer code gumming things up. And it seems to me that a lot of attribution tends to be like that computer code: It's best left invisible so that it doesn't get in the way of a story. There are certain kinds of stories you obviously can't do that with. But in a narrative reconstruction, if you really know where the information's coming from and that it's accurate, your reader is going to extend you a little trust and isn't going to demand to know, and in fact they're going to prefer that you don't put in too much attribution because it's going to slow things down.

How do you respond to people like the editor you mentioned, who wants it there and believes the reader deserves it?

I think that both that editor and I have the readers' best interests in mind, and I think we're doing the readers a service by not bogging down their reading of the story. I just don't think anybody's going to get through a 120-inch feature when you're slowing them down with unnecessary attribution.

The *St. Petersburg Times* will frequently display a box with narrative reconstructions that

will say the story is based on interviews, court records, and the reporter's observations. What might you say in a box accompanying the story about the operation on the trooper?

"This story was reconstructed from interviews and observations of people who were there."

In "The Legend on the License," an essay John Hersey wrote in *The Yale Review,* he said "There is one sacred rule of journalism. The writer must not invent. The legend on the license must read: NONE OF THIS WAS MADE UP." What is the license that readers grant you?

The license to drive them into this scene without the necessity for back seat driving or explaining everything that I'm about to do or that they're about to see. It's not really poetic license, but it's reportorial license I guess is what they're granting me, to report what happened, without them needing to know exactly where every single thing came from.

Do you think about this when you're writing?

Absolutely. If you didn't, you'd be a dangerous writer. I think I can talk to a doctor five weeks after the operation and ask him some of the routine things he said, or ask other people who were in that room with him what they heard, or do both, and when you hear the same sentences, then I think you can legitimize those sentences by putting quotation marks around them and give them that extra oomph of authority. But I don't think you can do that 20 years later.

Why do you want to recreate it?

Because in the tedium of our lives, there are moments that shine, that are crucibles, that have the possibility to turn into pearls. And this is one of those moments where from pain, you get pearls, and it is worth examining those times.

And what are the literary tools you use to do that?

Scenes held together by tension.

How do you get such a precise retelling: "Lemont, falling under the spell of Dr. Wang's anesthetics, coughs, and for the first time, blood spills from his bullet wound." Are there questions that help you get this kind of material?

When I'm doing an interview, I'm trying to picture what's going on. I want to hear it and I want to smell it and I want to know what the textures are. I'll actually ask people that: "OK, what did it feel like when it...,"

There was in me an almost unnatural curiosity of what a bullet wound looks like. They told me, "Well, you know, it isn't like what you see on TV." Typically, it was a little pink circle. And it was Bingham, the ER doctor, who explained to me that there was no blood until he coughed and then some came out and that was revealing to him because now he knew he had some serious internal bleeding. Where you get something like that is from curiosity.

How many times did you interview Leadbetter?

Once.

Did you talk to him again?

Briefly, to ask him if he would be willing to look at a graphic we were putting together and he said he would. There's no way I would have let him see the story. That's what I tell people. I say, "It's the *Journal*'s policy that the only person that edits the story is the editor." There's no such formal policy, but, damn straight, it's the policy. You don't want people going back in there and changing what they said to what they wish they had said.

Did you get it all right?

Yeah. I guess there were no iatrogenic injuries.

One thing I was proud of there was in the reporting when he was talking about the spleen and he said, "iatrogenically caused," and then he kept on going. And I actually flirted with the idea of nodding and pretending that I knew what that meant. But if I had, I would have missed a key thing, which was he thought that he had caused the injury. So I said, "Wait a minute, what's that ten-dollar word?" and he kind of smiled and said, "Oh, no, here comes a malpractice suit." And then he described to me that he thought perhaps he had injured the spleen, so, therefore, he was going to remove the spleen to determine whether it had been injured. And I really applaud him for his candor.

But if I hadn't stopped to say, "Hold it, what are you trying to tell me?" when he said "iatrogenically," if I had just let that slip by, I might never have understood what he was trying to tell me.

Is that a lesson you had to learn the hard way?

Yeah. When you sit down and look at your notes and you don't have it—I mean every reporter, particularly when you're just starting out, finds himself saying, "Oh, God, I've got to call this person back because I need to know..." And I really didn't have time to be making those kinds of follow-up phone calls here. I had to get as much of it right as possible the first time.

Where did you learn that details were so critical to this kind of writing?

It's weird. I decided in fourth or fifth grade that if I and somebody else were going to be looking at something, that I was going to see more. I just decided that, I don't know why. So I've kind of cultivated it.

What's the reason for being so specific, like when you say the doctors used "clear Ringer's lactate solution"?

The voice of a story has to ring true, and the authority is in the details. J. Anthony Lukas talked about using telling detail tellingly, not just using it for the sake of throwing it in to show how clever you are or that you did your homework, but to put it in places where it's going to enhance your story. And at the University of New Hampshire, John Yount used to talk about the importance of authority. When a reader sits down to read something, he wants to feel like he's in good hands, that the disembodied voice talking to him is an authority. And what gives you authority or credibility is well-used detail.

Did you interview Trooper Lemont for this story?

He didn't mind everybody else talking to me, but he didn't want to.

Did you hear from the doctor after the piece ran?

I heard from the hospital; they loved it. Everybody said that the doctor was satisfied with it, too.

What's your job with this story?

To inform, educate, and entertain.

You're giving people an update about a news event that happened in their town. "Here's some information that you didn't know."

And I think you educate them on what goes on inside of a hospital. They might see the hospital every day when they drive by it, and now you're taking them beyond the walls. As a reader, I like a story to tell me something I didn't know, and I think that this story tells people something they didn't know about how you're put together and how fragile you really are; that a hole the size of a penny going through you can do an awful lot of damage.

As for entertainment, well, you're not going to inform or educate readers if they don't get through the story, so basically you're trying to give them something to pass the time. "Here's something for you to do on Sunday morning. Have a look at this. And while you're at it, maybe you'll learn something you didn't know."

What looms largest of those three in terms of challenge?

Entertainment. How do you make it interesting? I think that's a challenge for the news business that we're not meeting very well. And in that desire to make it entertaining, we're forgetting the important tenets of educating and informing as far as the proliferation of tabloid journalism. It's empty entertainment without providing education and information. People still are turning to their serious newspapers for that, and it would be a mistake to abandon that role. But we also are obliged to do it in an entertaining way.

How do you make it so entertaining?

It is a conscious effort to do it. I guess one device that I use is what Joel Rawson [deputy executive editor] calls the spine, but I prefer to call a carrot. Ideally, the carrot is something you stick in front of the reader's nose—a little tension, a little piece of drama, a little conflict. And then you'd have a whole bunch of scenes and stuff and let them bite into that carrot until the very end. But it's kind of hard to have a carrot that you don't resolve for 120 inches. So what you do within each scene is begin it with a little carrot, then you have the characters going about their business as they work towards this resolution, then you reward the reader with a resolution, and then you move on to another scene and do it again.

What you need to do is establish a little tension and resolution in multiple places throughout a longer piece.

Do you formally plot out these stories?

No. I think this is the part where I'm kind of lucky, because I think all writers work hard and then we spend a lot of time thinking about writing when we're not doing it. I'm just lucky when it comes to the structure of a big piece, because I couldn't write an outline to save my life. If I committed to an outline, it would screw it up, it would make it rigid, and I need fluidity.

But on these stories, when I sat down to write, I basically knew where they were going.

So how do you go about writing?

Generally, it's like Humpty Dumpty said, I begin at the beginning, go on until I come to the end, and then stop. That's generally how I do it, but not always. Sometimes, there's a scene that just nags at me, I know it's good and I want to get it on the screen. That's the beauty of working with VDTs now. I can just write in that scene and insert it wherever and whenever I want.

Do you have to have a lead first?

I think the weakness in both the mountain and the Lemont stories is the lead. Carl Sessions Stepp recently came up to do a workshop on lead writing and he swears by the grab-them-by-the-throat lead, in which case maybe, "Shots fired, shots fired," would have been a better lead. But I hope that the reader would indulge me just a little bit, long enough to establish a scene. What I'm looking for in the beginning is a rather critical scene,

a time when the events are about to get hairy. It's
sort of the moment when you know you're going
to go over the waterfall.

**How long does it take you to write an 80- to
120-inch story? Is it one sitting?**

Both the Lemont and the mountain story were
two sittings. When I'm really happy with something on the notepad, those are really, truly the
best hours of my life, they really are. I mean
there's some tension there, but it's a good tension.
And, really, the good stories, the Lemont surgery
and the mountain, they truly are the finest hours
of my life because they're productive and they're
producing work that hopefully is good and it's
nice to actually be doing that.

I can remember the Lemont thing, and I believe
in the mountain one, too, I was writing uncon-
sciously in 40-minute blocks. I didn't say, "OK,
I'm now going to write for 40 minutes." What I
would do is I would write for 40 minutes and I'd
look up at the clock and say, "Well, I think I'll go
a little bit more, but I'll take a little break and then
I'll do maybe another half-hour and I'll go
home." I think I was originally targeting to go
home at 6:30 and got out the door about 9:30, so
I did several more of these blocks than I had anticipated doing.

**How did you get on the story about the moun-
tain climbers?**

It was basically a breaking news story. We had a
local kid who was dead on the mountain. I happened to be in the mountains the day that he died
and I didn't even know. It was super cold and I
was skiing up in Jackson, New Hampshire, with
my wife. We got to a place where you could see
the summit of Mount Washington and I pointed to
the meteorological station up there and I told her
what it was. I said, "It seems like every newspaper in New England every once in a while goes up

there and does a winter on Mount Washington story and I'd sure like a chance to do that, but it's been done so many times, it's kind of a cliché." Then I drove back home, went to work Monday morning, and "Oh, you've got to go to New Hampshire." So I had to get in my car, pick up the photographer, turn around, and go back up there.

The storm was on us and by the time I got to Portsmouth, we could see the cars coming down the Spalding Turnpike from the mountains with snow all over them. We asked people how it was and they said, "Don't try it." So that was a day wasted.

Tuesday morning, we finally got rolling, but the story seemed jinxed from the start because we finally figured out where Jeremy Haas would be coming down in the Snowcat. We rushed over there and we had missed him by like 90 seconds. The ambulance was literally driving away as we pulled up. It was an ugly beginning. So now I had to start talking to as many people as I could and I wanted to do as much in person as I could.

I did meet the meteorologists as they were milling around after they had dropped off Haas. And they said that I couldn't come back up the mountain with them because they just weren't expecting me and weren't geared for that. So I said, "Can I call you later up on the mountain," and they said sure, and that made me feel better. Then I went back down to Pinkham Notch where the lodge is. And I ran into Peter Collins, one of the mountain climbers who also had been stranded on top of the mountain with Jeremy for two days. And I really pumped him for information. I had him tell me everything, his story, and what it was like for him to be on the mountain, and what he had to go through to be up there.

I really grilled him, and also Bill Aughton. I bought a map and spread it out on this large cafeteria table and had both Aughton and Collins reconstructing what they knew of the trip, and they knew quite a bit.

When do you decide what narrative you will tell and what your characters will tell?

In the scene, it will always be the character; if the character's speaking, it's going to have quotes around it. But in the narrative, it's almost verbatim what's on my notepad of them telling me, with the quotes stripped away.

Why do you do that?

Because then you're telling the story in their voice and it's their story.

In 1985, I won the UPI Feature Writing Award for a White Mountain rescue story. I went back and I reread that story and it's all quotes. You know, sometimes I think that I'm no better at this kind of writing now than I was in my late 20s, but something like that is a reminder that you do improve, because I feel a little more comfortable with kicking off the quotation marks and making the sentences a little more readable, more confident in my ability to tell a story.

So how long were you up on the mountain?

I spent Tuesday night there, at Pinkham, and we came back Wednesday, and I went to a Providence College basketball game Wednesday night.

And when did you write?

Thursday.

You're an incredibly efficient reporter. If you had said you worked on this story for three weeks, I wouldn't have been surprised. Where did you get the detail about the mountain having "the worst weather on earth"?

I was standing at the Pinkham Notch Gift Center, waiting for something. And it was so damned cold out, you couldn't go outdoors. They had a book in there called *The Worst Weather on Earth.* So I started reading it and I said, "Well, hell, I'm going to start taking some notes out of this book."

There's a beautiful passage in here, "Below the treeline, the White Mountains in winter are a vision of heaven. Deep snow gives them the texture of whipping cream. Boulders become soft pillows. Sounds are muted by the snow. Wind in the frosted pines is a whisper, a caress."

Yeah, I just lifted that out of my notebook. I looked around and I said, "OK, what do you see?" and I just wrote it right down. I will always write down "Sight," and I'll look around and see what I'm seeing; and I'll write down "Sound," and then "Smell" or "Scent." And Tom Heslin [managing editor for investigations] suggested I add "Texture," and I'll do that frequently.

How did you organize this story?

I knew I wanted an opening scene that would introduce that something was wrong here. And then I knew I wanted to let people know that this mountain is a bear, not only in the winter, but also in the summer, because I thought that was really a redeeming part of this story. Hopefully it isn't just a voyeuristic peak at a tragedy, that there's a lesson here, and I knew I wanted to get in some stuff with Cormier and the rescue team.

You sort of block it out in your mind, how it's going to go, how you think it's going to go. And if it's working, you continue to follow that; and if it isn't, then you have the flexibility to change it around.

Do you find when you're writing, there are holes you have to fill and you have to call to check things or get more?

As you get more experience as a reporter, you have to make those follow-up calls less.

How do you keep from overlooking it at the moment?

You just keep thinking and asking yourself, "Do I have the raw materials to say what I need to say, what needs to be said? Do I have them?" And if you don't, what are you missing, and then you ask for it.

By Wednesday, I had a notebook full of great stuff and I knew it, I mean I was feeling the fission, I could feel that this notebook had some good stuff in it and I was very happy.

Can we talk a bit about your educational background?

I was in public school grades one through nine, prep school grades 10 and 11, and they kicked me out my senior year and I went back to Georgetown.

It was a tough place for me to be because I had just changed to that school when I was 15 and I got cancer and, in fact, had to have my thumb amputated, which they thought would keep the cancer away. But it didn't; it came back in a year and started marching up my arm and I could see tumors in my arm. It was kind of difficult to concentrate on homework, you know, when they told me I had three months to live.

What kind of cancer was it?

Some kind of a sarcoma, a lymph thing. It never did kill me. They wanted to chop my arm off and I said no. They already got my thumb, they weren't going to have my arm. So then they said, "Well, we'll give you chemo and your hair will fall out, you'll puke," and of course, having chemo was really primitive 20 years ago in the early '70s, so I passed on that, too.

My stepfather was a psychiatrist, and he knew this cancer researcher from M.I.T. who recommended I go to Switzerland. I went over there to the Lukakis Clinic near Basel and they have this extract of mistletoe. And they also really promoted a vegetarian vegan diet, and I thought that was so weird. I mean I wanted to check out of there as fast as I could and go eat Wiener schnitzel. And, of course, now I'm a strict vegetarian, but it took me a while to realize that that's a good healthy diet.

I still don't know if it was a misdiagnosis, the mistletoe, or a miracle, you know, one of those three. I don't know why I didn't die, but...

How did that influence your life as a writer?

That's when I decided I wanted to be a writer, really. When I was 14, before I ever had the cancer, I pictured myself being a hotel magnate. I was going to open a chain called Hospitality Hotels. I thought that was a good idea because hotels are always in nice places, so I'd get to live in a nice place and make a lot of money.

Then I got the cancer, and I guess even a 15-year-old reassesses what's important, and writing was important to me. And I thought at the time it was important to me because I wanted to leave a written record that I was here. But I know now that even writing gets crumbled into dusty tomes, and it isn't leaving the record that is important. It was Andre Dubus who pointed it out to us on one of our first days at Bradford College. He said, "We write not so that we'll be alive after we're dead, but so that we won't die while we're still living." And what he meant by that was that you write so that you pay attention while you're alive. I mean in order for you to write, you've got to pay attention, and by writing, you aren't letting yourself die.

So that's how that affected me. It gave me a desire to pay attention to my life and to record it, not so that there's a written record of it after I'm gone, but so that it's good while I've got it.

Why don't you tell readers about Andre Dubus.

He's a fiction writer who grew up in Louisiana. He became a Marine captain and then, at some point in his life, decided that wasn't really what he wanted to be doing, and he gave up the relative comforts of that to become a fiction writer, which was a very courageous thing to do, to turn in your uniform and your government-issued paycheck and write, while you're trying to raise a family. But he did it on the faith that he had the talent. And it wasn't easy, but ultimately, he was recognized as one of the best short story writers that our country's produced in this century.

A few years ago, he stopped to help a motorist at night and a car plowed into him and just ripped up both his legs. He lost one of them and the other one is useless. But he's writing again, you know, he's still writing because that's what he does. He's a writer.

One thing that he taught me is that writers are made, not born. He compared a writer to an Olympic athlete. You turn on your TV in the summer and you see the Olympic weightlifter there and he's throwing a whole bunch of weight over his head. And you know that he didn't just wake up one day with the ability to do that, you know that he's put in the time, that he's been in the gym, that this is what he thinks about, this is what he tailors his diet towards, this is who he is.

And a writer is the same way I think. You're not going to wake up one day and write the great American novel. You're going to do it letter by letter, sentence by sentence, writing frequently, and often not well, and eventually, if you're lucky, you're going to write something good. But Andre said you've got to work on it to do it well. He impressed upon us that if you don't think about it, then you aren't a writer. You can't just walk around and say, "I'm a writer." It's a state of mind.

And studying with him, even though he's a fiction writer for the most part, helped me a lot as a non-fiction writer because it taught me how to think like a writer. It taught me how to pay attention.

How did you get onto the story about Cam Lyman, the missing heiress?

At the *Journal,* besides having outside speakers come to talk to us, our own reporters will occasionally host a workshop. Tracy Breton was hosting one on how to cover the courts. And one thing Tracy said was, "There's a lot of neat things that go on in probate court that nobody ever gets." And so I was talking to the Hopkinton town clerk one day over the phone, and I parroted what Tracy said: "I bet there's a lot of interesting stuff that goes on in probate court." And she said, "Well, as a matter of fact, there is. We've got one right now..." and my ears just kind of perked up. She wouldn't tell me what because she's kind of a reticent New England type. But she said, "If you want to know more, you come in and look at the file." And so I did and I found out when the next hearing was going to be and I attended it.

How much revision do you do?

I kind of do it as I'm writing. I'll write a scene and I'll read the scene and I'll go through it, and then I'll write another scene and I'll read the first scene and that one. Then I'll write a third scene and I'll read all three, you know. So I don't know how many times I will read one of my scenes before the button's pushed on it.

A lot of times, because my wife is very interested in what's keeping me here until 10 o'clock at night, I'll do a printout so I can bring it home and either read it to her or else she will read it.

You read your story aloud to her?

I've done that, and that's helpful. When you're reading out loud, you know where a sentence begins to get awkward because you've got to get your mouth around it. And if it's gone on longer than it ought to or if it's got an unfortunate rhyme or alliteration that isn't good, your tongue will trip over it.

What would you tell somebody who said, "I'd like to do some good work in my bureau. What's your advice?"

This sounds corny, but the other day, I saw a headline that said, "Attitude is everything in career." I don't cop a Pollyanna attitude. I think anyone who knows me knows I'm a fairly skeptical person. But by the same token, I do think that if you sit around and complain about how bad things are, that becomes a self-fulfilling prophecy and that it's best really, instead of worrying about the opportunities you're not getting, to worry about the ones that you *are* getting and do the most with them. In fact, it becomes doubly important that you do that as there become fewer of them.

So, basically, seize the ones you've got and don't worry about the ones you don't have, because you can't control those.

There are sacrifices you make by being a reporter. People want to get into this field because they think they'll have some influence over what goes on, but you almost give up your ability to influence what goes on and agree to become a chronicler of it.

That's what you sacrifice. What do you gain?

The opportunity to see things that other people aren't going to see. I've been under the water in a nuclear submarine and I've been in a Newfoundland fishing village and I've talked to a doctor about being inside somebody's guts in the surgical suite. And most people don't get those opportunities. I basically get paid to go interesting places and that's not a bad job. It more than balances.

Ron Suskind

Finalist, Non-Deadline Writing

Ron Suskind is senior national affairs reporter in the Washington bureau of *The Wall Street Journal* where he writes about social, political, and economic issues in the United States. He was born in Kingston, N.Y., and raised in Wilmington, Del. He received a bachelor's degree with distinction from the University of Virginia and a master's degree from Columbia University Graduate School of Journalism. After running political campaigns for several years, he worked at *The New York Times,* the *St. Petersburg Times,* and was the editor of *Boston Business* magazine. For six years, he taught advanced journalism at Harvard University summer school. He has also been a commentator on National Public Radio's Boston affiliate. His freelance articles have appeared in *Harper's* and *The New York Times Magazine.* Suskind joined *The Wall Street Journal*'s Boston bureau in 1990, covering banking, finance, and general interest topics.

"Against All Odds," Suskind's indelible portrait of Cedric Jennings, a black Washington, D.C., high school student who dreams of attending M.I.T., and a sequel, "Class Struggle," drew nationwide attention to the plight of minority youth struggling for achievement by touching readers with their blend of empathy and literary skill. For these stories, Suskind also was awarded the Pulitzer Prize for feature writing.

Against all odds: In rough city school, top students struggle to learn–and escape

Cedric Jennings eyes M.I.T., but obstacles are steep; failure rules at Ballou

Physics labs, death threats

MAY 26, 1994

WASHINGTON—Recently, a student was shot dead by a classmate during lunch period outside Frank W. Ballou Senior High. It didn't come as much of a surprise to anyone at the school, in this city's most crime-infested ward. Just during the current school year, one boy was hacked by a student with an ax, a girl was badly wounded in a knife fight with another female student, five fires were set by arsonists, and an unidentified body was dumped next to the parking lot.

But all is quiet in the echoing hallways at 7:15 a.m., long before classes start on a spring morning. The only sound comes from the computer lab, where 16-year-old Cedric Jennings is already at work on an extra-credit project, a program to bill patients at a hospital. Later, he will work on his science-fair project, a chemical analysis of acid rain.

He arrives every day this early and often doesn't leave until dark. The high-school junior with the perfect grades has big dreams: He wants to go to Massachusetts Institute of Technology.

Cedric is one of a handful of honor students at Ballou, where the dropout rate is well into double digits and just 80 students out of more than 1,350 currently boast an average of B or better. They are a lonely lot. Cedric has almost no friends. Tall, gangly and unabashedly ambitious, he is a frequent target in a place where bullies belong to gangs and use guns; his life has been threatened more than once. He eats lunch in a classroom many days, plowing through extra work that he has asked for. "It's the only way I'll be able to compete with kids from other, harder schools," he says.

The arduous odyssey of Cedric and other top students shows how the street culture that dominates Ballou drags down anyone who seeks to do well. Just to get an ordinary education—the kind most teens take for granted—these students must take extraordinary measures. Much of their academic education must come outside of regular classes altogether: Little gets accomplished during the day in a place where attendance is sporadic, some fellow students read at only a fifth-grade level, and some stay in lower grades for years, leaving hardened, 18-year-old sophomores mixing with new arrivals.

'CROWD CONTROL'

"So much of what goes on here is crowd control," says Mahmood Dorosti, a math teacher. The few top students "have to put themselves on something like an independent-study course to really learn—which is an awful lot to ask of a teenager."

It has been this way as long as Cedric can remember. When he was a toddler, his mother, Barbara Jennings, reluctantly quit her clerical job and went on welfare for a few years so she could start her boy on a straight and narrow path. She took him to museums, read him books, took him on nature walks. She brought him to church four times each week, and warned him about the drug dealers on the corner. Cedric learned to loathe those dealers—especially the one who was his father.

Barbara Jennings, now 47, already had two daughters, her first born while she was in high school. Cedric, she vowed, would lead a different life. "You're a special boy," she would tell her son. "You have to see things far from here, far from this place. And someday, you'll get the kind of respect that a real man earns."

Cedric became a latch-key child at the age of five, when his mother went back to work. She filled her boy's head with visions of the Ivy

League, bringing him home a Harvard sweat shirt while he was in junior high. Every day after school, after double-locking the door behind him, he would study, dream of becoming an engineer living in a big house—and gaze at the dealers just outside his window stashing their cocaine in the alley.

SEDUCED BY FAILURE

Ballou High, a tired sprawl of '60s-era brick and steel, rises up from a blighted landscape of housing projects and rundown stores. Failure is pervasive here, even seductive. Some 836 sophomores enrolled last September—and 172 were gone by Thanksgiving. The junior class numbers only 399. The senior class, a paltry 240. "We don't know much about where the dropouts go," says Reginald Ballard, the assistant principal. "Use your imagination. Dead. Jail. Drugs."

On a recent afternoon, a raucous crowd of students fills the gymnasium for an assembly. Administrators here are often forced into bizarre games of cat and mouse with their students, and today is no exception: To lure everyone here, the school has brought in former Washington Mayor Marion Barry, several disk jockeys from a black radio station and a rhythm-and-blues singer.

A major reason for the assembly, though, has been kept a secret: to hand out academic awards to top students. Few of the winners would show up voluntarily to endure the sneers of classmates. When one hapless teen's name is called, a teacher must run to the bleachers and order him down as some in the crowd jeer "Nerd!"

The announcer moves on to the next honoree: "Cedric Jennings! Cedric Jennings!" Heads turn expectantly, but Cedric is nowhere to be seen. Someone must have tipped him off, worries Mr. Ballard. "It sends a terrible message," he says, "that doing well here means you better not show your face."

Cedric, at the moment, is holed up in a chemistry classroom. He often retreats here. It is his private sanctuary, the one place at Ballou where he feels completely safe, and where he spends hours talking with his mentor, chemistry teacher Clarence Taylor. Cedric later will insist he simply didn't know about the assembly—but he readily admits he hid out during a similar assembly last year even though he was supposed to get a $100 prize: "I just couldn't take it, the abuse."

Mr. Taylor, the teacher, has made Cedric's education something of a personal mission. He gives Cedric extra-credit assignments, like working on a sophisticated computer program that taps into weather satellites. He arranges trips, like a visit with scientists at the National Aeronautics and Space Administration. He challenges him with impromptu drills; Cedric can reel off all 109 elements of the periodic table by memory in three minutes, 39 seconds.

Most importantly, earlier this year, after Cedric's mother heard about an M.I.T. summer scholarship program for minority high schoolers, Mr. Taylor helped him apply.

Now, Cedric is pinning all of his hopes on getting into the program. Last year, it bootstrapped most of its participants into the M.I.T. freshman class, where the majority performed extremely well. It is Cedric's ticket out of this place, the culmination of everything that he has worked for his whole life.

"You can tell the difference between the ones who have hope and those who don't," says Mr. Taylor. "Cedric has it—the capacity to hope."

* * *

That capacity is fast being drummed out of some others in the dwindling circle of honor students at Ballou. Teachers have a name for what goes on here. The "crab bucket syndrome," they call it: When one crab tries to climb from a bucket, the others pull it back down.

Just take a glance at Phillip Atkins, 17, who was a top student in junior high, but who has let his grades slide into the C range. These days he goes by the nickname "Blunt," street talk for a thick marijuana cigarette, a "personal favorite" he says he enjoys with a "40-ouncer" of beer. He has perfected a dead-eyed stare, a trademark of the gang leaders he admires.

Phillip, now a junior, used to be something of a bookworm. At the housing project where he lives with both parents and his seven siblings, he read voraciously, especially about history. He still likes to read, though he would never tell that to the menacing crowd he hangs around with now.

Being openly smart, as Cedric is, "will make you a target, which is crazy at a place like Ballou," Phillip explains to his 15-year-old sister Alicia and her friend Octavia Hooks, both sophomore honor students, as they drive to apply for a summer-jobs program for disadvantaged youths. "The best way to avoid trouble," he says, "is to never get all the answers right on a test."

Alicia and Octavia nod along. "At least one wrong," Octavia says quietly, almost to herself.

Cedric tries never to get any wrong. His average this year is better than perfect: 4.02, thanks to an A+ in English. He takes the most advanced courses he can, including physics and computer science. "If you're smart, show it," he says. "Don't hide."

At school, though, Cedric's blatant studiousness seems to attract nothing but abuse. When Cedric recently told a girl in his math class that he would tutor her as long as she stopped copying his answers, she responded with physical threats—possibly to be carried out by a boyfriend. Earlier, one of the school's tougher students stopped him in the hallway and threatened to shoot him.

The police who are permanently stationed at the school say Ballou's code of behavior is much like that of a prison: Someone like Cedric who is "disrespected" and doesn't retaliate is vulnerable.

Worse, Cedric is worried that he is putting himself through all this for nothing. Scores are in, and Cedric has gotten a startling low 750 out of a possible 1600 on his PSATs, the pretest before the Scholastic Aptitude Test that colleges require. He is sure his chances of getting into the M.I.T. program, where average scores are far higher, are scuttled.

He admits that he panicked during the test, racing ahead, often guessing, and finishing early. He vows to do better next time. "I'm going to do better on the real SATs; I've got to," he says, working in Mr. Taylor's room on a computer program that offers drills and practice tests. "I've got no choice."

At his daily SAT Preparation class—where Cedric is the only one of 17 students to have completed last night's homework—Cedric leads one group of students in a practice exercise; Phillip leads another. Cedric races through the questions recklessly, ignoring his groupmates, one of whom protests faintly, "He won't let us do any." Phillip and his group don't bother trying. They cheat, looking up answers in the back of the book.

Janet Johns-Gibson, the class teacher, announces that one Ballou student who took the SAT scored a 1050. An unspectacular result almost anyplace else, but here the class swoons in amazement. "Cedric will do better than that," sneers Phillip. "He's such a brain." Cedric winces.

In truth, Cedric may not be the smartest student in his class. In a filthy boys room reeking of urine, Delante Coleman, a 17-year-old junior known as "Head," is describing life at the top. Head is the leader of Trenton Park Crew, a gang, and says he and "about 15 of my boys who back me up" enjoy "fine buggies," including a Lexus, and "money, which we get from wherever." There is a dark side, of course, like the murder last summer of the gang's previous leader, Head's best friend, by a rival thug from across town. The teen was found in his bed with a dozen bullet holes through his body.

But Head still feels invincible. "I'm not one, I'm many," says the 5-foot-3, 140-pound plug of a teenager. "Safety, in this neighborhood, is about being part of a group."

Head's grades are barely passing, in the D range. Yet Christopher Grimm, a physics teacher, knows a secret about Head: As a sophomore, he scored above 12th-grade-level nationally on the math section of a standardized basic-skills test. That's the same score Cedric got.

"How d'you find that out?" barks Head when confronted with this information. "Well, yeah, that's, umm, why I'm so good with money."

For sport, Head and his group like to toy with the "goodies," honor students like Cedric who carry books home and walk alone. "Everyone knows they're trying to be white, get ahead in the white man's world," he says, his voice turning bitter. "In a way, that's a little bit of disrespect to the rest of us."

Phillip tests even better than Head, his two F's in the latest quarter notwithstanding. On the basic-skills test, both he and Cedric hit a combined score—averaging English, math and other disciplines—of 12.9, putting both in the top 10% nationwide. But no one seems to pay attention to that, least of all Phillip's teachers, who mostly see him as a class clown. "Thought no one knew that," Phillip says, when a visitor mentions his scores.

Heading over to McDonald's after school, Phillip is joined by his sister Alicia and her friend Octavia, both top students a grade behind him. Over Big Macs and Cokes, the talk shifts to the future. "Well, I'm going to college," says Alicia coolly, staring down Phillip. "And then I'm going to be something like an executive secretary, running an office."

"Yeah, I'm going to college, too," says Phillip, looking away.

"Very funny, you going to college," snaps Alicia. "Get real."

"Well, I am."

"Get a life, Phillip, you got no chance."

"You've got nothing," he says, starting to yell. "Just your books. My life is after school."

"You got no life," she shouts back. "Nothing!"

The table falls silent, and everyone quietly finishes eating. But later, alone, Phillip admits that, no, there won't be any college. He has long since given up on the dreams he used to have when he and his father would spin a globe and talk about traveling the world. "I'm not really sure what happens from here," he says softly, sitting on the stone steps overlooking the track behind the school. "All I know is what I do now. I act stupid."

Phillip of late has become the cruelest of all of Cedric's tormentors. The two got into a scuffle recently—or at least Phillip decked Cedric, who didn't retaliate. A few days after the McDonald's blowup, Phillip and a friend bump into Cedric. "He thinks he's so smart," Phillip says. "You know, I'm as smart as he is." The friend laughs. He thinks it's a joke.

* * *

Cedric is on edge. He should be hearing from M.I.T. about the summer program any day now, and he isn't optimistic. In physics class, he gamely tries to concentrate on his daily worksheet. The worksheet is a core educational tool at Ballou: Attendance is too irregular, and books too scarce, to actually teach many lessons during class, some teachers say. Often, worksheets are just the previous day's homework, and Cedric finishes them quickly.

Today, though, he runs into trouble. Spotting a girl copying his work, he confronts her. The class erupts in catcalls, jeering at Cedric until the teacher removes him from the room. "I put in a lot of hours, a lot of time, to get everything just right," he says, from his exile in an adjoining lab area. "I shouldn't just give it away."

His mentor, Mr. Taylor, urges him to ignore the others. "I tell him he's in a long, harrowing race, a marathon, and he can't listen to what's being yelled at him from the sidelines," he says. "I tell him those people on the sideline are already out of the race."

But Cedric sometimes wishes he was more like those people. Recently, he asked his mother for a pair of extra-baggy, khaki-colored pants—a style made popular by Snoop Doggy Dogg, the rap star who was charged last year with murder. But "my mother said no way, that it symbolizes things, bad things, and bad people," he reports later, lingering in a stairwell. "I mean, I've gotta live."

Unable to shake his malaise, he wanders the halls after the school day ends, too distracted to concentrate on his usual extra-credit work. "Why am I doing this, working like a maniac?" he asks.

He stretches out his big hands, palms open. "Look at me. I'm not gonna make it. What's the point in even trying?"

* * *

Outside Phillip's house in the projects, his father, Israel Atkins, is holding forth on the problem of shooting too high. A lyrically articulate man who conducts prayer sessions at his home on weekends, he gives this advice to his eight children: Hoping for too much in this world can be dangerous.

"I see so many kids around here who are told they can be anything, who then run into almost inevitable disappointment, and all that hope turns into anger," he says one day, a few hours after finishing the night shift at his job cleaning rental cars. "Next thing, they're saying, 'See, I got it anyway—got it my way, by hustling—the fancy car, the cash.' And then they're lost.

"Set goals so they're attainable, so you can get some security, I tell my kids. Then keep focused on what success is all about: being close to God and appreciating life's simpler virtues."

Mr. Atkins is skeptical about a tentative—and maybe last—stab at achievement that Phillip is making: tap dancing. Phillip has taken a course offered at school, and is spending hours practicing for an upcoming show in a small theater at the city's John F. Kennedy Center for Performing Arts. His teacher, trying hard to encourage him, pronounces him "enormously gifted."

At Ballou, teachers desperate to find ways to motivate poor achievers often make such grand pronouncements. They will pick a characteristic and inflate it into a career path. So the hallways are filled with the next Carl Lewis, the next Bill Cosby, the next Michael Jackson.

But to Phillip's father, all this is nonsense. "Tap dancing will not get him a job," he says. It is all, he adds, part of the "problem of kids getting involved in these sorts of things, getting their heads full of all kinds of crazy notions."

* * *

As Cedric settles into his chair in history class, the teacher's discussion of the Great Depression echoes across 20 desks—only one other of which is filled.

But Cedric has other things on his mind. As soon as school is over, he seeks out his chemistry teacher Mr. Taylor. He isn't going to enter a city-wide science fair with his acid-rain project after all, he says. What's more, he is withdrawing from a program in which he would link up with a mentor, such as an Environmental Protection Agency employee, to prepare a project on the environment. Last year, Cedric had won third prize with his project on asbestos hazards. Mr. Taylor is at a loss as his star student slips out the door.

"I'm tired, I'm going home," Cedric murmurs. He walks grimly past a stairwell covered with graffiti: "HEAD LIVES."

The path may not get any easier. Not long after Cedric leaves, Joanne Camero, last year's salutatorian, stops by Mr. Taylor's chemistry classroom, looking despondent. Now a freshman at George Washington University, she has realized, she admits, "that the road from here keeps getting steeper."

The skills it took to make it through Ballou—focusing on nothing but academics, having no social life, and working closely with a few teachers—left Joanne ill-prepared for college, she says. There, professors are distant figures, and students flit easily from academics to socializing, something she never learned to do.

"I'm already worn out," she says. Her grades are poor and she has few friends. Tentatively, she admits that she is thinking about dropping out and transferring to a less rigorous college.

As she talks about past triumphs in high school, it becomes clear that for many of Ballou's honor students, perfect grades are an attempt to redeem imperfect lives—lives torn by poverty, by violence, by broken families. In Cedric's case, Mr. Taylor says later, the pursuit of flawless grades is a way to try to force his father to respect him, even to apologize to him. "I tell him it can't be," Mr. Taylor says. "That he must forgive that man that he tries so hard to hate."

* * *

Behind a forest of razor wire at a prison in Lorton, Va., Cedric Gilliam emerges into a visiting area. At 44 years old, he looks startlingly familiar, an older picture of his son. He has been in prison for nine years, serving a 12- to 36-year sentence for armed robbery.

When Cedric's mother became pregnant, "I told her...if you have the baby, you won't be seeing me again," Mr. Gilliam recalls, his voice flat. "So she said she'd have an abortion. But I messed up by not going down to the clinic with her. That was my mistake, you see, and she couldn't go through with it."

For years, Mr. Gilliam refused to publicly acknowledge that Cedric was his son, until his progeny had grown into a boy bearing the same wide, easy grin as his dad. One day, they met at a relative's apartment, in an encounter young Cedric recalls vividly. "And I ran to him and hugged him and said 'Daddy.' I just remember that I was so happy."

Not long afterward, Mr. Gilliam went to jail. The two have had infrequent contact since then. But their relationship, always strained, reached a breaking point last year when a fight ended with Mr. Gilliam threatening his son, "I'll blow your brains out."

Now, in the spare prison visiting room, Mr. Gilliam says his son has been on his mind constantly since then. "I've dialed the number a hundred times, but I keep hanging up," he says. "I know Cedric doesn't get, you know, that kind of respect from the other guys, and that used to bother me. But now I see all he's accomplished, and I'm proud of him, and I love him. I just don't know how to say it."

His son is skeptical. "By the time he's ready to say he loves me and all, it will be too late," Cedric says. "I'll be gone."

It is a Saturday afternoon, and the Kennedy Center auditorium comes alive with a wailing jazz number as Phillip and four other dancers spin and tap their way flawlessly through a complicated routine. The audience—about 200 parents, brothers and sisters of the school-aged performers— applauds wildly.

After the show, he is practically airborne, laughing and strutting in his yellow "Ballou Soul Tappers" T-shirt, looking out at the milling crowd in the lobby.

"You seen my people?" he asks one of his fellow tappers.

"No, haven't," she says.

"Your people here?" he asks, tentatively.

"Sure, my mom's over there," she says, pointing, then turning back to Phillip.

His throat seems to catch, and he shakes his head. "Yeah," he says, "I'll find out where they are, why they couldn't come." He tries to force a smile, but manages only a grimace. "I'll find out later."

* * *

Scripture Cathedral, a pillar of Washington's thriving apostolic Pentecostal community, is a cavernous church, its altar dominated by a 40-foot-tall illuminated cross. Evening services are about to begin, and Cedric's mother searches nervously for her son, scanning the crowd of women in hats and men in bow ties. Finally, he slips into a rear pew, looking haggard.

From the pulpit, the preacher, C.L. Long, announces that tonight, he has a "heavy heart": He had to bury a slain 15-year-old boy just this afternoon. But then he launches into a rousing sermon, and as he speaks, his rolling cadences echo through the sanctuary, bringing the 400 parishioners to their feet.

"When you don't have a dime in your pocket, when you don't have food on your table, if you got troubles, you're in the right place tonight," he shouts, as people yell out hallelujahs, raise their arms high, run through the aisles. Cedric, preoccupied, sits passively. But slowly, he, too, is drawn in and begins clapping.

Then the preacher seems to speak right to him. "Terrible things are happening, you're low, you're tired, you're fighting, you're waiting for your vision to become reality—you feel you can't wait anymore," the preacher thunders. "Say 'I'll be fine tonight 'cause Jesus is with me.' Say it! Say it!"

By now, Cedric is on his feet, the spark back in his eyes. "Yes," he shouts. "Yes."

It is a long service, and by the time mother and son pass the drug dealers—still standing vigil—and walk up the crumbling stairs to their apartment, it is approaching midnight.

Ms. Jennings gets the mail. On top of the *TV Guide* is an orange envelope from the U.S. Treasury: a stub from her automatic savings-bond contribution—$85 a week, about one-third of her after tax income—that she has been putting away for nine years to help pay for Cedric's college. "You don't see it, you don't miss it," she says.

Under the *TV Guide* is a white envelope.

Cedric grabs it. His hands begin to shake. "My heart is in my throat."

It is from M.I.T.

Fumbling, he rips it open.

"Wait. Wait. 'We are pleased to inform you...' Oh my God. Oh my God," he begins jumping around the tiny kitchen. Ms. Jennings reaches out to touch him, to share this moment with him—but he spins out of her reach.

"I can't believe it. I got in," he cries out, holding the letter against his chest, his eyes shut tight. "This is it. My life is about to begin."

Class struggle: Poor, black and smart, an inner-city teen tries to survive M.I.T.

Cedric Jennings triumphed over gangs, violence; now for the hard part

SEPTEMBER 22, 1994

CAMBRIDGE, Mass.—In a dormitory lobby, under harsh fluorescent lights, there is a glimpse of the future: A throng of promising minority high schoolers, chatting and laughing, happy and confident.

It is a late June day, and the 51 teenagers have just converged here at Massachusetts Institute of Technology for its prestigious minority summer program—a program that bootstraps most of its participants into M.I.T.'s freshman class. Already, an easy familiarity prevails. A doctor's son from Puerto Rico invites a chemical engineer's son from south Texas to explore nearby Harvard Square. Over near the soda machines, the Hispanic son of two schoolteachers meets a black girl who has the same T-shirt, from an annual minority-leadership convention.

"This is great," he says. "Kind of like we're all on our way up, together."

Maybe. Off to one side, a gangly boy is singing a rap song, mostly to himself. His expression is one of pure joy. Cedric Jennings, the son of a drug dealer and the product of one of Washington's most treacherous neighborhoods, has worked toward this moment for his entire life.

TICKET OUT OF POVERTY

Cedric, whose struggle to excel was chronicled in a May 26 page one article in this newspaper, hails from a square mile of chaos. His apartment building is surrounded by crack dealers, and his high school, Frank W. Ballou Senior High, is at the heart of the highest-crime area in the city. Already this year, four teenagers from his district—teens who should have been his schoolmates—were charged in homicides. Another six are dead, murder victims themselves.

For Cedric, M.I.T. has taken on almost mythic proportions. It represents the culmination of everything he has worked for, his ticket to escape poverty. He has staked everything on getting accepted to college here, and at the summer program's end he will find out whether he stands a chance. He doesn't dare think about what will happen if the answer is no.

"This will be the first steps of my path out, out of here, to a whole other world," he had said not long before leaving Washington for the summer program. "I'll be going so far from here, there'll be no looking back."

As Cedric looks around the bustling dormitory lobby on that first day, he finally feels at home, like he belongs. "They arrive here and say, 'Wow, I didn't know there were so many like me,'" says William Ramsey, administrative director of M.I.T.'s program. "It gives them a sense...that being a smart minority kid is the most normal thing to be."

STRANGER IN A STRANGE LAND

But they aren't all alike, really, a lesson Cedric is learning all too fast. He is one of only a tiny handful of students from poor backgrounds; most of the rest range from lower-middle-class to affluent. As he settles into chemistry class on the first day, a row of girls, all savvy and composed, amuse themselves by poking fun at "my Washington street-slang," as Cedric tells it later. "You know, the way I talk, slur my words and whatever."

Cedric is often taunted at his nearly all-black high school for "talking white." But now, he is hearing the flawless diction of a different world, of black students from suburbs with neat lawns and high schools that send most graduates off to college.

Other differences soon set him apart. One afternoon, as students talk about missing their families, it becomes clear that almost everyone else
has a father at home. Cedric's own father denied
paternity for years and has been in jail for almost
a decade. And while many of the students have
been teased back home for being brainy, Cedric's
studiousness has earned him threats from gang
members with guns.

Most worrisome, though, is that despite years
of asking for extra work after school—of creating
his own independent-study course just to get the
basic education that students elsewhere take for
granted—he is woefully far behind. He is overwhelmed by the blistering workload: six-hours
each day of intensive classes, study sessions with tutors each night, endless hours more of homework.

Only in calculus, his favorite subject, does he
feel sure of himself. He is slipping steadily behind
in physics, chemistry, robotics and English.

In the second week of the program, Cedric asks
one of the smartest students, who hails from a
top-notch public school, for help on some homework. "He said it was 'beneath him,'" Cedric
murmurs later, barely able to utter the words.
"Like, he's so much better than me. Like I'm
some kind of inferior human being."

A crowd of students jostles into a dormitory
lounge a few evenings later for Chinese food,
soda and a rare moment of release from studying.
Cliques already have formed, there are whispers
of romances, and lunch groups have crystallized,
almost always along black or Hispanic lines. But
as egg rolls disappear, divides are crossed.

A Hispanic teenager from a middle-class New
Mexico neighborhood tries to teach the opening
bars of Beethoven's "Moonlight Sonata" to a
black youngster, a toll taker's son from Miami.
An impeccably-clad black girl from an affluent
neighborhood teaches some dance steps to a less
privileged one.

Tutors, mostly minority undergraduates at
M.I.T. who once went through this program, look
on with tight smiles, always watchful. The aca-

demic pressure, they know, is rising fast. Midterm exams start this week—along with all-nighters and panic. Some students will grow depressed; others will get sick from exhaustion. The tutors count heads, to see if anyone looks glum, confused, or strays from the group.

"They're going through so much, that a day here is like a week, so we can't let them be down in the dumps for very long," says Valencia Thomas, a graduate of this program and now a 20-year-old sophomore at nearby Harvard University. "Their identities are being challenged, broken up and reformed. Being a minority and a high achiever means you have to carry extra baggage about who you are, and where you belong. That puts them at risk."

Tonight, all the students seem to be happy and accounted for. Almost.

Upstairs, Cedric is lying on his bed with the door closed and lights off, waiting for a miracle, that somehow, he will "be able to keep up with the others."

It is slow in coming.

"It's all about proving yourself, really," he says quietly, sitting up. "I'm trying, you know. It's all I can do is try. But where I start from is so far behind where some other kids are, I have to run twice the distance to catch up."

He is cutting back on calls to his mother, not wanting to tell her that things aren't going so well. Barbara Jennings had raised her boy to believe that he can succeed, that he must. When Cedric was a toddler, she quit her clerical job temporarily and went on welfare so that she could take him to museums, read him books, instill in him the importance of getting an education—and getting out.

"I know what she'll say: 'Don't get down, you can do anything you set your mind to,'" Cedric says. "I'm finding out it's not that simple."

Cedric isn't the only student who is falling behind. Moments later, Neda Ramirez's staccato voice echoes across the dormitory courtyard.

"I am so angry," says the Mexican-American teen, who goes to a rough, mostly Hispanic high school in the Texas border town of Edinburg. "I work so hard at my school—I have a 102% average—but I'm realizing the school is so awful it doesn't amount to anything. I don't belong here. My father says, 'Learn as much as you can at M.I.T., do your best and accept the consequences.' I said, 'Yeah, Dad, but I'm the one who has to deal with the failure.'"

By the middle of the third week, the detonations of self-doubt become audible. One morning in physics class, Cedric stands at his desk, walks out into the hallway, and screams.

The physics teacher, Thomas Washington, a black 24-year-old Ph.D. candidate at M.I.T., rushes after him. "I told him, 'Cedric, don't be so hard on yourself,'" Mr. Washington recounts later. "I told him that a lot of the material is new to lots of the kids—just keep at it."

But, days after the incident, Mr. Washington vents his frustration at how the deck is stacked against underprivileged students like Cedric and Neda.

"You have to understand that there's a controversy over who these types of programs should serve," he says, sitting in a sunny foyer one morning after class. "If you only took the kids who need this the most, the ones who somehow excel at terrible schools, who swim upstream but are still far behind academically, you wouldn't get enough eventually accepted to M.I.T. to justify the program."

And so the program ends up serving many students who really don't need it. Certainly, M.I.T.'s program—like others at many top colleges—looks very good. More than half its students eventually are offered admission to the freshman class. Those victors, however, are generally students from better schools in better neighborhoods, acknowledges Mr. Ramsey, a black M.I.T. graduate who is the program's administrative director. For some of them, this program is little more than résumé padding.

Mr. Ramsey, 68, had hoped it would be different. Seven years ago, when he took over the program, he had "grand plans, to find late bloomers, and deserving kids in tough spots. But it didn't take me three months to realize I'd be putting kids on a suicide dash."

A six-week program like M.I.T.'s, which doesn't offer additional, continuing support, simply can't function if it is filled only with inner-city youths whose educations lag so far behind, he says: "They'd get washed out and everything they believe in would come crashing down on their heads. Listen, we know a lot about suicide rates up here. I'd be raising them."

Perhaps it isn't surprising, then, that while 47% of all black children live in poverty in America, only about a dozen students in this year's M.I.T. program would even be considered lower-middle class, according to Mr. Ramsey. Though one or two of the neediest students like Cedric find their way to the program each year, he adds, they tend to be long shots to make it to the next step, into M.I.T. for college. Those few, though, Mr. Ramsey says, are "cases where you could save lives."

Which is why Cedric, more than perhaps any other student in this year's program, hits a nerve.

"I want to take Cedric by the hand and lead him through the material," says physics instructor Mr. Washington, pensively. "But I resist. The real world's not like that. If he makes it to M.I.T., he won't have someone like me to help him.

"You know, part of it I suppose is our fault," he adds. "We haven't figured out a way to give credit for distance traveled."

So, within the program—like society beyond it—a class system is becoming obvious, even to the students. At the top are students like the beautifully dressed Jenica Dover, one of the girls who had found Cedric's diction so amusing. A confident black girl, she attends a mostly white high school in wealthy Newton, Mass. "Some of this stuff is review for me," she says one day, strolling from physics class, where she spent some of the hour giggling with deskmates. "I come from a very good school, and that makes all this pretty manageable."

Cedric, Neda and the few others from poor backgrounds, meanwhile, are left to rely on what has gotten them this far: adrenaline and faith.

On a particularly sour day in mid-July, Cedric's rising doubts seem to overwhelm him. He can't work any harder in calculus, his best subject, yet he still lags behind other students in the class. Physics is becoming a daily nightmare.

Tossing and turning that night, too troubled to sleep, he looks out at the lights of M.I.T., thinking about the sacrifices he has made—the hours of extra work that he begged for from his teachers, the years focusing so single-mindedly on school that he didn't even have friends. "I thought that night that it wasn't ever going to be enough. That I wouldn't make it to M.I.T.," he says later. "That, all this time, I was just fooling myself."

As the hours passed he fell in and out of sleep. Then he awoke with a jolt, suddenly thinking about Cornelia Cunningham, an elder at the Washington Pentecostal church he attends as often as four times a week with his mother. A surrogate grandmother who had challenged and prodded Cedric since he was a small boy, "Mother Cunningham," as he always called her, had died two weeks before he left for M.I.T.

"I was lying there, and her spirit seemed to come to me, I could hear her voice, right there in my room, saying—just like always—'Cedric, you haven't yet begun to fight,'" he recounts. "And the next morning, I woke up and dove into my calculus homework like never before."

* * *

The auditorium near M.I.T.'s majestic domed library rings with raucous cheering, as teams prepare their robots for battle. Technically, this is an exercise in ingenuity and teamwork: Each three-student team had been given a box of motors, levers and wheels to design a machine—mostly little cars with hooks on the front—to fight against another team's robot over a small soccer ball.

But something has gone awry. The trios, carefully chosen and mixed in past years by the instructors, were self-selected this year by the students. Clearly, the lines were drawn by race. As the elimination rounds begin, Hispanic teams battle against black teams. "PUERTO RICO, PUERTO RICO," comes the chant from the Hispanic side.

Black students whoop as Cedric's team fights into the quarterfinals, only to lose. He stumbles in mock anguish toward the black section, into the arms of several girls who have become his friends. The winner, oddly enough, is a team led by a Caucasian boy from Oklahoma who is here because he is 1/128 Potawatomi Indian. Both camps are muted.

In the final weeks, the explosive issues of race and class that have been simmering since the students arrive break out into the open. It isn't just black vs. Hispanic or poor vs. rich. It is minority vs. white.

At a lunch table, over cold cuts on whole wheat, talk turns to the ultimate insult: "wanting to be white." Jocelyn Truitt, a black girl from a good Maryland high school, says her mother, a college professor, "started early on telling me to ignore the whole 'white' thing...I've got white friends. People say things, that I'm trading up, selling out, but I don't listen. Let them talk."

Leslie Chavez says she hears it, too, in her largely Hispanic school. "If you get good grades, you're 'white.' What, so you shouldn't do that? Thinking that way is a formula for failure."

In an English class discussion later on the same issue, some students say assimilation is the only answer. "The success of whites means they've mapped out the territory for success," says Alfred Fraijo, a cocky Hispanic from Los Angeles. "If you want to move up, and fit in, it will have to be on those terms. There's nothing wrong with aspiring to that—it's worth the price of success."

Cedric listens carefully, but the arguments for assimilation are foreign to him. He knows few whites; in his world, whites have always been the unseen oppressors. "The charge of 'wanting to be white,' where I'm from," Cedric says, "is like treason."

A charge for which he is being called to task, and not just by tough kids in Ballou's hallways. He has had phone conversations over the past few weeks with an old friend from junior high, a boy his age named Torrance Parks, who is trying to convert Cedric to Islam.

"He just says I should stick with my own," says Cedric, "that I'm already betraying my people, leaving them all behind, by coming up to a big white university and all, that even if I'm successful, I'll never be accepted by whites."

Back in Washington, Cedric's mother, a data-input clerk at the Department of Agriculture, is worried. She hopes Cedric will now continue to push forward, to take advantage of scholarships to private prep schools, getting him out of Ballou High for his senior year, "keeping on his path out."

"He needs to get more of what he's getting at M.I.T., more challenging work with nice, hard-working kids—maybe even white kids," she says. The words of Islam, which she fears might lead toward more radical black separatism, would "mean a retreat from all that." She adds that she asks Torrance: "What can you offer my son other than hate?"

She is increasingly frustrated, yet unable to get her son to discuss the issue. When recruiters from Phillips Exeter Academy come to M.I.T. to talk to the students, Cedric snubs them. "They have to wear jacket and tie there; it's elitist," he says, "It's not for me."

Still, in the past few weeks, Cedric has been inching forward. Perseverance finally seems to be paying off. He has risen to near the top of the group in calculus. He is improving in chemistry, adequate in robotics, and showing some potential in English. Physics remains a sore spot.

He also has found his place here. The clutch of middle- and upper-middle-class black girls who once made fun of him has grown fond of him, fiercely protective of him. One Friday night, when Cedric demurs about joining a Saturday group trip to Cape Cod, the girls press him until he finally admits his reason: He doesn't have a bathing suit.

"So we took him to the mall to pick out some trunks," says Isa Williams, the daughter of two Atlanta college professors. "Because he doesn't have maybe as many friends at home, Cedric has a tendency of closing up when he gets sad, and not turning to other people," she adds. "We want him to know we're there for him."

The next day, on the bus, Cedric, at his buoyant best, leads the group in songs.

Though he doesn't want to say it—to jinx anything—by early in the fifth week Cedric is actually feeling a shard of hope. Blackboard scribbles are beginning to make sense, even on the day in late-July when he is thinking only about what will follow classes: a late afternoon meeting with Prof. Trilling, the academic director. This is the meeting Cedric has been waiting for since the moment he arrived, when the professor will assess his progress and—most important— his prospects for someday getting accepted into M.I.T.

Cedric, wound tight, gets lost on the way to Prof. Trilling's office, arriving a few minutes late.

Professor Trilling, who is white, ushers the youngster into an office filled with certificates, wide windows, and a dark wood desk. Always conscious of clothes, Cedric tries to break the ice by complimenting Mr. Trilling on his shoes, but the professor doesn't respond, moving right to business.

After a moment, he asks Cedric if he is "thinking about applying and coming to M.I.T."

"Yeah," Cedric says. "I've been wanting to come for years."

"Well, I don't think you're M.I.T. material," the professor says flatly. "Your academic record isn't strong enough."

Cedric, whose average for his junior year was better than perfect, 4.19, thanks to several A+ grades, asks what he means.

The professor explains that Cedric's Scholastic Aptitude Test scores—he has scored only a 910 out of a possible 1600—are about 200 points below what they need to be.

Agitated, Cedric begins insisting that he is willing to work hard, "exceedingly hard," to make it at M.I.T. "He seemed to have this notion that if you work hard enough, you can achieve anything," Prof. Trilling recalls haltingly. "That is admirable, but it also can set you up for disappointment. And, at the present time, I told him, that just doesn't seem to be enough."

Ending the meeting, the professor jots down names of professors at Howard University, a black college in Washington, and at the University of Maryland. He suggests that Cedric call them, that if Cedric does well at one of those colleges, he might someday be able to transfer to M.I.T.

Cedric's eyes are wide, his temples bulging, his teeth clenched. He doesn't hear Mr. Trilling's words of encouragement; he hears only M.I.T.'s rejection. He takes the piece of paper from the professor, leaves without a word, and walks across campus and to his dorm room. Crumpling up the note, he throws it in the garbage. He skips dinner that night, ignoring the knocks on his locked door from Isa, Jenica and other worried friends. "I thought about everything," he says, "about what a fool I've been."

The next morning, wandering out into the foyer as calculus class ends, he finally blows. "He made me feel so small, this big," he says, almost screaming, as he presses his fingers close. " 'Not M.I.T. material'...Who is he to tell me that? He doesn't know what I've been through. This is it, right, this is racism. A white guy telling me I can't do it."

Physics class is starting. Cedric slips in, moving, now almost by rote, to the front row—the place he sits in almost every class he has ever taken.

Isa passes him a note: What happened?

He writes a note back describing the meeting and saying he is thinking of leaving, of just going home. The return missive, now also signed by Jenica and a third friend, tells Cedric he has worked too hard to give up. "You can't just run away," the note says, as Isa recalls later. "You have to stay and prove to them you have what it takes...We all care about you and love you." Cedric folds the note gently and puts it in his pocket.

The hour ends, with a worksheet Cedric is supposed to hand in barely touched. Taking a thick pencil from his bookbag, he scrawls "I AM LOST" across the blank sheet, drops it on the teacher's desk, and disappears into the crowd.

Jenica runs to catch up with him, to commiserate. But it will be difficult for her to fully understand: In her meeting with Prof. Trilling the next day, he encourages her to enroll at M.I.T. She shrugs off the invitation. "Actually," she tells the professor, "I was planning to go to Stanford."

* * *

On a sweltering late-summer day, all three air conditioners are blasting in Cedric's cramped apartment in Washington. Cedric is sitting on his bed, piled high with clothes, one of his bags not yet unpacked even though he returned home from Cambridge several weeks ago.

The last days of the M.I.T. program were fitful. Cedric didn't go to the final banquet, where awards are presented, because he didn't want to see Prof. Trilling again. But he made friends in Cambridge, and on the last morning, as vans were loaded for trips to the airport, he hugged and cried like the rest of them.

"I don't think much about it now, about M.I.T.," he says, as a police car speeds by, its siren barely audible over the air conditioners' whir. "Other things are happening. I have plenty to do."

Not really. Most days since returning from New England, he has spent knocking around the tiny, spare apartment, or going to church, or plodding through applications for colleges and scholarships.

The calls from Torrance, who has been joined in his passion for Islam by Cedric's first cousin, have increased. Cedric says he "just listens," and that "it's hard to argue with" Torrance.

But inside the awkward youngster, a storm rages. Not at home on the hustling streets, and ostracized by high-school peers who see his ambition as a sign of "disrespect," Cedric has discovered that the future he so carefully charted may not welcome him either.

Certainly, he will apply to colleges. And his final evaluations from each M.I.T. class turned out better than he—and perhaps even Prof. Trilling—thought they would. He showed improvement right through the very last day.

But the experience in Cambridge left Cedric bewildered. Private-school scholarship offers, crucial to help underprivileged students make up for lost years before landing in the swift currents of college, have been passed by, despite his mother's urgings. Instead, Cedric Jennings has decided to return to Ballou High, the place from which he has spent the last three years trying to escape.

"I know this may sound crazy," he says, shaking his head. "But I guess I'm sort of comfortable there, at my school. Comfortable in this place that I hate."

Lessons Learned

BY RON SUSKIND

Let go of your journalistic omniscience.

That's one lesson I've learned from this project. Happening across something unexpected and unplanned always beats the clever—and in some ways safer—effort to confirm what we already know or strongly suspect.

Of course, the latter is what I've often done as a journalist, especially in examining familiar subjects like the lives of poor inner city youths. There are stories written about such kids every day—like a sort of sociological weather report—full of the kinds of quotes I was getting from kids in my first days on this story: doing fine, looking forward to college, avoiding drugs, all is well.

I realized that the problem was me. I was overmanaging the reporting process. I needed to relax, just let things unfold toward whatever conclusions, grand or small. The students and I began talking about nothing in particular. I told them about my family. They told me about theirs. We reviewed cafeteria food and how teachers dressed, decided which students were cool and why. And that led, over time, to discussions of everything important.

In the process, I discarded some faults that I—like other world-wise journalists—had long ignored. For one: reflex condescension. One day, after a particularly tough exchange with a teacher, I asked myself a question: Do I think these students carry fewer innate gifts than my old high school classmates, many of whom went on to Ivy League universities? The unsettling answer: You bet.

Getting past that notion ended up being the most important breakthrough of this story's reporting. It allowed me to have faith in these students to be my guides to their odd, inverted universe. Sitting in countless classrooms, living with students from breakfast to bedtime, holding one's hand at a church service, and talking another through a pregnancy that even her mother was unaware of, helped me understand the rules of conduct on this bleak terrain. Why should a girl who knows, first hand, of the ravages of absent fathers and illegitimacy, repeatedly have unprotected sex? Why should a smart kid try to act stupid, condemning himself to a failed life in a place he hates? There are reasons—reasons every bit as compelling and sane as those that made it seem natural for me to go to college, on to a profession, and wait for marriage before becoming a father.

What drove the school's few honor students to flout to the dictates of their environment, making themselves targets, which, as class clown Phillip Atkins said, "is crazy at a place like Ballou"?

Phillip was right, and I had more to learn. What drove the most audacious honor student, Cedric Jennings, to such insanity? Who, really, was the smartest student at Ballou, where traditional measures of intelligence don't seem to apply? I was off on a journey.

Which brings me to another, overarching, lesson of this story: If the reporter goes on a journey, the reader will almost certainly follow. Don't worry too much about how it all will end, about whether the conclusions reached will necessarily fit with those you anticipated sitting at your desk in a faraway office. Any judgments arrived at back there—no matter how gifted a theorist you may be—provide little more than a sketchy, and maybe confused, map. There are times, during the reporting, when you have to throw that map away and draw a new one, or just proceed uncharted.

With this story, the map was constantly reworked. The story's first draft focused on several sophomore honor students grappling with the choice of staying on a path of dangerously conspicuous achievement or straying from it—choices Cedric and Phillip, both a year older, had already made. Editors were delighted, but no one could deny that the voice of the two older students—then minor characters—carried explosive resonance. So, back to school, for another three weeks of reporting with the older kids.

The same was true of the follow-up story at M.I.T. I suspected, going in, that Cedric would be overmatched. But the fierce racial dialogue that ensued among students, along with Cedric's collapse, rebound, and final deflation, was like riding a wild horse. I had no idea where it would take me. Again, the same rules applied. Don't dismiss actions that seem odd or foreign. Understand the underlying rationale—feel it—and a world will open up.

By the end of this project, I had lost my sense of distance. I found myself turning off an inner voice saying "step back, don't get too close." If caring about these kids made me less than objective, then I am guilty. I was indignant at what I saw, both at Ballou High School and later at M.I.T. I think we, as reporters, don't let such strong emotions inhabit us for fear it will cloud objectivity. This story taught me otherwise: The best stories are often driven by outrage.

And also by trust. What I learned from this story: Don't go out there collecting props—the faces and voices that will brilliantly illustrate your story idea. Great stories flow. They have their own mysterious course, just like our lives.

Brian Dickinson
Commentary

Since 1972, Brian Dickinson, editorial page editor and columnist for the *Providence Journal-Bulletin,* commented regularly about major national and international stories. In the last two years, his columns have shifted to a personal but no less significant focus: his battle with amyotrophic lateral sclerosis, better known as Lou Gehrig's disease. Dickinson's response is to challenge his illness as vigorously as he debated the weighty issues of the day. Paralyzed and robbed of speech, he continues to write columns using a specially equipped computer that he describes in his interview. (The conversation was conducted electronically. Dickinson responded to questions transmitted to his home computer in East Greenwich, R.I., via America Online.) In 30 years at the paper, he has worked as a reporter, bureau manager, state house reporter, and traveled widely, producing series of articles on South Africa, the Soviet Union, Eastern Europe, China, and Latin America. He is a past president of the National Conference of Editorial Writers, and in 1990 he organized and led a trip for more than 50 U.S. and Canadian editors to visit Eastern Europe and the Soviet Union. Dickinson graduated from Harvard College in 1959 with an A.B. degree in English, earned an M.A. degree in political science from Brown University, and did graduate study at the Woodrow Wilson School of Public and International Affairs at Princeton University. Before joining the *Journal-Bulletin,* he worked for *Newsweek* and *The New York Times.*

Dickinson shares with readers his fight with disease and his observations on life, enriching them with a vision marked by self-deprecating wit, eloquence, and undeniable courage. "Paradoxically, the more Dickinson's body betrays him," his colleague Gerald S. Goldstein wrote in the paper's Sunday magazine last March, "the more upbeat are his words."

In my illness, my three sons' true family values shine forth

JANUARY 23, 1994

Years ago, in the town where I live, there stood a modest restaurant named "Father and Son." It was the sort of establishment given to hot roast beef sandwiches, lemon meringue pie and massive white mugs of steaming coffee. A utilitarian lunch counter ran the length of the place, while a few wooden booths occupied the opposite wall. Its front window would steam up in winter. It is likely that a Coca-Cola calendar was hanging on a nail over the cash register, although I cannot be expected to remember all such details from that long ago.

For six months, I lunched at this spot nearly every day. Yet, even though I scrutinized the various countermen and fry cooks with care, I never did establish who might be the father and who, the son. Perhaps the restaurant's name had merely been inherited from years before, and bore no relation to present persons. Yet the name stayed with me: a sturdy title that evoked plain-spoken families and harmony among generations. The words are anything but unique; indeed, it was the prosaic familiarity of the name—"Father and Son"—that accounted for part of its reassuring appeal.

Several years later, before I would become a father for the first time, with a son of my own. And it would be less than two years afterward when I would become, through the marvel of twins, a father of sons for the second and third times. The acquisition of three sons in less than two years had quite some impact on their father (to say nothing of their mother). Now, more than two decades later, a riff through the memory files draws forth a jumble of images. Tears and laughter and rosy cheeks. Corduroy coveralls and fluffy snowsuits with many zippers. A first birthday, a first Christmas. A sandbox, jungle gym, excited shouts and skinned knees. School days. New friends. Swim team. Growing tall. High school, soccer practice, learning to ski, looking at girls. Vacation trips, raking the leaves, washing the dog, driving the car. Noisy parties and quiet talks. Family time. Then, in a wink: graduation and college, with years of hopes, hugs and phone bills of daunting dimension.

These three sons have been a lively and endearing (if occasionally bewildering) presence at the heart of our family. Andy will turn 26 soon. Jon and Matt, the unalike twins, are closing in on 24. Over our years together, these three lively characters have kept us alert and rather in awe of their energy and imagination. High jinks have not been unknown. These are, after all, males.

But they have also shown quite a capacity for rallying around and helping out in the family enterprise, and at no time has this been more warmly conveyed than in the months since I learned I have Lou Gehrig's disease. As the illness has advanced, now confining me to a wheelchair, our three sons have become what the medical world calls primary caregivers. All three have returned home to live for the time being, and have redesigned their lives around taking care of Dad. This is hardly a role that I would have wished for them—and certainly not one that they would have wished for themselves. They have put careers on hold. Girlfriends in distant cities are seen only occasionally. And each has told me that he will be around as long as he is needed.

Their contribution is beyond price. Indeed, if they had been unable to lend a hand, I'm not sure how my wife, Barbara, and I would have coped. As things stand, though, all five of us are united in this medical endeavor. My doctors, seeing our sons' unstinting support, call it remarkable. At various times each day, one or more of this trio might be acting as dresser, nurse, cook, driver, reader or simple companion. Since they're all strong, they can hoist me around with ease. Wheeling me out onto the deck for some sun, around the block for fresh air or into the car for a drive—my sons seem able to meet any request. If I could pay them based on what they're worth to me, they would soon get rich.

Each brings his own special qualities to the job of caring for his ailing father. Matt, something of an athlete, challenges me to reach, stretch and stand when my floppy muscles would rather not. Jon gives extra care to seeing that I get an attractive lunch and that my clothes fit comfortably. Andy has made a cottage industry out of fabricating accessories—ramps, handles and so on—to meet my needs. He also has a terrific sense of humor, which helps mightily to steer us safely through episodes where humor might be scarce.

The physical help that these three stalwarts provide is crucial: They make possible a day that offers me something more than just sitting in a chair. With my own team of roustabouts at the ready, I can go almost anywhere, even if not very fast. Yet it may be in the psychological realm where our three sons make their greatest contribution. They show something that had rather gone out of fashion: the timeless, sustaining strength that comes from family. By helping during this abnormal time, they are showing a devoted generosity of spirit. Their support is heartwarming to me. But the real winners may be my sons themselves, who at a challenging time can call upon values that had gone untested—until now.

Writers' Workshop

Talking Points

1) Study the opening paragraph of this column. Notice how Dickinson evokes a Norman Rockwell vision of the "Father and Son" restaurant. Focus on the details "hot roast beef sandwiches, lemon meringue pie and massive white mugs of steaming coffee" and consider how your mind creates its own picture.

2) Continue your examination. Notice how Dickinson then talks about his own fatherhood and provides a litany of details familiar to any parent. Only after that do we find out what the column is really about: Dickinson's illness and how his sons, now grown, have returned home, putting their own futures on hold to nurse their father. Could Dickinson have gotten to the point faster? Argue for and against that proposition.

3) By the column's end, Dickinson has reached his conclusion about the value of his son's help —"They make possible a day that offers me something more than just sitting in a chair"—and its larger meaning—"They show something that had rather gone out of fashion: the timeless, sustaining strength that comes from family." Discuss whether Dickinson's discovery is shared by the reader. Do you agree with his conclusion?

4) Dickinson often uses words that seem old-fashioned. Do you know what a "roustabout" is? Look up its origins. Discuss whether it's appropriate. Suggest a synonym.

Assignment Desk

1) Try this experiment with a fellow writer. Each of you write a fuller description of the "Father and Son" restaurant. Compare how your visions differ.

2) Guy de Maupassant, the French short story writer, had as his teacher Gustav Flaubert, author of *Madame Bovary.* "After repeating over and over again this truth, that there are not in the entire world two grains of sand, two hands or noses that are absolutely the same, Flaubert made me de-

scribe in a few sentences, a being or an object in such a way as to particularize it clearly, to distinguish it from all the other beings or all the objects of the same race or kind."

Visit a diner or restaurant and select a few details that reveal its uniqueness.

3) In paragraph three, Dickinson summarizes his sons' growth from infancy to manhood in 13 sentences, some of them fragments. Do the same for a period in your own life—your high school career, a courtship—or someone else's—a politician's career, a doctor's education.

4) Write your own column demonstrating what Dickinson calls "the timeless, sustaining strength that comes from family."

Spring break over, I resume my courses at Wheelchair U.

APRIL 6, 1994

Well, here we are again. After weeks of vile winter weather, which made southern New England seem more like the steppes of Siberia, the great ice sheet is melting. Actual flower buds have been seen. And I, after a restorative vacation under mostly sunny skies, am glad to be back at work.

The business of being handicapped—from getting around in public to making a word processor behave—has grown more interesting as it has become more of a challenge. It has now been 16 months since I was diagnosed as having Lou Gehrig's disease, and this period has offered a remarkable learning experience. Much of this learning comes with the necessary accepting of awkward reality. A year ago, before I had ever even sat in a wheelchair, the idea that I would become a permanent wheelchair user seemed outlandish. For the past seven months, however, I have been pretty much a wheelchair regular. The device has obvious limitations, but it does allow me to get around, which is the main thing.

A year ago, too, I might have regarded a wheelchair user as someone special, even extraordinary. But now, having joined the ranks of wheelers, I realize that it's not special at all. In the early days of this new life, I must admit to having been a bit self-conscious. After all, a wheelchair user on a city street, or entering a busy restaurant, is hardly inconspicuous. But I quickly came to see that everybody—well, almost everybody—was considerate and ready to help me move around.

At first, restaurants seemed to pose a formidable challenge. I halfway imagined that waiters might snoot me, or that my somewhat mumbled speech might prevent my ordering so much as a hamburger. But nothing like this has happened.

If anything, I've found that restaurants will go out of their way to accommodate me and my party. Whether in my own town or away on vacation, this has been invariably true. We are always given a table easy to reach from the entrance door. Waiters—am I imagining this?—are more attentive than usual. And it almost seems that we, having made a bit of an effort to reach their restaurant, bring about a reciprocal effort from the staff.

Initially, too, I was uneasy at the thought of being fed in public, rather the way an infant in a high chair is fed by a parent. After all, I reasoned, I had been feeding myself for more than 50 years: Would it not look bizarre to have a companion spooning minestrone into my mouth? Perhaps it does, but in my case, with hands that decided to stop working, such an adaptation was necessary. I need not have worried. No one has left my company in disgust, or has given me more than a sideways glance. I feel regarded as just another diner, albeit one who needs a bit of aid.

When using a wheelchair, I observe the world from about four feet up, instead of the six feet that I had been used to, and this does have certain disadvantages. Wheeling into a reception at a convention a few months ago, I found myself positioned considerably below the eye level of most other guests. For a time, my world seemed dominated by the wrinkled backs of navy blue blazers, with most conversations going on high above me. I soon realized, though, that much of this high-pitched chatter was boring, and that I was lucky to be out of the line of fire.

I found that my wheelchair status could lead to another uncomfortable situation in a large gathering. Because I cannot maneuver the wheelchair myself, I more than once found myself trapped in conversation with well-meaning (but long-winded) acquaintances. They could talk all night long, but I had no ready means of escape. Finally, working with a companion, I settled on "fresh air" as a code word signaling that I wanted to move away to new surroundings, and this worked well enough.

Writing has also required an interesting series of adaptations. In the early months of my illness, I was able to write easily using the computer at home, sending my copy to the office by way of a modem and a telephone hook-up. About last Christmas, however, when my fingers began to get floppy, I changed to a voice-recognition program that translated my utterances into words on the computer screen.

This worked fine until recently, when my increasingly gravelly voice began to confuse the computer. To compensate, I have acquired yet another computer program, which lets me select words and letters with a flick of a small switch that I hold in my hand. This is a remarkable system, which in time will become a fast friend. So far, though, it makes for very slow going, and to prepare this article I have lassoed a patient son who has taken my dictation.

As to the medical side of my illness, things stand about as follows: I continue to receive three injections a week of a drug called ciliary neurotrophic factor, which appears to slow the progress of the disease in laboratory animals. It may have slowed the progress of the disease in my body, too, although we have no way of knowing this with certainty. And as I have been doing for several months, I have four workouts with physical therapists each week, and each day I consume several dozen vitamin pills.

By now this routine has become familiar, shaping my days and giving a longer-term purpose to the weeks and months. It has not been the best of years, but I keep adapting to the changes at work simply because I have no other acceptable choice.

Besides, I keep getting letters from old friends, our crocuses have exploded with color, and baseball has returned to enrich the daily course of our lives. My son Jonathan and his friend Rachel took me to Fenway Park to watch the Red Sox bang out a victory on opening day. The old ballfield gleamed and a fresh breeze kept snapping the flag on the center field pole. It made a glorious afternoon.

Writers' Workshop

Talking Points

1) Dickinson's voice displays a sharpness of sensibility and a multi-layered tone that creates the strong mood evident in his columns. In the lead, he writes, "Actual flower buds have been seen." He follows that with the phrase, "The business of being handicapped...." What reactions do you think he seeks from the reader? Examine your own reaction and decide how his words prompted it.

2) Once again, Dickinson paints an unflinching portrait of living with a disability. When was the last time you read about the lives of the disabled in your newspaper? When was the last time you reported on the subject? Do the news media pay close enough attention to this segment of society? Why not?

3) Dickinson organizes this column around a series of revelations: assumptions that are jettisoned by unexpected realities. What are these assumptions and how they were overthrown?

4) Through all of the challenges of his illness, Dickinson remains stoical, featuring a dry understatement often associated with New England writers. "It has not been the best of years" is emblematic of his voice. Discuss the effect on the reader.

Assignment Desk

1) Write a column about an aspect of your life that contrasts expectations with a different reality. What you thought parenthood would be like. How your attitude changed toward a friend you had assumptions about before you knew her well.

2) Report and write a story about a disabled person.

3) The final paragraph offers a sharp contrast between the reality of life in a wheelchair and the joys of life perhaps overlooked by the able-bodied. Put yourself in Dickinson's place and write a passage celebrating the things in your life

that, like crocuses exploding with color, letters from old friends, and a fresh breeze snapping the flag on the center field pole, make it glorious.

4) Amyotrophic lateral sclerosis is better known as Lou Gehrig's disease. Who was Lou Gehrig and how did the illness get his name?

5) Pick a disability—blindness, deafness, paralysis—and brainstorm a list of your attitudes and assumptions about it. Present them to someone familiar with the disability from personal experience, either living with it or as a caregiver. How far off base were you? Write a column about the experience.

6) E.B. White, the *New Yorker* essayist, chronicled the realities of rural New England. White's essays are now in collected form. Read them and compare this New Englander's style with Dickinson's.

A traumatic new perspective, with some moments of joy

OCTOBER 2, 1994

Perspective, my father used to say. You have to see this in perspective. This was a favored piece of advice, which he would dispense on all sorts of occasions, such as the time I whacked my thumb with a hammer when I was building a tree fort in the big maple near our house. As a home remedy, his counsel wasn't of much use: I'm sure that at age 10 I had only the fuzziest idea what perspective even was, and my thumb smarted too much for me to guess.

In theory, people gain perspective as they grow older. The incident that seemed so traumatic at age 20 recedes to be barely a blip on our radar by the time we reach 50. And this is just as well: Imagine the fix we'd be in if middle-aged folks screamed at finding dog droppings on the rug, or fell into a fit of weeping every time they received a parking ticket.

Sometimes a fresh perspective forces itself on us abruptly, leaving our view of life permanently transformed. Marriage can do this, as can moving a family to a distant part of the country. So also can the intrusion of serious illness, as I have been learning over the past couple of years.

During this period, as my regular readers may recall, I was diagnosed as having a motor nerve cell disorder called amyotrophic lateral sclerosis (ALS), or Lou Gehrig's disease. It is incurable and historically fatal. In my case it has paralyzed my arms and legs, and destroyed my voice. More ruination is in the cards, no doubt; I have no wish to know details.

What the disease has accomplished, besides laying waste to my physical self, is to shake up my mental processes in ways that I can't yet define. But I do know that my own views of just about everything have been transformed in recent

months, and I suppose that this represents perspective of a sort.

Some of the change has come about, as one
might expect, in my awareness of time. I have no
idea how much I may have left, but it almost certainly will be a good bit less than I was anticipating before ALS paid me a call. Being seen as
scarce makes time more precious to me, as though
it were being measured in diamonds.

But even though I've become keenly aware of
the days slipping past, and although I make a
point of savoring each sunrise and rain shower, I
haven't set up any kind of crash program for fill-
ing each day with important activities. Having
shed all residual guilt, I now do pretty much as I
please. That thick history of Spain, taking up
shelf space all these years, will now not get read.
No matter: It probably wasn't going to get read
anyway.

I consider myself fortunate in still being able to
write; without this channel of communication, I
would feel totally isolated. My newspaper has
generously provided me with a gee-whiz home
computer, along with some remarkable software
developed by the SHARE Foundation at South-
eastern Massachusetts University, in North Dart-
mouth. Although I can effectively move only one
finger, that suffices to write with the computer,
using a single toggle switch that rests on my lap.

The medical fight against ALS remains frustratingly slow, although some researchers talk
optimistically of a possible breakthrough soon.
Several drugs are being tested, but so far none has
shown dramatic promise. In this quest for a po-
tentially life-saving drug, keeping a sense of perspective is not always easy for the patient. Your
malady seems inevitably to be advancing faster
than the research aimed at finding a cure. One
week you discover that you can no longer tie your
shoes. Another few weeks, and you realize that
you can barely drag your trembling legs up a
flight of stairs. You break a sweat. You know
what's going on: You have ALS. It's threading its
way among your billions of motor nerve cells,

crippling them as it goes, crippling you. You want to shout at those white-coated researchers in all those distant labs, shout and implore them to work harder, work faster—work overtime, work nights—to find a cure for ALS.

But then you take a breath and quiet down, because you realize that some of the world's best neurologists are working flat-out on the mystery of ALS, and have been for years; and if ALS was going to yield its secrets readily, this would have happened before now. Such is one sort of perspective.

Another involves the world of actual medical practice, or what some insist on calling the health care delivery "system." The past couple of years have allowed me close glimpses of this environment, including a recent hospital stay that seemed considerably longer than the five days of its actual duration. My findings, in brief:

Levels of knowledge and competence generally impressive. Nurses and aides do a usually superlative job of patient care, but report increasing stress as hospitals try to trim costs. Volume of paperwork is staggering. Local residents with minor health problems fill up emergency rooms, thereby strengthening the case for opening more neighborhood walk-in clinics. Insurance carrier readily covers pricey hospital visit but balks at paying for home care that is much less expensive. (And someone said our medical system is rational.)

This and various other perspectives have become known to me in the months since my world shrank and I adopted the wheelchair as my means of getting around. I have found new value in friendships, new joy in close family ties, new delight in the scent of a newly planed pineboard, new cheer upon hearing the voice of an old friend on the telephone. There is new freedom to ignore the flood of commercial noise that swirls around us every day, new puzzlement at the subtle turning of leaves on the big hickory, new wonder at the genius of Mozart. These are valued perspectives all. I'm lucky they came my way.

Writers' Workshop

Talking Points

1) David Finkel, an award-winning staff writer for *The Washington Post Magazine,* often reports "as if I were a photographer." In *The Complete Book of Feature Writing,* edited by Leonard Witt (*Writer's Digest,* 1991), Finkel says, "I not only stand near something, I move away for a long view. I crouch down, I move left and right. I try to view it from every angle possible to see what might be revealed." In much the same way, Brian Dickinson regularly steps back from his subject, literally and figuratively. What is the value of using perspective in reporting and writing?

2) This column marks one of the few times that Dickinson's reserve breaks down when he writes in paragraph nine, "One week you discover that you can no longer tie your shoes. Another few weeks, and you realize that you can barely drag your trembling legs up a flight of stairs. You break a sweat. You know what's going on: You have ALS.... You want to shout at those white-coated researchers in all those distant labs, shout and implore them to work harder, work faster—work overtime, work nights—to find a cure for ALS."

In the next paragraph, notice how he quickly regains control. Contrast these two passages and their effect. Discuss why Dickinson writes this passage in the second person, instead of the first.

3) In paragraph three, Dickinson lists several life changes that can alter perspective. Can you think of others? Can you conceive of a story that would explore these changes and their affect on you or someone else?

4) Dickinson waits until the last line to tell us his surprising conclusion: Even with all the challenges, the setbacks, the obviously painful aspects of ALS, he celebrates the joy of living, whatever its hardships, and declares himself "lucky." Did you expect that conclusion? What surprises you most about Brian Dickinson's columns? How has reading them changed your perspective?

Assignment Desk

1) Rent the movie *Pride of the Yankees* starring Gary Cooper as Lou Gehrig, and listen for echoes of Dickinson's conclusion in Gehrig's farewell speech. Do you think Dickinson is consciously echoing the movie?

2) Research and write a description of the onset of a serious illness, such as lung or breast cancer, its mechanisms, and its effects on the patient's body.

3) These columns could almost be subtitled "The Re-Education of Brian Dickinson." What are the lessons he learns through his experience with illness? What lessons does the reader learn?

4) Describe the point of this column in a single sentence.

5) In the final paragraph, Dickinson revels in the joy of his senses, "the scent of a newly planed pineboard, the voice of an old friend on the telephone, the subtle turning of leaves on the big hickory." If you were diagnosed with a terminal illness, what would you savor? Write a column about those pleasures.

Speechless, powerless, I strain to signal to the world

OCTOBER 30, 1994

The other day, I happened to glance into a mirror for the first time in several weeks, and saw my face.

We who can no longer shave ourselves or brush our own hair have little use for such accessories to vanity. But I looked for a few seconds at my reflected image, and was rather pleasantly surprised to find the familiar features intact.

The face was thinner, surely, than it had been a year previously (those 20 pounds that I lost had to come from somewhere). The eyes appeared a bit sunken, the corners of the mouth a trifle slack, and the entire assemblage could have stood a couple of days in bright sunshine. But it was unmistakably my face, and I found this fact somehow reassuring.

What image I had expected to see in the glass, I don't know—perhaps one of those twisted, inside-out Picasso faces, or the haunting, wasted visage of Dorian Gray. Either might have seemed an apt reflection of this writer, voice silenced and limbs sapped of their strength by Lou Gehrig's disease. Instead, I fancied that I looked nearly normal, even as I knew that this malady was annihilating my motor nerve cells by the millions.

Illness of any serious sort bends our vision, realigns our mind. Nothing is as it was. Whatever the stimulus—pain, fever, drug-induced haze or the hard-edged confrontation with one's own mortality—the sick person of necessity regards the world through different lenses than do those who are well.

In my own case, infirmity's visitation induced a fresh outlook toward many fellow humans, and I remember the first time this happened. It was nearly Christmas of 1992. I had just received confirmed diagnosis of Lou Gehrig's disease, an incurable neuromuscular disorder, and was at that point getting around with the aid of a cane. I had never especially noticed cane users as such, but on this particular afternoon, driving with a son around downtown Providence, I spotted five cane-brandishing pedestrians within the space of a few blocks. I felt the tug of a kinship bond.

"My," I said to my son, "there certainly are a lot of us out today."

This recognition had several facets. For one thing, my newly alerted eye was spotting cane-carriers as people who were just a bit unusual (because of the cane) and therefore deserving of special attention. A cane or crutch once might have been seen as a symbol of weakness leading to invisibility. (Shh! Something's wrong with that guy! See him limp! Why, he might even be contagious! We'd best stay away!) After using a cane myself, though, my fellow caners came to appear as just regular folks who had recently had a bad day with an ankle injury or whatever. It was okay for them to be out in public on their own. Some of them were probably even nice.

Gazing at the cane contingent, I further realized that I was now numbered among them. Hey, lookie here! I've got a cane, too! I even managed a twinge of pride at this new kernel of awareness, although the honor was one that I could have cheerfully foregone.

Several weeks into winter, as I was negotiating a treacherous icy downtown sidewalk with the help of my cane, I learned that this distinction had its downside. A man of middle years and motley clothes approached me, glanced at the cane and at me, then bawled in my face:

"Move it, cripple freak!"

This got my attention briefly, and I quickly understood that my illness had propelled me into the ranks of the incapacitated, the disabled—all those whom circumstances have rendered less than physically whole. Members of this large aggregation—one estimate places the number of "disabled" Americans at 40 million—are not often addressed as I was that winter afternoon. Until recently, however, handicapped people encountered more damaging treatment in the form of job discrimination, limited access to public buildings and, across much of the population, a general indifference to their needs.

Now, many of those needs are being addressed; and the healthy majority has learned that, with a bit of help, many disabled people function well and lead rich lives. Yet folk myths die hard. The idea that many of the disabled are incompetent or severely retarded seems hard to dispel, as I discovered during a recent hospital stay.

I was in for minor surgery, a few days only. Most of the nurses learned quickly that I could neither move nor speak, and were really quite wonderful in working out eye signals so I could communicate. On the last night of my stay, however, I was visited by a young nurse and an aide who hadn't gotten the word. They tended to their tidying routine, and there then ensued several minutes of blocked communication between the nurses and me. All I could really do was blink my eyes and murmur an unvoiced "hum" (my family says that I sound like a space alien from *Star Wars*). The room was warm; when I tried to get the nurses to turn on a small table fan, I got no response. I signaled that I wanted them to leave the bed elevated for sleeping; they cranked me down flat. When I indicated that I would prefer the covers left off, the two tucked them snugly around my shoulders. And, when I tried to get the wall light left on, a nurse turned it off.

Trivial matters certainly, and no harm was done. But, as the departing nurses stood in the half-light of the doorway, gazing blankly at me as I tried to mouth "please," I caught a glimpse of what it must be to have truly no voice at all in today's world—to be immobilized, powerless, invisible. You strain and ache and try to reach out, in the hope of being understood or at least heard. But then you meet deafness, or a refusal to listen, and you have learned a smidgeon more about things that matter.

Writers' Workshop

Talking Points

1) Robert Love Taylor writes, "The self, I began to understand, was as spacious as a continent—more so, I understand now: It is a territory without borders, depthless, its history is infinite, its language is memory." The self is every writer's territory. Discuss Dickinson's territory and that of other writers you admire.

2) Again, Dickinson explores the impact of the lens through which life is viewed. He switches back and forth between persons who are sick and those who are well. As a reporter, do you make these kinds of mental and psychological shifts that enable you to empathize with the criminal and the crime victim or both sides in the abortion debate?

3) Several of Dickinson's columns end on a positive note, focusing on his appreciation of life's simple pleasures. How does the ending of this column differ? What do you think gives it such a special poignancy?

4) Dickinson's focus is relentlessly "micro," zeroing in on his condition, its effects on him and his family, and his attempts to reconcile life with a terminal illness. In this column, however, he steps back and relates his personal situation to the estimated 40 million "disabled" Americans. Consider why he made that choice in this column and whether his other columns would be strengthened or weakened if he placed his illness in a larger context every time.

Assignment Desk

1) In paragraph three, Dickinson describes his image in the mirror. With a few brush strokes, he sketches the vision of a man living with a terminal illness. See how long you can go without looking in the mirror, as he did, and then describe yourself in the looking glass.

2) This column conveys the indignities that persons with disabilities face on a daily basis. Interview several persons with various disabilities and write a column based on what they tell you.

3) Describe your territory as a writer. Start visiting it on a regular basis.

4) Ride in a wheelchair for a day, and write a column about the experience, focusing on other people's reactions to you.

Take a deep breath, decide to enjoy life, feed the birds

DECEMBER 18, 1994

Time to take a deep breath—a deep breath, then pause. There. Feel better already, don't you? Close your eyes. Tight. Count to 10. Slowly. Afterwards—eyes still closed, mind you—think of a particularly upbeat something that you did this year. Call up an image of this episode. Why is it memorable? How long will you remember?

You say 1994 wasn't an especially upbeat year for you? That happens. No problem. Go back two, three years—more if you need to—until you come upon an image that makes you smile. The important thing is to stay in the game.

When in doubt, feed the birds.

Write a letter. The exercise will benefit your immortal soul and absolutely floor the recipient, who probably hasn't received a letter from anyone since Earl Butz was secretary of agriculture. Teach yourself to tie a few good knots. While you're at it, knit up the raveled sleeve of care. Allow 10 minutes extra for everything. When worried, just remember the words of Bernard de Clairvaux: "Hey, babe, chill. Things could be worse."

Feed the birds.

Listen as the tea kettle whistles. Watch it steam up the kitchen windows. Write down Grandmother's recipe for potato pancakes Parmesan, before you lose it again. Avoid throngs. Laugh out loud when you feel like it. For one day, leave your wristwatch at home. Learn to whittle; throw shavings into the fireplace, where they will do some good.

Break the mold.

Drive a different route to work. Say "good morning" to those glowering faces in the elevator (don't worry: Most people don't bite). Be aware of the fact that rock salt on sidewalks can kill grass. Watch dawn arrive; see how many colors the sky turns.

Take a deep breath.

Count your blessings.

Harboring a grudge against someone? Has it helped? (Didn't think so.) Sing, if only in the shower. Get older family members to tape their reminiscences. Wiggle your toes. Next time you make chili, add extra spice. Whistle while you work. Go for a good long walk; stretch those legs, including those important Achilles tendons, so easily forgotten in the hectic pace of today's living.

Take the dog.

Remember what my father used to say. When I was a boy, and about to head off somewhere or other, my father always used to say, "Don't do anything dumb!"

Remember to feed the birds.

Take a chance now and then. Look for a new friend. Telephone an old friend. Seize the moment. Believe in yourself. If you keep kicking yourself, you're going to fall down. Davey Crockett, he of the long rifle and wild frontier, said: "Make sure you're right, then go ahead," which put it nicely. A carpenter says: "Measure twice, cut once."

Take your choice.

Breathe deeply. Let your memory slip back to that summer when you were quite small, at the beach with your family, and your father hoisted you onto his shoulders and waded into the lake until his knees were covered. You had never seen so much water. You trusted your father totally.

Close your eyes. Squint hard, relax. How long ago was that first date with the person you later married—25 years? 30 years? More? Certainly a long, long time. Just as certainly, a very short time. How can it be both?

I've no idea. But it is.

Smile. Give a loved one a good, strong hug, just on general principles; because we never can tell, can we?

Don't forget to feed the birds.

Think about this for a moment. Humans are said to be the only creatures with a time sense, including an ability to contemplate such a thing as a future. Does it follow that humankind is the only species able to deal with the concept of hope? I suspect that we are. I do believe that the capacity for hope can help us meet stiff challenges.

Open the bedroom window a crack at night; sleep in fresh air.

Take a time-out now and then as a way of reducing stress. It works for sports teams, long-distance truckers and troublesome toddlers; so why shouldn't it work for you?

Seize the moment. Make it your own. One never has quite enough moments, although we don't know this when we are young. Then, if we look ahead, we see an endless stream full of moments, so many that we could never count them, and all of them ours for the taking. Before we know it, though, the stream has shrunk dramatically and the available moments are growing scarce; and we wish that we had gone after them more assiduously when the stream was full.

So, we say again: Seize the moment—while you can.

As long as you are seizing moments, use the opportunity to divest yourself of all that residual guilt you're carrying around. Guilt gives us warts and yellow teeth, among other things, and never did anyone any good. Gather up your guilt, wrap with care and send it Federal Express to my cousin Pearl in Bayonne, who can never get enough of the stuff.

Forgive. Smile. Walk. (Oh, do walk when you can.) Share. Reach. Laugh. Teach. Learn. Run. Believe. Lift. Climb. Understand. Explore. Give. Appreciate. And, since you can never do it all, savor the small moments that, aggregated, become great. Stay in the game—oh, and do remember to look after the birds.

Writers' Workshop

Talking Points

1) What's most powerful about this column are the things left unsaid. This is written by a man who can't speak, who can't feed the birds, who can't move anything but his thumb, and yet he doesn't mention his illness. Every other column refers to Lou Gehrig's disease except this one. Why? Discuss the impact of that omission.

2) Dickinson urges readers to "Gather up your guilt, wrap with care and send it Federal Express to my cousin Pearl in Bayonne, who can never get enough of the stuff." Do you think he really has a Cousin Pearl in Bayonne? Does it matter?

3) Discuss the freedom columnists have compared with news reporters. Should the rules be different?

4) There are two refrains in this column. What are they? How many times do they appear? What is the effect of this repetition?

5) Compare this column with Dickinson's other pieces. What are the elements that set this column apart? Consider the effect of differences in sentence length and structure. Which is your favorite column? Discuss why.

Assignment Desk

1) With Brian Dickinson as your inspiration, write a column celebrating the joys of your life.

2) Write an insert to this column, trying to approximate Dickinson's voice, that provides the information about his illness. Assess whether it dilutes or strengthens the piece.

3) Rewrite this column in the first person.

4) Dickinson clearly savors words, like a wine connoisseur rolling an aged vintage around the tongue. Itemize every verb in this column, separating active from passive verbs. Do the same thing with some of your own stories.

5) Read the final paragraph aloud, slowly, stopping at every punctuation point. Try to give each verb the spirit of its meaning. After the last sentence, sit quietly, and then write for five minutes, without pausing to edit yourself. Build a column from your thoughts.

6) It takes Brian Dickinson hours to finish his column, using a computer that he controls with one thumb. As an experiment, change the means by which you normally write and see how it affects your writing voice. Draft your next story with a pad and pencil instead of a word processor. Dictate it to a friend. How does changing the technology change the craft of writing?

A conversation with
Brian Dickinson

CHRISTOPHER SCANLAN: How did you get started in journalism?

BRIAN DICKINSON: Mine has been a typically unplanned journalism career. After graduation from Harvard in 1959, I worked a few months doing research at *Newsweek.* I joined *The New York Times* staff, spending about two years as a news assistant. I spent two years in Washington doing publicity for the Army. During one year of law school, I worked in *The New York Times* Washington office. That was the year JKF was killed, and journalism became more interesting than law as a career. I asked the advice of James Reston, then head of the *Times*'s Washington bureau; he told me to get started on a quality newspaper of medium size in a town that had a good university.

Could you sketch your career at the *Providence Journal-Bulletin*?

In October 1964, I went to Providence and signed on with the *Journal.* I spent a few months on the state news staff, a year on the night city staff, a year-and-a-half running the Cranston office, a year on the day city staff. In 1969, I took a year off for graduate work on a fellowship to Princeton. Back in Providence, I spent two years covering politics and the legislature.

In mid-1972, I accepted an offer of an editorial writing job, and have remained on the editorial side since then. I've felt little regret about the move away from news reporting. Writing opinion pieces has allowed me an unlimited range of topics and considerable flexibility as to style, especially with the column. I was an editorial writer for several years, and I became editorial page editor in 1981. In 1986 or '87, I asked to do the column full time; it has remained my main responsibility at the *Journal* since.

Did you ever write pieces as personal as these before?

The columns growing from the ALS experience have had the most intensely personal focus of any I've written, but I've done plenty of other pieces with personal subject matter; most of the latter have come from family experiences.

How have readers responded to them?

Reader response to my ALS pieces has been terrific—very moving, supportive, 100 percent positive. I've received more mail on these columns than on anything else that I've written. People seem interested in the subject, but astonished at my perseverance. This is very gratifying to hear, but I'm not certain what people expected. The disease has cut me off from most activity; but fortunately, I can still write, and so I do.

You make it abundantly clear what you have learned about life from your experience with Lou Gehrig's disease. It struck me that the columns could almost be retitled "The Re-Education of Brian Dickinson." What has the experience of writing these columns taught you about your craft? What is the value of writing to you?

The past two years of writing under physical limitations have shown me the power of the personal tale to grab readers; the tremendous importance of choosing every word with care; the need to avoid the cliché trap; the value of thinking ahead as a sentence takes shape, planning where it's headed, as though the writing process were a chess game; the wisdom of the old saw, "write what you know"; the amazing riches of the imagination that lie waiting to be tapped, but are often hidden in the daily noise of instant news.

You write your column in a very unusual way. Could you describe the technical process.

I write from home on a Compaq Presario 486 computer that is connected by modem with the *Journal*. Since I can neither speak nor operate a keyboard, I have turned to some remarkable software that lets me write—in fact, operate almost every computer function—by clicking a sensitive on/off switch that rests on my wheelchair table. I can click by moving a single fingertip a small fraction of an inch.

The program divides the screen into halves. One half holds text as it is being written. The other half has an eight-column grid containing letters of the alphabet, numbers 1-9, and several operational functions (shift, back space, margins, etc.). A blinking cursor hops continuously from one column to the next; a click moves it down a particular column; another click brings the desired character to the screen.

Fortunately, not every word has to be composed in this laborious manner, letter by letter. The program contains a list of about 7,500 basic words; I can get any of them with just four clicks. I can modify the list to meet my needs. I can store and recover files, transfer files to floppy disk, etc. The program also runs a voice synthesizer, which will speak out loud anything that I write on screen.

It's a remarkable machine, although it's slow: Writing one column will take me at least 15 hours. But I'm lucky to have it. Without some such machine, I would have trouble communicating with anyone about anything.

Technology aside, could you describe the craft process that produces these columns. Where do you get the ideas for them? How do you report them? How do you decide what it is you want to say? How do you plan them: with a formal outline, or a mental plan? How do you write them: in repeated drafts, line by line? How do you revise?

There's almost an embarrassing absence of any formal organizing routine. Sometimes I will mentally outline a piece before I begin writing, but on the really personal pieces I will often just dive in and see where the first few sentences take me. This approach, which I call "instant immersion," usually gives me a fix on the subject after a couple of paragraphs.

Writing with this computer program is so time-consuming that I avoid revision unless it's absolutely necessary. Since I can only write at a rate of about six lines an hour, any false start or wasted word means considerable time lost. So my *first* draft is usually the *final* draft, except for minor tinkering. I've been at this for long enough that editors seldom change my copy.

The bright side of this rather plodding approach to writing is that I'm forced to think ahead as I work. I suspect that this may have helped the sentences flow, since I usually think through an entire clause at a time before writing down any of it. As I am building a sentence, I find that I make more of a mental stretch in search of just the right word; I am less inclined than ever to settle for the first word that jumps into my head.

Your style is casual and discursive, belying the fact that each column takes 15 hours to write, one letter at a time. How do you make so painless a reading experience from such a grueling process?

The process shapes the product. It's ironic, I suppose, but the labor-intensive nature of my technique has made me more careful, more reflective, if you will, rather than less.

Are you a better writer today because of the way you have to write? Do you express your thoughts differently because you must write so deliberately?

Yes to both. I've touched on this earlier. The technique forced on me by this illness, while frustratingly slow, affords time to think; it imposes its own crude requirements for discipline, economy, and focus. The technique demands alertness and precise timing to click the switch on the correct letter or word. This forces a level of concentration that benefits the whole process.

What lessons have you learned—or re-learned —from writing these columns that you wish you had known when you were just starting out as a writer?

Language is everything. Make each word count. And stamp out anything that smells even remotely like a cliché.

Should journalists write more about themselves?

I wouldn't presume to make such a pronouncement. My pieces developing out of my illness have drawn attention partly because ALS is a rarity. I try hard to write them from a position of some detachment, which helps me avoid getting maudlin and, I suppose, adds to the credibility of the pieces.

You have become a voice for the disabled. Is this a voice that is adequately heard?

My illness gave me an entirely new perspective on what it means to be disabled. I have become one of them, and, no, our voices are not adequately heard. Facing the hard fact of someone's disability makes some people uncomfortable; it is easier to look away than it is to deal with it.

What surprised you most about the writing of these columns?

If I was surprised, it was by the powerful—and, so far as I could tell, entirely positive—reaction from readers. Most people with serious illnesses do not take them public, I guess; and in fact I was hesitant in the beginning about going public with my ALS. The idea seemed like selfish opportunism at first, but the warmth of the reader response encouraged me to write further on the theme.

What shaped your writer's voice?

Writing columns helped shape whatever voice I may have acquired; and I probably sought out the column's flexibility to counter the institutional constraints, real or imagined, that surround much editorial writing.

Who are the writers you admire, who influenced you?

James Reston, Henry James, Daniel Boorstin, E.B. White, Ray Bradbury, Stephen Hawking, John Updike, Willa Cather.

What advice would you give someone trying to write about a challenge in their life, whether it's illness or emotional or psychological challenges?

Decide how candid you should be, what your goal is in writing, and how much staying potential you have. The act of *sharing* intensely personal information can be stressful, leaving a writer feeling vulnerable. On the other hand, the experience can be entirely positive, as mine has been, strengthening my spirit and inspiring many readers. I've found a tremendous hunger out there for responsible medical journalism.

What does the writing of these columns mean to you?

Writing these columns has been a gift to me in several respects. Seeing them in print, I am showing that I'm still able to function and produce. I'm finding the creative process more fun than ever. I get a kick out of astonishing people who haven't seen me in some time, and are amazed to find me sitting up and clicking away on my computer. The outpouring of warm support from readers has given me a tremendous, almost spiritual, sense of the universality of the human condition. I don't know quite how to put it; I feel *enhanced.* Readers write to say I've inspired them—what a kick to read this! Also, by continuing to write, I feel that I'm showing that I have some tiger in me. That's a good feeling.

Your column, "Take a Deep Breath, Decide to Enjoy Life, Feed the Birds," is a wonderful litany of advice for almost anyone. Could you compose a similar list of advice for writers?

Read, read, read. Write one true sentence, as Hemingway advised, then chew it over and make it better. Say your sentence aloud, the better to feel cadence, rhythm, stress. Play around with different genres of writing. Take some risks. Stretch your working vocabulary. Believe in yourself.

Susan Trausch
Editorial Writing

Susan Trausch won the ASNE award for editorial writing in her first year on the job. She came to *The Boston Globe*'s editorial page in January 1994 from the op-ed page where she wrote a column from 1989-1993. Trausch joined the *Globe*'s business pages in 1973, writing news, features, and "Out to Lunch," a humor column. She went to Washington for the paper in 1982, and wrote a book about her experiences, *It Came From the Swamp—Your Federal Government at Work,* that should be required reading for every newcomer to the capital. Says H.D.S. Greenway, the *Globe*'s editorial page editor, "Susan's 'Just a minute!' style brings a freshness to our pages as well as that rarest of editorial page qualities—humor. Underneath the laughter lies an editorial razor blade, and there is never any doubt on which side she comes down."

Trausch has a delightful sense of the absurd, revels in the music of language and the power of words to inform, illuminate, and impale bloated thought. Even on a page without bylines, her editorials stand out with a witty, wise, and caring voice of their own.

A summons from history

SEPTEMBER 23, 1994

The past came to claim Aleksandras Lileikis this week. It knocked on his door on Sumner Street in Norwood, shattering his quiet present and shocking the friends and neighbors who thought they knew the man in the yellow house. It knocked on all of our doors, pointing to the genocide of more than 50 years ago, demanding that we hear the stories and seek the truth.

Lileikis says the truth is that he did not sign the death warrants for 40,000 Jews in Lithuania during World War II and that the Justice Department has no right to try to remove his citizenship or deport him.

As always, the evidence should be carefully weighed before a person is convicted of committing crimes against humanity. But the weighing must be done, and the search must continue for the foot soldiers and generals who carried out the Holocaust. Some people ask why, feeling that hunting down old men is an exercise in hate, that the past is best forgotten and that Lileikis, who is 87 years old, should be left to live out his days in peace.

The answer is that there is no statute of limitation on murder. Whether one person is killed or 6 million are lost, the memory of those lives must be honored by society's insistence that guilty parties answer for the crime in a court of law.

Not to insist is to share the guilt, to become part of that long, silent, immoral line of people who "just followed orders" or looked the other way, or who now deny that the Holocaust ever happened. If Lileikis is innocent, his story will be heard and his name cleared. Innocent or guilty, he is obligated to stand and tell that story.

The past is never dead, no matter how long it may lie buried in shallow, unmarked graves. Eventually it will be answered for. The butchers in Rwanda, Bosnia, Iraq, Cambodia and other killing zones should remember that. Someday there will be a knock on the door. Not in the dead of night, but on a bright September afternoon.

Writers' Workshop

Talking Points

1) Notice how Trausch begins this editorial—"The past came to claim Aleksandras Lileikis this week. It knocked on his door on Sumner Street in Norwood..."—and then returns to the same point at the end—"Someday there will be a knock on the door. Not in the dead of night, but on a bright September afternoon." What are the advantages of such a circular structure?

2) Talk about the placement of each point of argument within a Trausch editorial. How has she anticipated the reader's position and countered it?

3) News and opinion are the raw material of editorials. Separate what is news and what is opinion in this editorial, and discuss the balance between these two elements. If you were writing this editorial, would you shift the balance to either side?

4) Rhythm and repetition are vital to the power of Trausch's writing. Read aloud the third paragraph: "As always, the evidence should be carefully weighed before a person is convicted of committing crimes against humanity. But the weighing must be done, and the search must continue for the foot soldiers and generals who carried out the Holocaust." Discuss the effect of this paragraph and isolate the elements that give it strength.

Assignment Desk

1) Pick a topic on which you have passionate, personal feelings—abortion, drunken driving, animal experimentation, racial or sexist discrimination. Try to write an editorial that will make a person who holds exactly opposite views read and think.

2) Write an editorial that follows the example of Trausch's circular structure. What were the challenges facing you and how did you overcome them?

3) Take an essay, speech, argument, or magazine article of at least 3,000 words and write a brief, tight, to-the-point

editorial. To do this you have to select one aspect of the subject, limit it, and then develop it. Write a paragraph on how you did this.

4) In the editorial's final paragraph, Trausch refers to "the butchers in Rwanda, Bosnia, Iraq, and Cambodia." Research and write an editorial about one or more of these atrocities.

The sea around us

A ferry sinks in the Baltic, killing more than 800 people, reminding us how fragile all our boats are on life's seas. That fragility isn't confronted too often. If it were, people wouldn't leave the house in the morning. Living requires us to set forth confidently every day with agendas and shopping lists, much like those nearly 1,000 passengers who boarded the *Estonia* in Tallinn on Tuesday night. One must assume the destination will be reached.

Seeing the photographs of empty life vests and rafts awash in giant waves, one remembers just about every ferry trip taken over a lifetime, usually in a holiday mood, or, if the ride is part of a regular commute, with barely a thought to the potential ferocity of the elements. "I'll be on the 6 o'clock boat," says the hurried commuter, newspaper tucked under arm, briefcase stuffed with work. "See you at the dock."

People get into planes, trains and automobiles just as routinely, blocking out whatever disaster has been in the news, focusing instead on luggage, lunch and laptop computer, rarely stopping to consider that such nonchalance is an act of faith.

After all, the world is so advanced and transportation is state-of-the-art. Procedures are in place to handle any emergency. What is there to fear?

People have the same attitude about modern medicine and are shocked to hear about the plague in India. The plague was supposed to be extinct, a nightmare confined to the Dark Ages. How can it be taking lives in 1994?

Earthquakes, fires, random shootings and other disasters, manmade and natural, crowd into the consciousness for a brief, terrifying time and are then shut out, ordered back into the shadows. People wince, fold the newspaper into the wastebasket, turn off the television and again launch their boats, however small. The sun is out. The winds are fair. The journey continues.

Writers' Workshop

Talking Points

1) Trausch gets right to the point in the lead of this editorial, merging news and commentary in her very first sentence: "A ferry sinks in the Baltic, killing more than 800 people, reminding us how fragile all our boats are on life's seas." Study her other editorials and determine how and when she differentiates between the news and her commentary.

2) Read the ending of this editorial aloud: "The sun is out. The winds are fair. The journey continues." Many newspaper stories trail off, but the last line is often the most important one in an editorial. Study the endings of Trausch's editorials. Discuss their style, differences, and impact.

3) Discuss the role of the editorial in the newspaper. How does the editorial serve the reader? The paper? The community?

Assignment Desk

1) Effective writing creates a conversation between the writer and reader. Imagine the dialogue that lies beneath the text of this editorial. Create the other half of the conversation, writing what she heard the reader saying before she wrote the following paragraph in response to it. Example: "Did you hear about that ferry boat sinking?"

2) Write about how this editorial made you feel and what aspects of the editorial prompted your reaction. Be as specific as possible as you record your impressions and the resonant elements of the editorial.

3) When you read the paper tomorrow morning, identify the news story that seems to strike the deepest chord inside you. Follow the method Trausch describes in her interview and quickly jot a list of your thoughts on the topic: questions, interview possibilities, your opinions, possible leads, and endings. Write a 400-word editorial.

4) Read the news stories about the event Trausch is commenting on in this editorial. What information did she focus on? What did she leave out? Discuss the possible reasons

for her decisions. Rewrite the editorial by focusing on different elements within the story.

5) Write editorials on a serious subject and a humorous one. Which one do you find more challenging to write?

Easy pickings for plaintiffs

OCTOBER 4, 1994

If lawyers had lived in the Garden of Eden, Eve
would have sued the owner for negligence. Counsel for the aggrieved party would have argued that
paradise was not well maintained—if it were, it
would not have had a snake problem.

Sound absurd? Not to farmers running pick-
your-own apple orchards. They and their counterparts at berry, pumpkin and Christmas tree farms
have had the litigious public descending on their
profits like locusts. The same people who head
out to the country to escape the sterility of super-
markets are the first to cry "whiplash!" if they
slip on an apple peel.

Turned ankles, bee stings, poison ivy and
strained backs—usually caused when a customer
hefts too much produce to the car—have all translated into losses and increased liability insurance
for farmers. Even the new state law stipulating
that owners are responsible only for preventable
injuries caused by wanton negligence probably
won't do much to stop the aggressive attorney.

The problem is not simply greed but the sense
of entitlement some people have about the natural
world. They enter forest or field with a theme
park mentality and assume there will be no risks.
They walk into an orchard the same way they
would enter a pavilion in Walt Disney World.

That's why Massachusetts now requires farmers to post this reality check at their gates: "Under Section 2E of Chapter 128 of the General
Laws, the owner, operator, or any employee of
this farm, shall not be liable for injury or death
of persons, or damage to property, resulting out of
the conduct of this 'pick your own' harvesting
activity in the absence of willful, wanton, or reckless conduct."

Ah, nature. That's what most customers still
want, too—fresh air and fresh fruit, not a day in

court. But a persistent minority is causing a problem so big that many farmers are thinking about
selling their land to developers. Once again everyone is being hurt by a few rotten apples.

Writers' Workshop

Talking Points

1) Writers use similes to compare two things that are essentially different but are considered to be alike in one way or another. Discuss why Trausch compares the "litigious public descending" on the profits of farmers running pick-your-own orchards to "locusts." Would it have been as telling a simile if she had compared them to vultures?

2) We usually talk about voice in terms of the individual, but the voice of the editorial is the voice of an institution. Discuss how this helps and limits the writer. Trausch is able to convey a personal voice within the institutional voice. How does she do it?

3) In an editorial of just six paragraphs, Trausch uses one to quote a section of state law verbatim: "Under Section 2E of Chapter 128 of the General Laws, the owner, operator, or any employee of this farm, shall not be liable for injury or death of persons, or damage to property, resulting out of the conduct of this 'pick your own' harvesting activity in the absence of willful, wanton, or reckless conduct." What is the effect? Do you agree with her decision?

4) "An occasional short sentence can carry a tremendous punch," William Zinsser notes in his classic writing text, *On Writing Well*. Notice how Trausch follows up that passage of legalese with a two-word sentence that carries a wallop of irony: "Ah, nature." Describe the effect.

5) Editorial writers, columnists, and reporters write about news in distinctly different ways. In her career, Susan Trausch has worked in all three roles. Discuss the differences among editorials, columns, interpretive news stories.

Assignment Desk

1) Take a story you have written and write an editorial on the same subject. Then write a paragraph describing the differences you felt as a writer as well as some of the significant differences in the editorial form compared with a news story.

2) Rewrite the legalese in paragraph five for a lay reader. Compare it with the verbatim transcript of the section of state law. Which would be preferable in a news story on this issue?

3) Identify and describe the target of Trausch's criticism. How persuasive is the case she makes against them? Write an editorial that takes their side.

4) Rewrite this editorial as a column and as a news story. What elements are missing from the editorial that should appear in these two other forms?

Goodbye, Columbus

OCTOBER 10, 1994

Love him or hate him, Christopher Columbus represents a time when a person could get into a boat and sail off to a new world. Americans living in 1994 can envy that. Not that they condone plunder and pillage, nor would they trade the conveniences of the late 20th century for the primitive lifestyle of the 15th, but the planet did seem a lot bigger in 1492.

Stuck in rush-hour traffic, or in a dead-end job, or in line at the fax machine, citizens of the modern world often wish for that ancient sense of distance. Today's globe feels like a tennis ball in the palm of the hand. No spot is considered unreachable. No land remains untouched. No war, famine, coup, scandal, innovation or summit meeting goes unreported. It's right there in the living room.

Even vacations that are supposed to take a person away from it all can turn into a crowd. Plan a trip to Katmandu and the Sherpas are booked for months. Awake in the splendor of Yosemite to hear the beep of a cellular phone in the next tent.

Adventure on the high seas is reduced to a weekend "cruise to nowhere." Searching in vain for an unblazed trail, today's bushwhacker compensates by driving a Ford Explorer or investing in the Magellan Fund.

Outer space was supposed to be America's next frontier, but budget cuts have given earthbound projects precedence. The bold exploration of geography and moonscape has evolved into quieter journeys into cyberspace, genetic engineering, AIDS and brain research and world population planning. All vital pursuits, but the going is incremental and painstaking, often involving committees and confusing ethical considerations.

Today the world hangs on America's door, asking for relief, military intervention or political asylum. Desperate sailors head for our shores on flimsy rafts but are denied entry. There are too many, and a country must set limits. Columbus Day reminds us of the days when there were no limits. We wouldn't go back to the ignorance or brutality, but recalling the positive energy of one explorer may help us go forward.

Writers' Workshop

Talking Points

1) In this editorial, Trausch provides a thoughtful and engaging commentary that makes the reader take notice of what Columbus Day really means. Suggest other contrasts between exploration and frontiers in 1492 and 503 years later.

2) Embedded in Trausch's editorials are observations that create unforgettable moments of recognition for readers, whether they have experienced them personally or not. An example from "Goodbye, Columbus" appears in paragraph three. "Awake in the splendor of Yosemite to hear the beep of a cellular phone in the next tent." Look for other examples in the rest of her editorials and discuss their impact.

3) A single theme dominates an effective piece of writing, bolstered by evidence supporting that central idea. Is there one sentence in this editorial that captures the theme? Discuss the reasons for your choice.

4) Notice how Trausch marshals the evidence for her argument in paragraph two: "Stuck in rush-hour traffic, or in a dead-end job, or in line at the fax machine, citizens of the modern world often wish for that ancient sense of distance. Today's globe feels like a tennis ball in the palm of the hand. No spot is considered unreachable. No land remains untouched. No war, famine, coup, scandal, innovation or summit meeting goes unreported. It's right there in the living room." Discuss the strengths of her logic and style, including sentence length, repetition, and imagery.

5) Like their counterparts in the newsroom, editorial writers also get stuck with cliché assignments—Christmas, Thanksgiving, V-E Day, Memorial Day, Spring, Columbus Day. Study what Trausch did with this assignment and apply its lessons to a similar assignment.

Assignment Desk

1) Write your own editorial commemorating Columbus Day.

2) On Feb. 14, 1991, Philip M. Boffey, deputy editorial page editor of *The New York Times,* wrote an editorial that was a touching Valentine's Day love letter to his wife, lawyer Ronda Billig. Look up and read Boffey's editorial and then think of the holiday that carries the most meaning for you and write an editorial about it. Keep in mind what Jack Rosenthal, then-editorial page editor at the *Times,* had to say about personalized editorials: "The test is not whether it's personal or freaky or frivolous. The test is whether it has something to say to a large audience."

3) Find Columbus Day editorials published in three other papers and compare them with the one written by Trausch. Which one did you prefer and why?

4) Interview local editorial writers and write a report on what they feel are the greatest problems of their craft and how they solve them. Compare their responses to the comments in Trausch's interview. Discuss those points where the local writers and/or Trausch disagree.

Water, water everywhere

NOVEMBER 7, 1994

America's obsession with chic bottled water is getting worse. Moving way beyond "Perrier with a twist," the truly trendy are seeking the ultimate H_2O experience from big-name fashion designers, who give away private-label stock as a promotional item in their stores.

Buy a $1,500 Donna Karan original and take home a bottle of DKNY water to drink while wearing it. Talk about a fashion statement. At those prices they should be handing out Dom Perignon.

Water "just seems so right," Patti Cohen, public relations executive for Donna Karan, told *The Wall Street Journal.* "Water is international. It's real. It's part of you."

It's also becoming a pain in the glass. The Gap offers it as an accessory to expensive jeans. Ralph Lauren is thinking about bottling it, and Chanel makes a $1,200 tote for carrying it. Maxfield, the Los Angeles boutique, floated it in aquariums with tropical fish at a "water launching party" last summer to announce that the clothier was marketing the stuff to hotels and restaurants.

Enough! Bring back the days when water was boring, when a person could go into a restaurant and order it straight from the kitchen tap for free and when people did not discuss the relative merits of glaciers versus natural springs.

Have we no backbone to stand up to the status marketers? Has the fear, or guilt, about what human beings have done to the environment made us fanatics about finding the clearest and the purest while ego demands the classiest?

One wonders what Rudyard Kipling might have made of the madness had he been around to create "Gunga Din" in 1994. Perhaps his poem would have gone something like this:

It was "Din! Din! Din!
"Bring the haute couture on ice to keep us thin.
"Pour the Evian and Blass,
"Give our lives a shot of class.
"Do you sell it under your name, Mr. Din?"

Writers' Workshop

Talking Points

1) Editorials are too often filled with generalities. Examine this editorial, noting the specific details and the generalities and the balance between the two, and discuss the effect of these elements.

2) Trausch's editorials display a variety of voices: the storyteller, the preacher, the teacher, the satirist. Contrast Trausch's voice in this editorial with her voice in "The Sea Around Us." Identify what makes the two pieces sound so different. How and why does subject matter require a shift in tone?

3) Apart from subject matter, identify the major differences between this editorial and "A Summons from History." Consider such elements as sentence length, word choice, and balance of fact and opinion.

4) *In Best Newspaper Writing 1994,* Michael Gartner, last year's ASNE editorial winner and a finalist this year, called "facts" the most important element of an editorial. "A lot of editorial writers try to get by on their writing or their outrage, not on their reporting. That just doesn't work.... In an editorial, you use facts to persuade as well as inform." Retrace the reporting Trausch had to do for this editorial.

5) Writers use parody to poke fun by imitating, as Trausch does here with her spoof of "Gunga Din." Look for other examples in your newspaper reading.

Assignment Desk

1) Pick the editorial you like the most and describe, paragraph by paragraph, the writer's problem and how she solved it.

2) Read Rudyard Kipling's poem "Gunga Din." Why did water play such an important role in that story? Rent *The Player,* Robert Altman's film satire on Hollywood that also features a running gag on bottled water. Discuss the dif-

ferences and similarities between Trausch's treatment and Altman's.

3) Most pop culture trends have a short shelf life. Who still wears mood rings today? What is the latest trend you're aware of and what does it say about society? Write an editorial about it. Try to include a parody as Trausch did.

4) Play around with clauses, setting up a sentence that starts in one direction and ends going in the opposite direction. You can do it within a phrase as in "She had a whim of iron." Notice how Trausch achieves comic effect by starting in one direction and then gives you a surprise by going the opposite way, as in "a pain in the glass." It should be unexpected, but also on target.

A conversation with
Susan Trausch

CHRISTOPHER SCANLAN: I have been having a great time reading *It Came From the Swamp,* the book you wrote about covering Washington for the *Globe,* and one passage in particular: "Why do I do this to myself? Because I refuse to accept life without frivolity. So I keep trying to reach out, as the phone company says, and jab someone in the ribs with a well-placed elbow. It's a dirty job, but somebody's got to do it. And it does help preserve one's sanity after a day at the office."

Is that what you're still doing?

SUSAN TRAUSCH: I suppose I'm addicted to that. I always have tried, as a writer, to go for the common ground, and the most common ground we have, I think, involves humor and allows us to, in learning the lessons about ourselves, enjoy it more than the traditional editorial scolding stance: "It would be prudent if we all did this..." I try to make it more human and make it about "us," rather than "them" or "you."

Writing, or any art, touches that universality in us. And it makes you go, "Oh, yeah! I've done this, I've felt this." It should touch us where we're most real. The topics I like the most are the ones that either say something funny about human nature or the fragility of life or something we all feel as people.

Traditionally there's so little of what you're talking about on newspaper editorial pages. So little humor, certainly. Do you have that sense, as a reader of editorial pages?

The tendency is to be serious about public policy. There's nothing wrong with that. It's a real important part of editorial pages. But I think along with that, along with bashing the president, you've got to have a spot where we're just being people. We get overwhelmed with the serious. We look at Newt Gingrich and think, "It's time to write a hard-hitter." There's so much that's deadly serious going on—welfare cuts and kids going without their school lunches—the world cries out for a lot of serious treatment and that's good.

But we need a little relief from all of that.

Are you the "relief pitcher" then?

I'm considered the relief pitcher, yes. Although I write serious ones, too.

Do you have a beat or a specialty on the page?

I asked not to have a beat and (editorial page editor) David Greenway agreed that I would just be a floater and write about whatever grabbed me. So I don't really have an official thing that I follow. Everybody else does. And I've fought that. I've always fought it. I've been in the business for over 20 years and when I was on the business pages or when I was in Washington, I tried very hard to avoid a "beat."

I try to pick the most interesting story in the news, not necessarily the biggest story—for instance, in Saturday's paper there was a story about some entrepreneur who has invented a parking meter that will no longer make it possible for us to pull up to the parking meter and use the other guy's time as he pulls out. In other words, there's 20 minutes left on the meter and that car pulls out, it'll just automatically, through the magic of infrared computers, go back to zero.

This to me goes to the very Soul of Man. We want our freebies. Life is bad enough, you're going to take our 20 minutes' parking away from us? So that kind of thing grabs me in that it's something we can all relate to, but it's also something we can say something bigger about how we are as personalities and how automated and impersonal the world has become, and it's funny.

When did you become an editorial writer?

January 1994, so I've been at this game a year and two months.

So you won the ASNE editorial writing award for the first editorials you had written.

Beginner's luck.

Last year the winner for headlines was Ken Wells of *The Wall Street Journal,* and he had just joined the Page One desk.

Maybe this business needs fresh eyes.

What is it that you brought to the editorial page as someone who had never been an editorial writer before?

If I had been told to write dead-serious stuff, I wouldn't have brought anything. So I guess what I brought was my wacky view of the world. And I didn't have to bury it and say, "It would be prudent if we ____ ." Fill in the blank.

Do you think that writers on newspapers should be flexible enough to be able to write humor and then, the very next day, do a serious piece?

It's hard to write humor. It's really one of the hardest things to do, and you should never force humor on a writer. It's either in your soul to write humor or it ain't. And generally, if it ain't, people just don't gravitate toward it. If it is, you can't *not* write it. It's just got to come out. And I think that's part of the reason there isn't a lot of humor in papers, because it can be really bad. I've written some really bad stuff; I'm familiar with the process. When I was doing the column, I would write one and always gave myself several days before it ran so I could come in and read it after the weekend and throw up for a while and then start over. Because your first pass at a humor piece is often just perfectly wretched. Every cliché you've ever been taught comes out, and you think it's riotously funny and then you read it on Monday and it's not.

So what do you do then?

With a column, you just start over. With an editorial, you don't have that luxury.

What's the secret of being funny?

I think it's keeping it human. And not writing down to the reader, or making fun of the reader. It's sharing the joke. In other words, you've been there. It's not trying to be too erudite and use words like "erudite," you know? It needs to be real and very down-to-earth, without being pedestrian.

Where did you learn to write humor? And who did you learn it from?

I always wrote it. I don't know where I learned it. My father had a great sense of humor. His day job was insurance salesman, and he wrote by night. He wrote tons and tons of short stories that got in places like *Outdoor Magazine* and *Fly Fisherman.* I do remember him typing madly. I have his typewriter. An old Underwood. It's in my office at home next to the computer.

He also told me not to go into writing. Of course, then he was very proud that I did. He said, "No, do something easy."

Whom do you write for?

I write for the reader. And that's probably an old-fashioned, bizarre notion. I always visualize the guy on the subway, really busy, and I either have to grab him in the first three words or he's going to turn to the comic page or the sports page. I want to tell that person, "There's something we can share here." I guess I also write for myself.

My favorite quote about writing was from O. Henry, who said, "Write what makes you happy." And I think that's so true. There's nothing more leaden than a subject you're not into. You can make the sentences come out all right, but it will have no fire. And no joy.

Where did you learn about writing?

In the seventh grade, I read Benchley and Thurber, and I just went out of my bird. I said, "You can earn money doing this? I want to do this! How do I do this?" They were my heroes. I remember reading *The Thurber Album,* and he wrote about his aunt who used to put everything of value outside her bedroom door, wrapped up in a great big scarf, because she figured if the burglars came then they wouldn't kill her. You know, only Thurber would have these crazy relatives. And I can't remember if it was Thurber or Benchley who had an uncle who was the only human being ever to have Dutch elm disease. It's hysterical. Benchley's titles just put me away, "20,000 Leagues Under the Sea, or David Copperfield." I would just roll on the floor in the library.

What advice would you give someone who wants to write editorials like yours, which are sometimes funny and sometimes very serious?

I'd definitely read Don Murray. He wrote a wonderful book on writing, (*Writing For Your Readers,* Globe Pequot Press, 1992) and I'm reading an absolutely stupendous series of books that have been around forever that I didn't know about, *The Paris Review Interviews.*

It's so good. Thurber's in there. He's in my living room. They tell me what he looks like and what he said and how he wrote when he was blind and it was just incredible. So I'd read tons of books on writing, but I'd mostly write. You have to write. You have to put words on paper every single day. And you have to give yourself an assignment and do it.

You have to do it and find your voice, and I suppose if somebody said to me, "Oh, I want to write like that," I would say to them, "First of all, have you written anything?" and if they had never written anything I'd say, "You've got to start writing to figure out what your voice is. You have to keep putting the words on paper and find out who's there."

You described *The Boston Globe* as a writer's paper. What does that mean?

It means an editor will go with your ideas. There's nothing worse than an editor that lays it on you from the top and just says, "No." And believe me, I've worked for that kind of person. And it is the most stultifying thing you can imagine. It's not that you don't accept assignments. I don't mean that you always come up with it and the editor just sits there. I mean, he comes up with ideas too, but it's a collaborative effort where you're both interested in the best possible writing you can get, or best possible story, and you're not interested in whose ego is on the line or who's bucking for a promotion or who's trying to make points with four editors up. You really are concentrating on the product.

How often do you write editorials on deadline?

Oh, almost all the time.

And what is a deadline, for you?

A deadline is 4 o'clock, and it's a very tight deadline. You come out of the meeting at 11 or 11:15, and you've got to have it—it's a rigid 4 o'clock deadline.
Eight of us on the editorial board meet every day at 10:15, and go around the room and talk about what ideas we've got. And we decide do we want to say something about this, do we want to say it now, is it better to wait for more news de-

velopment on it. We have what we call "feeding the goat." You have this big blank space every day, it's usually four editorials, 35 lines each, and the goat is always hungry, and Friday in here is the pits because you've got to feed the goat for Saturday, Sunday, and Monday—also Tuesday, if it's a long weekend. So you need to generate copy, is what I'm saying.

So you come out of that 11 o'clock meeting with an assignment that you didn't know about when you came to work that day.

You can never plan a lunch, you know? And you have to write fast. And I'm often frozen for the first hour, "Oh, God, what am I going to say?" I will do a library search, depending on the topic, to see if there's anything in there.

How do you start the writing?

I usually start out just writing down a bunch of ideas on a legal pad, before I start to type, just free associate. What points would I want to say about all of this. Somehow the mechanical business of putting down those ideas helps me get my wheels going. I'll write the topic of the editorial at the top and then anything that occurs to me.

It's like a ritual. I can't just stare at a blank screen and start to write. I've discovered over the years that I have to break down what's trying to come out of my head. So the way I do that is to just take individual ideas and write them down. And that helps me organize it, too, because I can see themes emerging, like, this clump of stuff could all go together, and that clump of stuff would be part of another idea. When I write down all these things, when I go to write my lead, it's easier. Somehow I know what my head is trying to say, as opposed to having it all jammed there at the opening. I pick out the little threads of thought first.

If a beginning journalist came to you and said, "I'm having a real problem on deadline," or an editor came and said, "This reporter is just not cutting it on deadline," would you suggest this approach?

I would just say, "Sit down and go through your notebook. Just write something as simple as, 'Good quote on fire engines,' and then circle that in your notebook or put a '1' next to it." You have to know what's in the notebook. You have to stop rummaging through your notebook in a panic. You have to know what's in there. And then know what's in your mind. It all depends on what kind of story you're doing, but you have to go through that notebook and know what goodies are in there.

After you do your work on the pad, what then?

Somewhere in there eat lunch, usually eat at my desk, because I find it really breaks my concentration to go up, have lunch, have a conversation for an hour, and then come back. I eat my salad, and I'm either reading what I got out of the library queue, or thinking of more little points, this is all by way of putting off that moment, you know.

So then I have to come up with it, and you can just hear the clock ticking. I mean, if it's 2 o'clock and I don't have a lead, I'm screaming, "What am I going to write?!" Sometimes it's 3 o'clock, I don't have a lead.

Is getting that lead first critical?

I have to have a lead or I can't write anything. I have to have my first sentence, because that's my whole piece. That's the tone, that says what is this piece about, it's the theme, the thing by which everything hangs. If I don't have that first sentence, I just can't keep going forward. Especially on something that's only 35 lines long, boy, if I don't have the first sentence...

How do you get the lead?

Just trial and error. I've got these ideas I've written down, and some of them I'll put stars next to if I think that could be the lead, or the main essence of the piece, and then I'll work with that idea and I'll write it over and over and over 50 times until I get it. And once I get the first sentence, then I can keep going.

I keep going to the top and rewriting it. I'll write the first sentence and then I'll write the second sentence and then maybe I've got a paragraph and I'll go back and say, "There's something not right here," and I'll do it over and over and over. And then I go to the second paragraph. It's a matter of always going from the top down, and it's like you hear the rhythm—especially if it's humor, there's a rhythm to these words. One word off, you've lost the tap dance. It's not funny.

It's just instinctive. You just know it's off.

Are you reading it aloud to yourself?

I'm not saying it, but in my head I keep reading it. I hear it.

"The past came to claim Aleksandras Lileikis this week." When you write that sentence in the editorial about the man accused of being a Nazi death camp guard, do you know, "Ah, this is it"?

I hope it is. There is always doubt. I've changed leads right before I've hit the send button. And I've gone in the queue before the editor reads it and I go, "No, no, it's something else." So I'm always wary of it. I always hope it's the right lead. But I'm always looking at it suspiciously, thinking, "You may think you're the right lead, but we don't know yet."

For all your wonderful wit, there's nothing funny in "A Summons From History." Do you remember writing that piece?

It was a front-page story, and I went into the meeting and I said, "We've got to write about this." We talked about, "Well, you know, is it another Nazi hunter story and what do you say that's new?" I felt what we had to say was that there would always be this hunt and that it's not a vindictive ripping apart of lives. It is justice for the injustice, and it has to go on for all of us. The world has to know that a crime like that, whether it was committed in Dachau in the '30s or San Salvador in the '80s, that humanity is going to come back and demand retribution. And that was the story, I thought.

Was it written that day?

Yes. It was written on deadline with a lot of sweat. When I have to do a lot of research on an editorial, then it's twice as hard. This one I just sat down and wrote, but even then it was a sweat.

Did it go through a lot of revision?

That ran basically as I wrote it. I had covered the gathering in Washington when the Holocaust survivors returned to the capital and found each other, in some cases for the first time since the war. There were just thousands and thousands, busloads of Jewish folks from all over America, and I spent three days interviewing them. It's one of the most moving things that I've ever experienced. By the end of the three days, I was so exhausted I couldn't hear another story. There was a man who clawed his way through a train on the way to the camps, women meeting each other, showing each other their numbers.

For another story I interviewed Elie Wiesel about what was it like to win the Nobel Prize and how did his life change. He was in this apartment in New York where all the furniture was black and he was sitting in shadow, and he just said, "There was no champagne."

When I read about Lileikis, those people came back to me. People with their numbers and those wonderful warm people who had carried their burdens for so long.

What is the value of the editorial writer?

I guess it's much the same value as the reporter. It's somebody who's going to ask questions, and if you're the mayor or the governor or the president, it's the double purpose of the editorial page to grab the power structure by the lapels and say, "Hey, you! Enough!" And if you're the mayor of the town, you pay a lot of attention to the local paper —we like to think they do, anyway. And if you're the President of the United States, it comes in an agglomeration; your aides tell you, "Well, 500 newspapers just said you're wrong, Mr. President."

How do you develop your topic within strict limitations of space on the editorial page?

That's probably the great teaching discipline of editorial writing. You really have to boil it down and that's why pad writing is crucial in this job because every word counts. You've got an idea and you boil it down to its smallest space. And try to make it powerful space. I think everybody should do editorial writing, because it's a real discipline. You really learn economy of language and making it strong. There isn't any editorial I've written, and probably isn't any that's appeared in print, that I couldn't go through and still take out the extraneous words.

What is it like to write for an institution like *The Boston Globe*?

You have to get used to not having a byline. You're anonymous. You are the voice of the *Globe.* And it's not like seeing your name in print the next day, although you see your voice in print.

If you have dedicated followers, they will send you a message on the computer saying, "You wrote that one, right?" You know, it's sort of a guessing game, "Guess who wrote the editorial."

What are the advantages?

The advantages are a fun group, several other people going, "Yeah, that's a good idea you have," or they are glad you came up with one for Saturday because we're one short, and so you've got that group sharing of the loneliest part of writing, which is coming up with the idea. It's interesting meeting different people. I mean the mayor likes to have breakfast with us, or the governor comes in for lunch—we had Daniel Ellsberg in here, we've had George McGovern. We have the Right come in, too. You get to talk to people.

What are the limitations?

The limitations are that you may have an idea and it may not fly, and when you did a column you could always do it. Sometimes when my little electrical impulses are going off as a writer, I know something's there. Sometimes I have trouble articulating it and I haven't made my list on the pad yet, I haven't formed it, I just know there's something there. So I'm groping for what it is I think is there, and it may not fly with the group, whereas if you're a lonely columnist, you'll get to go down that road.

What's the hardest part of being an editorial writer?

Focusing one's thoughts quickly, and also condensing big ideas into a little space. And you can never ramble. Sometimes you feel like you're not telling the whole story, either. It's really condensed down to its bare bones: what is the opinion in here, what is it we want the world to do or not do, or people to think about. Things get boiled down to their very essence like distilling a chemical or something into its purest form, and that's real hard.

You raised two issues—time and space.

The enemy of all of us who labor in the journalistic vineyards.

What strategies and techniques are most effective for dealing with the issue of time? Getting it done in a day?

Putting my thoughts down. Doing real fast library work. I go to the library, usually the first thing, and see what's in there. And reading those things fast, and getting my basic thoughts down as quickly as possible, and trying to get a lead written before lunch because it seems like once I eat food my mind goes slower. The brain cells must have to go down to the stomach and work on the salad or something.

What about space? How do you write so tight?

I keep shortening my sentences. I'll get a thought down and I'm becoming really good at turning two sentences into three words.

In "Easy Pickings for Plaintiffs" you quote a long passage from the state law followed by a paragraph with just two words, "Ah, Nature." What were you doing there?

I picked it for its very stiff legalese, as against the flow of why we allegedly go to these farms. Showing how the lawyers had intruded themselves on the natural experience. I felt the language was just so wonderfully stiff that it was funny. It made me laugh.

I wanted the juxtaposition of the stiff legal idiots against poetry, which is what you really go to an orchard for. And why you want to cut down your own Christmas tree and you want to leave your stuffy apartment and walk in the woods. And, unfortunately, you know, this is 1995, so you've got liability insurance following you through the woods.

How conscious are you of your voice?

I just write what feels natural. And what sounds funny, if I'm writing a funny one. And what I think will resonate with most people. I try not to use big words, and also I can't spell them anyway, so why use them. When you're on a 4 o'clock deadline, you don't have time to go to the dictionary, so you use the short ones. But when I'm writing, I'm working with the material. I don't sit there and think, "Now, what is my voice?"

Your editorials display a wide range of voices. There's the storyteller's voice, there's the preacher, the teacher. In the letter accompanying your nomination, your boss called it your "Just a minute!" style. Are you aware that there are different voices in your pieces?

I just go with the material. If you're writing about the Nazi officer, there is no humor. You just have to be absolutely straight—it's a dramatic event and there's just nothing funny in there. But when you're writing funny, I'm aware of trying to be more flip. It entirely depends on the subject. That dictates the tone.

What has editorial writing done for you as a writer?

It's made me much tighter. I had to write tight when I wrote a column. It was only 70 lines. But there still was a lot more elbow room than there is here. And I guess it also really makes me focus on what it is I want to say, because there's no room for anything more.

Do you ever get blocked when the 4 o'clock deadline is looming?

I always break through the block. I just say, "Well, it's not great but that's my lead," and I just write through it. And then somewhere when you're getting down toward line 35, a better lead may come to you.

You have to go with what you've got. You have to get it down. You have to tell the story as best you can in the time limits. You have to say, "OK, you know, this one is not going to be deathless prose. It's just going to be the best I can do." The worst moment of panic is the first paragraph, the first 15 lines are always the hardest. We're not Hemingway. So you just have to get it out there and make it as clear as you can.

What role do editors play for you in the writing of these?

There's very little changing, probably because our time is so tight. I find the editing much more sensible and very often an editor will make just the right change on a word or say, "Well, why don't you turn this sentence around."

How does an editor hinder a writer?

The worst thing an editor can do is dump on your ideas so that eventually you don't think of any. An editor should nurture in a writer the ability to come up with stuff. Because every writer is unique. Every writer has a voice and a certain way of looking at the world, and that should always be encouraged because that's where you get your best stuff. If a writer comes up to you and says, "God, I just saw the wildest thing on the way to work," or, "I read this story in the paper and boy, we could do a great big take-out on this," unless it's the looniest idea you ever heard or we've just done 10 of them, I would always say yes. Grab that enthusiasm because that's where you'll get the best copy.

You've been a business reporter, business columnist, a columnist, a magazine writer, op-ed page columnist, Washington reporter. What did you learn from each of those roles and how do those lessons apply to your job today?

In business reporting, I learned that no question was too stupid and that no matter how much this business expert might know, I was not afraid to ask what the Dow Jones was. It didn't matter how stupid I appeared in front of this person. And I have to say that most business people were pretty savvy about answering questions. I found much more of that snobbery in Washington. "You don't know? Here, read this seven-pound mountain of material and then ask your questions." Nobody wanted to explain anything in Washington. They all wanted to use their knowledge as a weapon against you. But business people didn't do that. They wanted to talk about their business. So I learned to ask questions and to explain complex things.

Washington taught me that you have to believe in a good idea. You have to believe that the place is nuts. Washington taught me to believe in myself because what I saw was funny. And my ideas were good.

Magazine writing taught me how to organize vast amounts of material, to do three weeks of interviewing, and to be able to boil it all down.

From column writing I learned to really go deeply inside myself and constantly ask myself, "What did I think of that?" or, "What did this thing in Washington mean?" I was always looking for that human thing that we could all relate to.

How do you want people to react to the editorial about the ferry?

I want them to share that human moment of a common event that turns into a tragedy and know that we all walk on the edge. And we can all get on the wrong ferry any minute. I want people to feel at once how fragile life is and how precious, and to enjoy those days they have.

What reaction do you want from "Water, Water Everywhere"?

How silly we can get about fashion and how complex and expensive life has become.

You decided to make up your own version of "Gunga Din," didn't you?

It was in the middle of writing it. I was looking for an ending or something. It was on my pad of paper. I wrote everything I could think of associated with water, and one of the things I wrote down was "Gunga Din, check poem." So I went down to the library and decided to end with old Gunga.

Are there any rules or principles you write by?

I try always, I hope, to be fair and not to savage somebody. Because you have such power as the media that you can always make a person look stupid. I'm thinking of some political profiles I've read where the intent from the beginning was to rip the person's face off, and I have consciously tried not to do that. I always feel that everybody has a story, everybody has a reason, and you can write strongly without being mean.

Is there anything that I haven't asked you that you really think should be said about writing?

Try always to find your voice as a writer and don't be afraid to be different. Don't think any kind of writing, whether it's editorial writing or writing out of Washington, or magazine writing, has a formula written in stone. It's so important to find a new way to say it, or let's say "your" way to say it, and to never feel like, "This is how I write because I'm in Washington." "Dateline: Washington. The State Department said yesterday that 40 more people would be going to Bosnia." The State Department doesn't talk, you know. Always try to break through the cliché and say it as though your reputation as a writer depended on that sentence.

Michael Gartner

Finalist, Editorial Writing

Michael Gartner is co-owner and one-person editorial page of *The Daily Tribune,* a 10,000 circulation newspaper 38 miles from his hometown of Des Moines. The son and grandson of Iowa newspapermen, Gartner has been in the news business for four decades. He is a former Page One editor of *The Wall Street Journal,* former editor and president of *The Des Moines Register,* former editor of the *Courier-Journal* of Louisville, former general news executive of Gannett Co. and *USA Today,* and, most recently, former president of NBC News. In 1994, he became the first past president of the American Society of Newspaper Editors to receive its Distinguished Writing Award for editorials. Gartner began his newspaper career at age 15 when he took a job answering phones and taking dictation in the sports department of *The Des Moines Register.* He writes a regular column for *USA Today* and for the last 15 years, he has written a syndicated column on language.

From his desk in the center of the *Tribune* newsroom, Gartner teaches his young staff with a combination of exhortation and example, reporting and crafting editorials that hold powerful institutions in their community accountable while also reminding readers of the wonders of the world around them. Phone to his ear, fingers on the keyboard, he collects the facts, figures, and colorful details that make his editorials sparkle with the joy of a man in love with language.

The return of spring

MARCH 17, 1994

It won't be long.

It won't be long till the orioles and warblers are back in McFarland Park.

It won't be long till the silver maples are blossoming along the highways.

It won't be long till the wildflowers are blooming along the hiking trails.

And it won't be long till you'll be mowing your lawn.

Yesterday was such a beautiful day that we called around—to Steve Lekwa at the conservation board, to Jim Carpenter at the Department of Transportation, to Harry Hillaker at the state climatology office and to Professor Jim Dinsmore at Iowa State University—to talk about spring.

Is it really here? we asked.

Is the snow gone for good? we asked.

Yes and no, they said.

"I'm not going to dump the gas out of my snowblower for another month," Steve Lekwa said, and he reminded us of an April blizzard that shut I-35 for three days 21 years ago. "We'll probably have some more snow," agreed Harry Hillaker, who said March 28 is the average last day for an inch or more of snow. "But you don't have to worry about it sticking around," he said cheerfully.

The signs of spring are everywhere, they agreed.

"I had bluebirds singing over my head when I went to get in the car Tuesday morning," Lekwa said. "And I heard a robin singing Monday evening in Ames, which was a wonderful sound."

The bluebirds and robins and geese spend the winter just south of the snow line, in Missouri and Arkansas. Our local Canada geese—perhaps a hundred of them—are back already, selecting and defending their nesting territories. Within a couple of weeks, they'll be incubating eggs, and you'll see goslings on the lake at Hickory Grove Park by the first of May.

(Geese are monogamous for life, and many return to the same nests year after year, Lekwa says, though even to him "it's hard to recognize one Canada goose from the next." A pair will stay together as long as 20 years, and each spring they'll raise from one to seven goslings. Of course, if they want to make it back to Missouri they have to survive the fall hunting season.)

The neo-tropical birds, the thrushes and grosbeaks and orioles and other birds that go way South, won't be back until the trees begin to leaf out, which will be a few more weeks. And that's probably when the hummingbirds will come back, too.

And what a winter they've had! The tiny hummingbird flies all the way to Panama every winter. It starts with a leisurely, 900-mile trip to the Gulf Coast of Texas, then stocks up for a grueling, 300-mile, over-water leg to the Yucatan Peninsula and then a final several-hundred-mile trip to Panama.

The bird that makes this trip—the ruby-throated hummingbird that hangs around your flowers in the summer—weighs just three grams, about a tenth of an ounce. (In case anyone ever asks you, it would take 288,000 hummingbirds to outweigh a cow.) And it makes this round trip every year. ("How long does a hummingbird live?" we asked Dinsmore, an ornithologist in the department of animal ecology at Iowa State. "After 5 or 6, it's a pretty ripe old hummingbird," he says. Still, he adds, "they see a lot of the world" in their lifetime.)

The wildflowers will be blooming by the time the hummingbirds get back. The first of the flowers, the white and pink and blue hepatica, are already showing buds. But it will be June, probably, before you'll be seeing the black-eyed Susans along the interstates, says Jim Carpenter, whose department is about ready to replant from the heavy flood damage of last year. But as we drive along we should see some silver maples leafing out by May, then the green ash, he says.

And each day we have more time to see all this. Although the equinox isn't until Sunday, today is the day we come closest to 12 hours of day, 12 hours of night. (Actually, night gets an extra minute.) Each day, too, we're getting more sunshine—the sun is shining 55 percent of the daylight hours now, up from 52 percent in January.

Besides more sun, we'll probably be getting more rain in coming weeks, a bit more than normal, Hillaker says. Oh, oh, we thought. What does that mean for the grass? Well, Lekwa said...

It won't be long.

Before it's long.

Lessons Learned

BY MICHAEL GARTNER

The best thing about being a newspaperman is that you can call up people and ask them questions about whatever interests you that day. And, in my town at least, they'll patiently explain almost anything you want to know.

One pretty morning in March, I wanted to know about spring.

Let me pause here for a minute, and take you off on a couple of tangents.

The first tangent: My editorials are usually long leisurely essays, filled with facts that make my case for me. Rarely do I have to call anyone a jerk or any program idiotic. I just report and report and then present my brief, dropping in a rising chorus of one-sentence comments every few paragraphs. I'm sort of the opposite of Richard Aregood. Anything he can say in 10 words, I can say in 800.

As I said, it was a pretty morning, so I thought I'd write about spring.

Oh, first, the second tangent:

I've edited great writers over the years, and along the way I've become a pretty good writer myself. The one lesson I've learned, from others and from myself, is that good writing can mask lazy reporting. A sentence can be so lovely, a paragraph so pleasing, that you don't realize until too late that they said nothing, that they had no facts and no opinions. So I insist, of others and of myself, that you gather a bushel of facts before you sit down to peck out the story, even if the story is an editorial. Besides, that makes the writing easier.

Now, back to spring.

It was a pretty morning, as I've told you twice already, but repetition helps drive home the point in editorials, so I sat down to gather some facts. What do I want to know? I asked myself. What do I want to say?

I wanted to know the usual, the how and the why and the when and the whether of the weather. So I called a man who knew about wildlife, a man who knew about weather. I asked each man one question: Is spring here?

And then I listened.

The wildlife man started right off about geese. The bird man started right off about hummingbirds. The flower man started right off about hepatica. And the weather man started right off about snow.

They talked, and I typed. I'd interrupt, sometimes, to ask a detail—like "How long does a hummingbird live?"—but mostly I just listened as these men talked about the things they love. (Another lesson: People love to talk about things they know about to anyone who is even slightly interested. Never be reluctant to make the phone call.) Apparently, not a lot of people call these men to ask about hummingbirds or Canada (not Canadian—another lesson learned) geese or black-eyed Susans or the percentage of sunshine on an average January day.

By the end of the morning, I had my bushel of facts, and a couple of great quotes. (Geese are monogamous for life, the wildlife man told me, though "it's hard to recognize one Canada goose from another." "After 5 or 6, it's a pretty ripe old hummingbird," the bird man told me. Still, "they see a lot of the world" in their lifetime.)

Now that I know what I know, I said to myself, what do I want to say? This isn't one of those editorials where you come out for or against something—who could be against spring, for heaven's sake? I just wanted to talk about spring.

I wanted to say "yes, maybe, no." Is spring here? Well, yes, sort of, maybe, not really. But it won't be long till it is.

"It won't be long" became the chorus, and, as it turned out, it worked it's way into a little gimmick at the end that, upon rereading, I'm not sure worked.

I wanted the editorial to bring a smile, because the world is grim and the reader ought to be sent a smile every few days. I wanted it to be just a refreshing pause from the diet of politics and taxes and world woes. But, most of all, I wanted it to inform, because editorials—be they on schools or taxes or politics or spring—must always inform.

Which gets me back to facts.

Which gets me to my favorite fact in the editorial, which is how many hummingbirds it would take to outweigh a cow.

That's in there because there was a fellow at my desk that day, talking to me about this and that, and I told him about hummingbirds. A lesson that he knew—that everything must be relevant and understandable—prompted him to ask, "How can you make the reader understand the tininess of a hummingbird?" As a little inside joke for him and a smile for the readers, I put the answer—yet another fact—in the editorial.

The larger lesson is that editorials, even editorials about spring, must have facts. The smaller lesson is that it takes 288,000 hummingbirds to outweigh a cow.

And that's more than you learn in some editorials.

George Vecsey
Sports Writing

Three times a week, George Vecsey offers the readers of *The New York Times* literate and provocative columns that the ASNE judges called "a regular demonstration that sports writing at its best is not only a lot of fun, but illuminating of the human condition." Vecsey began his career in 1960, writing sports for *Newsday* for eight years before joining the *Times*. In 1970, he became a national correspondent, opening a Louisville, Ky., bureau and spending three years covering everything from coal mining to country music to the Kentucky Derby. He covered religion for three years (a beat not at all unlike sports, he says in his interview) before returning to the sports beat. Vecsey has been writing the "Sports of the Times" column since 1982. Two of his three children are sports writers.

In addition to his newspaper work, Vecsey has been a prolific writer of books, about the Mets

The New York Times

and Appalachia, and has written or edited best-selling biographies of sports and entertainment figures Martina Navratilova, Loretta Lynn, and Bob Welch, as well as *A Year in the Sun*, which chronicles his own life as a sportswriter. His columns appeal to the passionate amateur who cares more about Vecsey's trenchant observations on games and their players than the scores.

Decision means the Mick might make it to 65 or 70

JANUARY 30, 1994

I always figured there was only one column left about the Mick—the one about his being found dead in a hotel room, or blown away by some tough guy who didn't appreciate Mantle's behavior in a bar, or maybe even tumbling down a hillside in a pickup after going out for drinks on Christmas Day, just to match his old pal Billy Martin.

Maybe that gloomy column will never get written quite that way. Or at least in the meantime, there is this hopeful column about Mickey Mantle, age 62, checking himself into the Betty Ford Center, the rehab clinic to the stars.

They deal with celebrities out at Betty Ford. The counselors try to break through the chemical haze and the arrogance and the denial, to persuade the performers and the political figures and the athletes that they really do have a lot in common with the skid-row drunk or the street junkie. Sometimes the lessons stick. Up to now, the Mick has been a tough case.

* * *

He started admitting he had a problem with alcohol years ago, but all that meant was that he was allegedly controlling what he tossed down— wine coolers instead of the hard stuff, as if that made much difference to his liver.

His agent says the blackouts started to worry Mantle, as well they should. The blackouts are a sign that alcohol is short-circuiting the brain wires. They are nature's way of telling you you're going to die or get killed soon.

Somebody persuaded the Mick of this danger. Whoever it was was a better friend than all the rest of the ball players and the Broadway wise guys and the old-time sportswriters and the golfers who laughed at him and encouraged him over four decades, letting him know he could get away with anything because he was the Mick.

Not that Mantle needed much help in his desperation. His father, Mutt Mantle, died of Hodgkin's disease when he was 41, and that's what Mantle felt was ahead of him after he came down with osteomyelitis in his left leg at the age of 19. He was surprised when he kept on living.

"If I knew I was going to make it to 50, I would have taken better care of myself" was a line he used over and over again at card shows, autograph shows, home-shopping network performances, public appearances, wherever there were people willing to plunk down money to gawk at the Mick.

To his own amazement, he became a legend all over again in his 50s. He went through years wandering around hustling plaid-pantsed rich guys on the golf course, men who considered it an honor to get conned into losing money to the Mick, and then buying him a few rounds afterward, and then a few more rounds. The difference was, a lot of them knew how to stop.

Everybody who has been around Mantle has a favorite story. Somebody told me recently about watching Mantle absolutely sloshed in a bar somewhere, and doing the usual drugstore cowboy things, but being relatively charming about it, like an actor playing the role of Mickey Mantle. Suddenly he was aware of his wife, his long-suffering wife, Merlyn, arriving.

"You could see the Mick straighten up," somebody described it. "You could see his clothes get neater, you could see his face get sober, and he turned to everybody at the bar and he whispered, 'Don't nobody say nothing.' And he walked a straight line to Merlyn."

So he was a legend, and he was a character, and he was also something of a joke. I didn't think he was all that funny because I've got too many friends who've struggled to stay sober day by day, and I've never felt like glorifying a guy who was basically defying the odds.

Besides, I felt like a collaborator. When I was a young reporter, Mantle was about two-thirds surly and one-third funny, which was his right, and he could scare some of the young reporters with his glare. We were around when he slinked into the clubhouse at noon for a day game, reeking of alcohol, and his face just plain ugly, and teammates would look the other way, but usually he would be in the lineup.

One day he couldn't start, but he pinch-hit a home run and made jokes later about how hung over he was, and we did write that. Most of the time we just wrote about his bravery, and his bad legs, and how much other players admired him, and his bad temper, but it was the early '60s, and what the heck, we had a president who was burning it at both ends, too, and nobody wrote about him.

Different time. Nowadays, people can't say they weren't warned about what a beer or a wine could do to their reflexes. Up to now, Mickey Mantle shrugged off the warning. It was too easy banging down the alcohol, to hide the fears and the insecurities that sober people learn to acknowledge.

* * *

A lot of people will say Mickey Mantle has been an alcoholic for a long time, but the Betty Ford Center will tell him that nobody else's opinion matters, only his. If Mickey Mantle can walk sober out of Betty Ford, he's got a chance. When he gets back to the restaurant with his name on it on Central Park South, he'll discover that most bartenders these days are very conscientious about keeping a glass filled with club soda for anybody who asks.

I hope Mantle asks for club soda. I'd admire him more than I ever did for the home runs, even more than the times he came back from injuries, even more than the times he was funny and decent. He might be more funny, more decent now, with a sober personality. It's a new feeling, rooting for Mickey Mantle.

Writers' Workshop

Talking Points

1) From his opening paragraph, Vecsey is almost cruelly blunt with his take on a golden-haired sports idol and his fall from grace. "I always figured there was only one column left about the Mick—the one about his being found dead in a hotel room, or blown away by some tough guy who didn't appreciate Mantle's behavior in a bar, or maybe even tumbling down a hillside in a pickup after going out for drinks on Christmas Day, just to match his old pal Billy Martin." But Vecsey quickly changes gears in the next paragraph. How successfully does Vecsey balance the gloomy with the hopeful?

2) Alcoholism is the true subject of this column. Mantle's struggle is but a vehicle. Notice how Vecsey weaves details about the effects of alcohol on the body and spirit.

3) Diction refers to a writer's choice of words and puts an indelible stamp on a piece of writing. Notice the tough-guy stance that creates the harsh tone of this piece about Mickey Mantle, such as his reference to "The Mick," "wine coolers instead of the hard stuff." Look for other examples and discuss their effect.

4) Vecsey also goes beyond the games, most obviously in this piece on Mickey Mantle's alcoholism, but in other pieces about the alcohol and drug problems of contemporary players such as Dwight Gooden and Darryl Strawberry. Discuss the larger values and perspectives he returns to. How would you assess Vecsey's attitudes towards individual accountability?

5) Vecsey is tough on himself too. "Besides, I felt like a collaborator," he writes, describing how Mantle showed up "reeking of alcohol, his face just plain ugly." But the sportswriters didn't write about it. Contrast the coverage of Mickey Mantle in the 1960s with the reporting on alleged cocaine use by the late basketball star Reggie Lewis in a front page article in *The Wall Street Journal* written in 1995 by ASNE non-deadline finalist and Pulitzer Prize winner Ron Suskind. Discuss whether this is a positive change.

6) Vecsey is not afraid to bring himself into his pieces, recalling himself as a young sportswriter. What is the effect of such self-references?

7) In his columns, Vecsey mentions former Yankee managers Billy Martin and Charles Dillon (better known as "Casey") Stengel, without identifying them fully. Do you think Vecsey should have provided more background? Given their passionate and often well-informed audience, do sports columnists have more leeway than other columnists? Are sports columnists, almost by their very nature, writing for insiders? Should they broaden their sense of audience?

Assignment Desk

1) Report and write a column about the seamier side of professional sports—gambling, drug and alcohol abuse, domestic violence—that explores the issue of heroes with feet of clay.

2) Consider how often in your reporting you focus on the foibles of your sources: the council member who falls asleep at meetings, the racist or sexist jokes made by the police detective. If you're not, are you doing your readers a disservice? Discuss why reporters might shy away from reporting these aspects of their sources' characters.

3) Research and write a column about the effects of alcoholism on the human body.

4) Alcohol and writers don't mix well. Read *The Thirsty Muse,* a book by literary historian Tom Dardis, which analyzes in graphic detail the effects of drinking on the lives of William Faulkner, F. Scott Fitzgerald, Ernest Hemingway, and Eugene O'Neill.

5) One truism of fiction is that a character must be transformed by the end of the story. Contrast the opening paragraph of this column with the last line, "It's a new feeling, rooting for Mickey Mantle." What makes Vecsey's transformation from a critic to a fan of Mantle believable?

6) Write a column that explores your changing attitudes towards someone. Make sure you provide enough support for the transformation.

The survivor won't
let time slip by

FEBRUARY 26, 1994

HAMAR, Norway—Nancy Kerrigan had already skated a gold-medal performance. The people running the figure skating championship did not even have the Ukrainian national anthem at hand, but it is a safe guess they knew exactly where "The Star-Spangled Banner" could be found. And then the hauntingly gifted young woman from Odessa began to skate.

She is different, this young woman with the circles below her eyes, this young woman with grief lines on her face. It is impossible to stop staring at her. She knows how to express herself with her hands at all times and her slender body gyrates with emotions no instructor can supply. She was in pain from a dreadful collision in practice on Thursday, but Oksana Baiul is no stranger to pain.

She began to skate and the entire audience gazed at her, and so did the nine judges, even though all nine of them had just voted Nancy Kerrigan first, up to that moment. She skated, and within the Olympic Amphitheater of Hamar, the mystery of art asserted itself over the practicality of science. She made everybody stop and think that maybe Nancy Kerrigan's by-the-numbers, totally competent performance was not quite enough.

* * *

The name of the Ukrainian national anthem, by the way, is either "The Ukraine Has Not Died" or "The Ukraine Has Not Perished," depending on the translation. There has been much death, much perishing of joy and hope, in the 16 years of Oksana Baiul, but last night she was alone on the ice, and she skated to negate the pain of her mother's death, and her grandparents' death, and the defection of her first beloved coach, and perhaps even the political disruptions and the deprivations of her homeland.

She skated with all the intense feeling of Eastern Europe, the region that raises ballerinas and figure skaters the way America raises rock stars. She is only 16, and the laughter and the tears come bubbling out of her, but she is also a survivor, wily enough to know that nearly four minutes of skating were not quite enough.

She had not been perfect, because genius cannot be perfect; it must live on the edge. But this is also an athletic performance, with points added for this jump, with points detracted for that omission, and Oksana Baiul was not yet satisfied.

Seeing her mother die of ovarian cancer three years ago, sleeping in the rink for a while, now living in a borrowed bed in somebody else's apartment, she has learned to make the most of every chance. Last night she still had a few seconds until the music stopped.

She was due to perform one more double axel, but instead she tossed in a triple toe, and then she did a combination of a double axel and a double toe, a very demanding performance for anybody at the end of four minutes, particularly a girl who has been run down by another skater in practice 32 hours earlier, particularly a girl operating on three stitches and a pain-killing injection, a girl living on nerve.

* * *

Tonya Harding, America's alleged survivor, had not been able to get on the ice with proper boots on her feet. Harding and her advisers had looked like Curly, Moe and Larry living out a hideous nightmare, but Ukraine's survivor made time stop. Then she looked to the heavens in much the same way Dan Jansen of the United States had recalled his dead sister a week earlier.

"This difficult life gave me the strength to excel," she said later. "Yes, my mother was with me at the moment of victory." And she claimed she had not thought that she was pulling out a gold-medal performance.

"Certainly not. I could not think of the gold medal after that performance. I never do. My goal is to do well and give joy to the spectators and show myself to the judges. Tonight, judging from the applause of the audience, I thought I had done that."

She did more than that. Five judges from nations with links to the vanished Soviet bloc gave her higher grades than they had given Nancy Kerrigan. The Ukrainian judge is the father of her former coach. Much will be made of that in days and years to come, but I submit that all the old political favors are long gone, and that we are left, in moments like this, with feelings.

Five judges felt the gifted young woman from Odessa had skated the best last night, and so did I. This takes nothing away from Nancy Kerrigan's grace under pressure in these last two ugly months, but the young woman from Odessa also had courage, and she had genius, besides. And then somebody located the national anthem of the Ukraine, and a gifted young woman's face showed tears and laughter, at the very same time.

Writers' Workshop

Talking Points

1) Writers on deadline can't always nail down every fact. Smart ones like Vecsey use such difficulties to their advantage. Notice how Vecsey reports confusion over the name of the Ukrainian national anthem: "...is either 'The Ukraine Has Not Died,' or 'The Ukraine Has Not Perished.'" Consider how it supports his theme that Oksana Baiul seemed an unlikely winner of the gold medal.

2) Notice how Vecsey alludes to Oksana Baiul without identifying her until the end of the second paragraph. Instead he refers to her as "the hauntingly gifted young woman from Odessa." Consider why he uses this indirect method and its impact on readers.

3) Study the structure of this column carefully. Notice how Vecsey uses the Ukrainian anthem as a thread that he weaves throughout the piece. How many times does he use the theme? What is the effect?

4) Vecsey deftly handles the technical details of figure skating as in this paragraph about Baiul's performance. "She was due to perform one more double axel, but instead she tossed in a triple toe, and then she did a combination of a double axel and a double toe..." But more important than technical details is his feel for the inside of a sport or a game, baseball's history and romance, "the mystery of art" in Oksana Baiul's skating, Charles Oakley's performance as an "old pro" on the basketball court. Study his craft, how he manages to describe a sport's science as well as its art with a few deft strokes rather than with purple prose.

5) The columnist has the opportunity to use himself as a lens through which to view his subjects. By the end of this column, Vecsey makes a value judgment about the outcome of the competition. How and why has he earned the right?

Assignment Desk

1) Sportswriters need to know the rules of the games they cover. What are a double axel and a double toe? Under what

circumstances would a further explanation of the terms have been necessary?

2) In this column, Vecsey sketches the painful childhood of Oksana Baiul, skillfully weaving biographical details. Isolate the elements and rewrite them in a single paragraph as if you were writing a profile of her. Contrast this approach with Vecsey's delivery.

3) Vecsey quotes his subjects sparingly. Study several of your stories. How heavily do they rely on quotes? As an experiment, revise the quotes into narrative and compare which is more effective.

4) Using Vecsey's thread of the Ukrainian national anthem as a model, select a detail in your reporting of a story and deliberately weave it through the piece as a structural and thematic element. Limit yourself, as Vecsey does, to using the detail just three times, at the beginning, middle, and end of your story. Discuss the effect of such a device on structure, pacing, and tone.

Italy's coach seems straight from Fellini

JULY 10, 1994

FOXBORO, Mass.—If any team in this World Cup has the right to be an apparition out of Fellini, it is, of course, the team from Il Maestro's homeland. The Italian team confounds and confuses and frustrates and frightens its own supporters, but in some bizarre, goofy, weird, Fellini-esque way, it keeps winning.

"E La Nave Va." And the ship sails on. That was one of Fellini's films, a tottering cruise ship loose out on the high seas—dying elephants, absurd sopranos, pudgy princes, the whole thing—but somehow, through divine intervention or what, the ship did not sink. And that's all that matters.

"We are lucky," said Giorgio Chinaglia, who once played for Italy and later the New York Cosmos. "It is better than being unlucky."

Giorgio has that right. The Italians looked as if they were going to self-destruct in the first round, but here they are in the semifinals—worth all that skill and collective experience, but no set lineup or recognizable attack or a game plan that I could tell you about. The Italians beat Spain, 2-1, yesterday, on the usual late goal by Roberto Baggio, intervention from Il Divino Codino (the divine pigtail) himself.

* * *

What makes this team really Fellini-esque is its coach, Arrigo Sacchi, who always seems to be smiling at something only he knows. This grin makes me a trifle nervous. Sacchi would be right at home in one of Fellini's epics about a man trying to get a grip. Sacchi could be the harried ringmaster, keeping all the women in his life at bay with a whip and a chair, except that Sacchi has 22 players going round and round in circles. He even benched Il Codino during a game in the first round. Il Capitano Hook.

The smokestacks tremble. The sides bulge. The reel rolls from side to side. And meanwhile, the Italians are in the semifinals for the first time since 1982, which is of some significance, because they survived a dismal first round that time, too, and they kept getting better.

That year Paolo Rossi came scampering down the left side on the counter-attack like the scamp in *Bicycle Thief* from an earlier era of Italian cinema. This time it is the introverted little man with the pigtail who keeps getting better, perhaps playing out of a controlled rage that Sacchi dared sack him in the midst of the Norway game.

"E La Nave Va." The Fellini hero struggles to control his anarchic world. Sacchi has been running the national team—basically a dream team, an all-star team—for three years. He has called up so many players that the count has become obscured somewhere in the low 70s. And in the high seas of the World Cup, with the entire globe paying attention, Arrigo Sacchi is still dreaming, still manipulating, still cogitating, still flashing that preoccupied, most unmerry smile of his.

Italy has now played five games here in this continent that an Italian allegedly discovered. ("Chris going to America; Chris going to find a striker!" to paraphrase Flip Wilson's classic tale of Columbus going to America to find Ray Charles). Sacchi has now used 20 of his 22 players in five games, which isn't easy, considering he can substitute only two field players and one goalkeeper per game. The result of all this convening, all this coming and going, is that Italian fans question Sacchi's sanity, and the Italian players often act like passing strangers.

Early yesterday, Daniele Massaro dumped a back pass and Billy Costacurta was nowhere in the vicinity, and the two of them raised their arms at each other in classic operatic gestures. The joke is that Massaro and Costacurta play on the same Milan team—the very team Sacchi used to coach. You'd think they'd know each other by now, but 70-odd players in three Fellini-esque years will addle anybody.

"I am never afraid of being unpopular, or else I wouldn't have done 99 per cent of everything I have done," Sacchi was quoted as saying.

It is a wonderful philosophy for a man who changes players the way a Fellini hero changes mistresses. But Sacchi is looking, always looking. And yesterday, in the immortal words of the notoriously Fellini-esque Charles Dillon Stengel, he done splendid.

* * *

Some of Sacchi's machinations were forced when Gianluca Pagliuca, his goalkeeper, was sent off in the second game for stopping a potential goal with his hands, out of the goalkeeping area. Pagliuca was subsequently suspended for two more games. Yesterday he was eligible to play again, and Sacchi started him because "he was disqualified, and it was only fair."

Pagliuca recognized the risk the coach was taking. The goalkeeper from Sampdoria in Genoa said later, "Had we lost, I might have been blamed." Instead, Pagliuca made half a dozen acrobatic saves under heavy fire in the second half, including the rarely used knee save on Julio Salinas, after Pagliuca had committed to leaping off the ground in anticipation of a high chip shot. The goalkeeper either made a genius out of his coach—or vice versa.

Either way, the ship sails on. I've got the feeling I've seen this movie before.

Writers' Workshop

Talking Points

1) Vecsey's columns are laced with humor, sometimes sardonic. This trait is perhaps most obvious in this column about the Italian soccer team playing in the World Cup and what he describes as its Fellini-esque coach. He builds on an extended metaphor. Does he overdo it? Even if he does, do you think readers would mind?

2) Allusions can be hazardous, forcing the writer to choose between over-explaining or leaving the reader in the dark. What are the omissions that signal Vecsey's confidence in the literacy of *The New York Times* audience?

3) Vecsey admits to being a true fan of just one sport—soccer. How does his passion come through in this column?

4) Vecsey drops allusions to Italian films without seeming at all pretentious. For one thing, Vecsey doesn't try to tell us everything he knows; for another, he includes a few American in-jokes—like "Il Capitano Hook." Consider how, as a result, he captures a kind of circus atmosphere on the Italian squad, but conveys a genuine appreciation of the team's energy and artistry.

Assignment Desk

1) Vecsey likens the Italian soccer team to a movie by Fellini. Write a column that links another aspect of pop culture—a movie or song—with another sports team. Explain why the movie or song reminds you of this team with as much specific detail as possible.

2) Vecsey writes for a specific audience, readers of *The New York Times*, that he expects will understand his allusions without explanation. Make any changes you think a less sophisticated audience might need to fully appreciate the humor of this piece.

3) In America, soccer is a minor player in professional sports. Yet Vecsey's enthusiasm for the game is contagious. Report and write a column about a sport that is overshad-

owed by football, baseball, or basketball (lacrosse or field
hockey come to mind) that effectively conveys its charms to
readers unfamiliar with the game.

No Mookie, no Maz, no Fisk, no nothing

The rage kicks in when you least expect it. You think you're fine. You can do without baseball. You have a life. Then with absolutely no warning, reality kicks you right in the backside. The dirty so-and-sos have killed the World Series.

No Country Slaughter steaming from first with the winning run. No Babe Ruth taunting the Cubs and hitting one over the wall. No Bob Gibson glowering in the shadows. No Bill Mazeroski heading for home with all of Pittsburgh about to climb on his back. No World Series. Just twitchy Bud and rigid Don. Just rage.

Both sides now. First it was the owners you hated, or maybe the players, but now it's both. Selfish, stupid, arrogant, boorish, pig-headed un-American whining weasels. They robbed us of the 1994 World Series.

* * *

It would have begun last night, much too late for fans in the East. The dopes who run baseball didn't even run it right when they were working. But at least you could have woken up this morning in Montreal or New York or Cleveland, or wherever the World Series might have been extra important this year, and mumbled, "Who finally won that game?"

No Reggie Jackson hitting three dingers in one game. No Kirk Gibson hobbling around the bases late on a Saturday night. No Grover Cleveland Alexander lurching out of the bullpen. No nothing.

I didn't mind not going to the World Series, grumpy writers like me standing around the batting cage in raincoats, waiting for 8:38 p.m. October has been a delight in New York. I never watched a second of the Ken Burns series. Nostalgia for what? Baseball doesn't want me, I don't want baseball. That's my theory. My friends Rob and June held a softball game on their own field of dreams. Expos vs. Indians "for all the marbles," he said. I played third base. I could still make the throw to first. Excuse me, but I thought about Brooks Robinson in 1970. Rob hit a shot over the left-field fence and I thought about Joe Carter in 1993. October. Memories. World Series. Rage.

Rage isn't good for anybody, so I did the most pacific thing possible. I called Mookie Wilson, whose gentle wisdom was a delight when he played for the Mets. He still works for them as a roving minor league instructor and community-relations specialist, which means people can look at him and say, "Here, this is what baseball can be, at its best."

The reason I called Mookie Wilson, of course, is that eight years ago this Tuesday, he was the central figure in the most stupendous sequence I ever saw at a sporting event, a World Series turning completely around on two freak plays, both nubby little incidents, altered by millimeters. What made them so stunning was that they happened on the potential final pitch of a World Series.

"I guess we won't have any memories like that this year," Wilson said with his high-pitched Southern voice.

I asked Wilson about his earliest World Series memory. "I wasn't what you'd call a baseball fan when I was growing up," he admitted, "but in 1975 I was in junior college in Spartanburg, S.C., and I watched every game in our dormitory. I was rooting for the Big Red Machine of Cincinnati. Foster. Morgan. Perez. Rose. Griffey. Concepción. Bench. They had a great team."

Is there one 1975 moment Mookie Wilson remembers best? He chuckled at the other end of the phone line. "Fisk's home run," he said. "Naturally." He meant the 12th-inning shot down the left-field line that Carlton Fisk made stay fair by waving his arms like a carnival magician performing hocus-pocus. It is one of the defining moments in all those World Series. It won the sixth game. Eleven years later, Mookie Wilson would also have a defining sixth game.

"During the season, you always say, 'We can come back tomorrow and win,'" Wilson said the other day. "But during the post-season, the atmosphere is different. You get to a point, it could be your last game. You don't want to play catchup ball in the World Series. The tradition, the media, the atmosphere, make it different. I was so excited being there, it made me more relaxed."

On the night of Oct. 25, Mookie Wilson became immortal—although he doesn't act immortal. He was due up sixth in that 10th inning, the far side of the moon, the way it appeared. Two quick outs. The Red Sox moved up the dugout steps, ready to roll. "It's funny," Wilson said, "but the only thing I can remember from that inning is Oil Can Boyd on the top step, his foot on the dirt, another player looking at him. That's the only picture in my mind."

Three straight singles. Oil Can Boyd removed his foot from the dirt. The Red Sox began to edge down the steps. Mookie Wilson levitated himself to avoid being hit by Bob Stanley's inside pitch; some Boston fans still blame Rich Gedman for not stopping it. By ducking the wild pitch, Wilson allowed the tying run to score from third. Had he been hit by the pitch, the bases would have been loaded, the Mets still down a run. (Trivia question: Who was on deck? Answer: Howard Johnson. Supply your own alternate ending.)

With the winning run on second, Mookie Wilson slapped a magical mystery grounder toward Bill Buckner, who was playing deep behind first base. The ball squibbed through (I always like to write it this way) the gnarled wickets of Buckner. The game was over. Revisionist history is starting to say that Wilson would have beaten Buckner to first even if Buckner had fielded it.

"The pitcher was pretty well out of it," Wilson said. "We'll never know, will we?"

* * *

We only know that 1986 is remembered best for Mookie Wilson's at-bat. We only know that 1975 is remembered for the Carlton Fisk body-English home run. We only know that 1947 is remembered for Cookie Lavagetto breaking up Bill Bevens's no-hitter, and Al Gionfriddo robbing DiMaggio with a great catch in left-center, and dog-gone it, the Yankees still won the Series and the Brooklyn Dodgers had to "Wait 'til next year," as always.

Back then, "Wait 'til next year" had a romantic notion to it, like the Lost City of Atlantis or Brigadoon. Now we are totally out of romance. This year will produce no Mookie Wilson, no Carlton Fisk, no Joe Page, no Mickey Lolich, no Sandy Koufax sitting out the Jewish holy day and then pitching the Dodgers to the world championship, no Mantle hitting one off Barney Schultz, (my man Taxerman waded through all this Met stuff just to make sure Koufax and the Mick got their due).

This year will be remembered for nothing. No valuable lessons, no moral victories, nothing. The two sides colluded, in their own dance-of-the-morons, to have no World Series. Wait 'til next year? Who cares? The owners and the players will either work it out next year, or they won't. Baseball will never be the same. They stole a year from us, they stole the World Series, they stole baseball. We try to shrug it off, and then the rage kicks in.

Writers' Workshop

Talking Points

1) In this column about the baseball strike, Vecsey doesn't take a side, but simply labels the owners *and* the players as "morons." Consider how much freedom of expression the columnist enjoys. Could Vecsey have written with such sharp invective had the subject been the Arab-Israeli or Bosnian conflicts? Does it make a difference that he's writing about sports, not politics? Does a sports columnist have a wider latitude than a political columnist?

2) This piece scorns "nostalgia." But notice how Vecsey, in the middle narrative section on the 1986 World Series, evokes the history and romance of baseball in a more tough-minded way. Baseball, in general, seems to bring out sentimentality in many writers and readers (what Kevin Kerrane of the University of Delaware calls the "*Field of Dreams* syndrome"). Study the gritty details that ground this and other Vecsey columns.

3) Vecsey's editor says Vecsey can write as a kind of Everyman. Notice how he begins by referring to himself as "you," conveys his own reactions as "I," and by the end of the column has transmuted this into "we." Discuss why his emotional response, though strong, doesn't seem merely personal; it articulates the frustration of millions.

4) Vecsey is writing as a sports insider here, addressing an audience with a deep knowledge of World Series long past, an audience that knows who Bob Gibson and Bill Mazeroski are and when their World Series games were played; that knows exactly who "twitchy Bud and rigid Don" are. What are the advantages and disadvantages of such an approach?

5) Columnists reveal themselves to their readers in a variety of ways—word choice, subject matter, self-references. Notice how Vecsey engages his readers by addressing them directly—"(Trivia question: Who was on deck? Answer: Howard Johnson. Supply your own alternate ending.)"—and acknowledging his own presence—"The ball squibbed through (I always like to write it this way) the gnarled wickets of Buckner."

6) Discuss the differences in the relationship between a news reporter and a columnist. Should news stories reveal to readers more information about their authors? Why/Why not?

7) Pacing is clearly important to Vecsey. Examine how the pace changes throughout this column. Where does it slow down? Where does it speed up? What is the value of alternating the rhythm of a piece?

Assignment Desk

1) Vecsey says he has a researcher—his memory. With its devotion to World Series trivia, this column could only have been written by someone who knows the game of baseball well. What topic could you write about with such passion without looking up anything ? Make a list of the references you'd want to make.

2) Reorganize this column, beginning with Mookie Wilson instead of the author's rage over the baseball strike. How does that change the piece? Which is more effective?

3) Unlike many of his columns, this one seems written for the diehard baseball fan who doesn't need or want any explanation for most of the allusions. Rewrite the column for a high school newspaper or a paper in South Africa. Could Vecsey's theme—the way both sides in the strike have robbed the fans—be explored as effectively for readers who don't know the history as well?

4) Vecsey also writes the headlines for his columns, unlike a news reporter. Rewrite the headline for the *New York Post,* a tabloid known for its pungent urban style.

A conversation with
George Vecsey

CHRISTOPHER SCANLAN: What is your job? How do you describe your beat?

GEORGE VECSEY: There are a few limitations, but they are to some degree self-limitations. I have very little interest in pro football. I write about it, I criticize it, and somebody says, "Some of the best writing you do is about pro football because you don't like it." I just find it boring and presumptuous and all that, so therefore when I write about it, I think I have an edge to what I write.

I'm an abolitionist about boxing, which means I almost never do anything about boxing. I did do some stuff on Riddick Bowe when he was the champion, because it interested me that he was from Brooklyn. I didn't feel hypocritical about it. Usually the only time I write about boxing is when somebody's in a coma.

I don't write anything about golf. I have no interest in golf. On the other hand, I have a lot of freedom to jump in and out of stuff. My job is to write about sports in general, about big-time professional and big-time college sports because that's what the traffic demands these days. I tend toward the human side of sports, the big issues, the themes, the money, the politics, the drugs, the personalities, the people, the cities, the way people feel about sports. I try not to write about why teams are winning games, or who's got the hot team, or what's wrong with the Mets, what's wrong with the Jets, what's wrong with the Nets, all this stuff.

What is the average work day for you?

Having an idea or having made plans for something and then having the demands of daily journalism intrude on what you thought would be a nice, reflective, personal, sensitive, intelligent column.

In other words, you're going to write something you've thought about for a week, and you work on it much of the day, and then at 3 o'clock the office calls and says, "I don't know if you heard, but there's been a trade."

A manager gets fired at 4 o'clock, you're expected to have an opinion on it by 4:45.

An example of the worst kind of day: I had a column on college basketball last Saturday for the Sunday paper. I was writing about surprise teams and teams being tired and kids playing above their ability. I was sitting in a press room at noon with a 3 o'clock deadline, when all of a sudden, I get a call from the office that Michael Jordan was indeed playing in Indianapolis on Sunday and could I, A) come up with a Jordan column right away for a 3 o'clock deadline, and B) could I get myself from Albany to Indianapolis for the next day's game.

As it turns out, I think I wrote an OK column. I wound up using an anecdote I'd remembered from somebody's book and other impressions of Jordan. I wasn't exactly happy with anything I'd done, but it was done so fast that you almost don't have time to think about it.

One of the columns that I won this lovely award for was done literally in 25 minutes.

Which one was that?

The Oksana Baiul column—which is about as fast as you can type 800 words. Fortunately I took typing in junior high school.

To be able to type fast is an asset to writing a sports column these days. I used to do a lot of thematic planning. But you can't do that these days because you have to react to things much quicker.

It started with my wife two or three years ago saying, "I can't stand Kerrigan, Harding's a klutz, Yamaguchi's pretty, but this little girl from the Ukraine..."

I started to pay attention to Baiul, and I already had been told by somebody who I think has exquisite judgment on artistic trends that this little girl from the Ukraine was special. So I paid

attention, and indeed she was...artistic, child-
like, her story was a tear-jerker. So I began to
watch her and then through the Olympics—this
was the culmination of two months of nuttiness. I
mean, maybe one of the nuttiest things I've ever
covered.

I was there in Detroit when the knee-whacking
happened and at first, you wonder, "Why did
Nancy Kerrigan get hit in the knee?" and then
you get worried that it could have been serious,
when you didn't know if her career was over, if
she'd ever be able to skate again, if there were lu-
natics on the loose.

Then Nancy's knee was better, she was going
to perform; then Tonya became more interesting
than Nancy. So we had these two characters, and
then we get to the Olympics and Kerrigan is
whiny and Harding is just a slob. She shows up,
she can't get her laces tied, she whines and cries,
and it's all like total nuttiness.

And in the middle of it all, Baiul just kept skating. She got hurt out in practice the day before
with six of 'em practicing at the same time. We
heard this thud and all of a sudden there were
these two women on the ground.

What was your reaction to that?

I was so sad for her. I saw her get up and she was
almost crying, and she's a little kid and part
woman at the same time. There was this sense of
her being endangered.

She was also delightful to watch because she
really was creative and flamboyant in that kind of
Eastern European, emotional way, and Kerrigan is
so unemotional. I just assumed that this was the
'going to Disneyland, born in the U.S.A. Olympics' where Kerrigan would win—not out of sympathy but it was her time—the forces were in
place. She got knee-whacked, she came back, she
was brave, she was in first place after the first
night, and I had already written a column for
Thursday's paper saying Kerrigan is in first place
after the compulsories. She deserves it, she's been

disciplined, she's kept her head, blah-blah-blah-blah-blah.

Had you prepared anything for this column on the figure skating competition?

I certainly hadn't put anything in my machine. Sometimes I do. Even if you think you can make deadline, you must have one ready to roll in case there's an overtime or rain-out, or something happens that you can't make an opinion by deadline. You've got to have another column. And sometimes you write a column for the first edition and change it for the second.

We still had no real sense of what we were doing by 9, 9:30, and then they skated. And what happened, as the column points out, is that Baiul improvised in her last 30 seconds; she threw in a couple of extra jumps. Kerrigan had been OK—but Baiul just went past her. Even though the judging is controversial and I don't even claim to understand it, emotionally I agreed with it. Emotionally, professionally, I thought Baiul was better that night. I thought she looked better, she reacted better.

Baiul came out relatively late into the press room and there's this crowded scene and there's an interpreter interpreting. I guess she speaks Russian rather than Ukrainian, or maybe she speaks Ukrainian, I can't remember. I'm sitting next to a Russian guy and I say to him, "Wait a minute now. What's the name of the anthem that they couldn't find?" And he tells me, and then a Ukrainian person says, "No, no, it's slightly different." So now I've got a Russian and a Ukrainian telling me two slightly different things, and of course there's English going on and French and back and forth, and it's crowded, and I'm looking at my watch and I'm saying, "Oh, damn, I've got an hour to finish a column—I've got 58 minutes to finish a column."

And finally she came out. She talked, she smiled. I went back to my machine probably with 45 minutes to file.

What happened that made you able to write with such grace and conviction and speed?

Somewhere along the line from the time that she was hurt the day before to the time she performed to the time she actually won it, my respect for her as a performer and as a story had jelled into a very sympathetic point of view. Not only was she beautiful and graceful and artistic, but she was also courageous. You could say it's a fan's reaction, and I say, "Well, it is." I think a lot of writing about sports is feeling: feeling yourself, feeling the event, feeling the personality, feeling the mood of the crowd, the good and the bad. It is very personal, certainly more than reporting on news and even maybe more than writing columns on political events.

Baiul was the story of that event to me, and I know that in writing that column I don't think I had the words that I wanted. I do believe in writing things in advance to help if you don't know what you're going to have. On the other hand, I don't believe in writing something off what you think will happen, how you think you're going to feel when it happens.

So I don't think I had anything in my machine that would've been any help to me to write that column. There was nothing that had happened before 10 o'clock that night that could've predicted that I would write that column on Baiul.

One of the things that impressed me about this column is the patterning. You piece together disparate pieces of information into a mosaic that present a theme.

It was important for me to make it as emotional in print as it was in reality: who she was, where she'd come from, what had happened the day before, all the nuttiness of the two months previous. It was important to get all that as well as I could, and then to set the scene. One of the problems that I have with writing a sports column is that I don't get as much chance to describe and to report and to be lyrical as I did when I was a reporter.

There's so much opinion, that you don't get to stand back, in fact, it's not *courant* these days. Your marching instructions are, "Go out there and kick butt." That is what a sports columnist does these days, I guess. But I don't know if there was any butt-kicking to do that night. That was not the time to do that. It was more time to say, "This is what you folks need to know about this young performer."

Do you deliberately say the detail of the anthem is something I can use in this?

It's a columnist's technique, one of the tricks of the trade, to latch onto details, things you can see and prove. I mean, I can't prove that they had a hard time finding the anthem. It may very well be that Baiul just was sobbing in her room, which later turned out she was, and that Kerrigan was making snide remarks—"What's the matter? She's only going to cry anyway. Why do her makeup?" We didn't even know about that that night; that came out like a day later, which is great gossip, and of course then you have a column the next day on why was Kerrigan so whiny. But at that point, all you knew was that they were saying they couldn't find the anthem.

Do you make a note of it?

I'm sure I scribbled down a lot of notes—what else do you do with your hand while somebody's talking? It's better to take notes than not, I think.

I don't use my notes except for details, but in a situation like that, I trust my memory. I write down as much as I can, but there's only going to be a couple of quotes coming out of something anyway, and I trust my memory enough. A lot of times I don't even have time to go to my notes—literally don't have time to look down and say, let me find that. You have to remember. Or you turn to the person next to you—sportswriting is very inbred—if you've both heard the same quote, you'll turn to the guy from the competitor or the woman from the competitor and say, "Did she say that she *did* have trouble with the double or she *didn't* have trouble with the double?"

Over the years as I've gotten older, I've learned to discipline myself better for the act of writing— less panic, knowing myself better. And it helps, too, when you've been doing a job longer. And what I've learned is that if you think you have 40 minutes, you actually can do it in 30 minutes, and so don't rush to start just for the sake of typing.

What helps you make the deadline?

Another part of the routine is to learn to shut it all out when you get in front of the machine. Whether I put my head down, or I put my hands in front of my eyes—meditation would be too strong a word—but something short of that, which is taking a deep breath, making sure the oxygen gets as far into your lungs and your brain as it can, and knowing that you have the time to do it. If I didn't have the time, if there were other things going on, I could panic like anybody can. But if you know that you can type that fast, you can write a column. If you've been doing it long enough, you know how fast your fingers work; there's no excuse to not have something into your office on time.

I mean, if somebody had said, "Write a column in six minutes," I would say, "I can't write a column in six minutes." But I can write one in 25 or 30 minutes.

How do you start?

Sometimes you have the headline before the column, since we write our own headlines.

So you wrote "The Survivor Won't Let Time Slip By?" Why do you write your own headlines?

I went back to sports 12 years ago to write long, flowery features and travel around and just sort of dress up the sports section—and they said, "Well, would you do a column once in a while?" And, "What about the headline?"

"Headlines! Man—I hate copy-editing. That's one of the reasons I left *Newsday* 20 years ago, was to get away from copy-editing." And they said, "Well, here our sports columnists write their own headlines."

The challenge of writing your own headline is that I know what I'm trying to say, and also after a while you learn to take the leap into the creative.

So that's what you write first?

No, not always. Sometimes you don't even have a good headline.

The first thing generally is to get a lead, and here we're getting into the glories of technology and the glories of the computer, which I am not good at and I resisted and grumped about when we first started to use computers. It's a wonderful tool. Every time I hear people talk about not being able to write the same and the process of hand to pen to paper, I say, "What are you talking about?" To be able to type fast and clearly and cleanly and then to move paragraphs around—I mean, how many books would've been different? Would *War and Peace* have been different if the guy could've moved his paragraphs around instead of having to rewrite them?

I read about people, real writers and serious writers, who say that every word has to be perfect before they can go to the next one, and every sentence and every paragraph, things have to build off each other. That's fine and if it works for them and if that's how the best writers do their best writing that I pay money to read, then thank goodness they do it that way.

But for me hacking out a sports column, the technique is to just type as fast as you can, knowing your material because you don't have time to screw around. Electronically what that means is you can write the ninth paragraph and you'll say, "Now, that's really what I'm trying to say here." So you press a button, you move the cursor, you press another button, you move the cursor up, you press another button, and you move the paragraph. That simple. On deadline. You've saved your ass.

How do you plan your stories? Is it in your head or on paper or on the screen?

It's certainly not on paper. If you have time, you think about it while you're asleep at night. Really. I mean like today, I guess I didn't know that Kentucky won last night, but I needed an early column today. So I went to bed last night. I was tired; I have been very busy. But I'm sure that I thought about if Kentucky wins this second game and they're going to play North Carolina on Saturday, am I going to write something about it?

It certainly was in my mind last night. My daughter, who's also a sports columnist, was here with a colleague of hers who is a journalist, we were watching this game, and I'm sure I was thinking about it while I was asleep. Waking up, it was in my mind, the theme.

Do you have a reader in mind when you write?

She's a little old lady who lives by herself up on the Upper West Side and the *Times* is very important to her. When she taught or was a librarian or was a civil servant, the *Times* covered things she did. Now she's retired and she reads the *Times* every day and she goes out for lunch or breakfast and she reads the paper.

Our local sports radio crazies would say, "You know, as a sportswriter he's not writing for the real fan." If you're talking about my target, it's the average *Times* reader, not the hard-core sports fan.

Do you make a distinction between journalism and sportswriting?

I hate the word "sportswriter." The implication is some childish doof in a sweatsuit eating free food and kind of lumbering in and writing clichés and getting things wrong. I don't wear sweatsuits to work. In fact, I wear jackets and ties almost all the time to work just to make the point I'm a serious person. I work for a serious paper, I'm in a serious business, I'm at work, I'm going to work. Dress is important.

What do you want to be thought of as?

A journalist.

What advice can you give about sportswriting?

Journalism is only the first line of defense: anybody who expects the daily newspaper to be everything is missing a lot of other stimuli. But having said that, that you can't get all your information from a newspaper, what's better? What's protecting us more? Is it government? Is it television? Is it private industry? Is it medicine? Is it law? What other force in society as silly and crass and limited and superficial as journalism is, what other force in society is lumbering along, making mistakes, arrogant, foolish, but sort of doing the right thing more often than not?

You went from covering religion to writing about sports? What are the differences?

None. It's exactly the same. They do it on weekends, and they do it in big places, and they celebrate, and they've got their heroes and their gods and their fallen deities, their devils and their angels, and their celebrations. You couldn't possibly have more respect for a real deity than they do for "these wonderful, stellar athletes coming here tonight..." You know, it's the same.

What role have editors played, good and bad, in your career?

With editors, the first thing they can do is to recognize talent. If an editor says to you, "You've got talent, you're my kind of person," then you go into it with a sense of excitement. I think journalism is a kind of compulsive, addictive behavior. We have to be pushed and pulled and challenged every day, and if we're not, we don't perform well.

In 1970 I got a call from Gene Roberts, [now managing editor] and in essence what he said was, "You don't know me, I don't know you, but I like the way you write. Would you want to be an Appalachian correspondent for the *Times*?"

I don't even think I answered his first call. It seems to me my reaction was, oh, probably some guy looking for tickets to the Giant-Jet game or something. But once he explained it to me, Roberts just sold me on covering Appalachia.

Here was somebody making it sound like fun. Journalism isn't fun a lot of times. There are so many rules, so many "nos," but here was somebody who wasn't talking about rules at all. He was talking about freedom. Go down there, take a look around.

Did you work out of your house?

I had a closet at the *Courier-Journal* Building, literally a closet that Barry Bingham scoured up. "Well, this is all we have, but we're proud to have you in our building."

Why did you become a journalist?

It was a job. It was the only thing I knew how to do. I saw my father doing it. He worked full time for the Associated Press. It probably saved me from a life of crime or a life of dereliction.

When did you become a writer?

When I was in high school. It was a very big and very elite public high school in Queens called Jamaica High School, and there were so many bright kids in that school, and I fell through the cracks and was in the general classes rather than the Honors classes.

And I remember turning in an essay and it came back with an A-plus on it. Then the teacher, whose name was Irma Rhodes, had me read it in class, and she told her class, "Listen to this." It was the first praise that I'd gotten. I then wanted to perform for her, and I would write, and I would get plenty of reward in the class. I mean, people thought I was neat. There was even a girl in the class who liked me.

Let's talk about the column on Mickey Mantle. Was this a deadline piece?

No, but it probably was a four-hour piece. I certainly didn't need more than a couple of hours. I know how I felt about Mantle.

The real trick was to get it right, to write it well, because by that time my rule of "know how you feel" certainly was in play. The trick was to liberate how I felt and make it vaguely literate as opposed to just reciting things about him or being maudlin, to try to get the tone right.

How do you do that?

I knew how I felt about him. I was already in the mode of doing it. But how do you get to that point is to consciously say, "What do I really feel?"

Do you know if Mickey Mantle saw that column?

No idea. One of the things working for the *Times,* I always operate on the assumption that nobody sees anything, that they don't read the paper, and that it doesn't matter. I'm not writing for them. I'm not writing for my subjects.

Do you want to hold athletes to a higher standard of behavior that's as high as their salaries?

No, I absolutely do not. I think that's unfair. I only want to hold them to standards for themselves and their families, and to not get away with things.

I don't want to hold Darryl Strawberry or Dwight Gooden or anybody else up that they should be idols to America's youth because America is going to be disappointed as hell if they do.

Let it evolve. Let somebody grow up to be Julius Erving first and then he can be an idol. Let him survive 15 years in the NBA and come through it with his head high and with a religious or at least a moral point of view, and never having been in a scandal and being a role model as a husband and a father. And then, *then,* we'll call him a role model. But not at 23.

You use yourself as a lens in several of these pieces, and you bring in enough self-history to give authority to your conclusions. By the end of that, you feel as a reader, that this guy has earned the right to this opinion. Is that a big part of what you do, use yourself as the lens?

I think by now, it's the only way to keep sane about this stuff. And because I do know who I am, and sometimes I don't even mind being foolish, like pointing out that this is a minority opinion or this is a cranky opinion or I'm going to sound like a jerk here. If I write something about football, I will say, "This is just a cranky person who likes to be obstinate or different, so you don't have to take it all that seriously. You're going to think I'm a jerk in the next paragraph, so let me prepare you for it."

Let's say a young journalist came to you and said, "George, I've just been given a column. And I want to be good. Can you give me some advice?"

If that person is being given a promotion, it probably means that there's a reason for it, that it's not an accident. You have to say, "I must be OK, I must be pretty good," and to trust yourself but not in an egotistical way, but to listen to your best instincts. The things you think are right probably are right.

You do have to rely on yourself. As a columnist particularly, you are Han Solo, you are the Lone Ranger. You have to trust yourself before you can trust anybody else, because once you let somebody else into your brain, you're taking a chance. Once you ask for permission or once you rely on somebody else, possibly somebody will say no. Know what you want first, and particularly for a column, because it is your column—it does have your name on it, and a column implies opinion and personality, so you have to know yourself and you have to know what you want to do under optimum circumstances.

Get good advice and listen to the people at the paper, but deep down, listen to yourself. You are on your own as a columnist.

The Boston Globe

Dan Shaughnessy
Finalist, Sports Writing

Dan Shaughnessy is a sports columnist for *The Boston Globe.* He was born in Groton, Mass., graduated from Holy Cross in 1975, and worked at the *Baltimore Evening Sun* and the *Washington Star* from 1977-81. He joined the *Globe* in 1981 and covered the Celtics from 1982-86 and the Red Sox from 1986 until 1989 when he became a sports columnist. He has been named Massachusetts Sportswriter of the Year in each of the last five years, and three times has been voted one of America's top three sports columnists by Associated Press Sports Editors. Shaughnessy has written four books: *Seeing Red* (the Red Auerbach Story), *The Curse of the Bambino, Ever Green,* and *One Strike Away.* He makes regular appearances on WEEI sports radio and WBZ-TV *Sports Final.*

When his daughter, Kate, was diagnosed with leukemia, he resisted the urge to write about it. Fortunately, he changed his mind, producing a piece that resonates with a parent's love and pain and the concern for a child whose story brought out the best in others.

A ball sails, emotions swirl

APRIL 18, 1994

My daughter, Kate, threw out a first ball before yesterday's Red Sox-White Sox game at Fenway Park. Kate has leukemia.

Kate and 6-year-old Philip Doyle of Weymouth, another Jimmy Fund patient, were first-ball tossers for the Sox' second annual Kids Opening Day. I cannot speak for the Doyles, but I expect yesterday they felt very much like my wife and myself.

Watching Kate walk to the mound, I thought about all the bad times she's endured in the last five months. I thought about the spinal taps, bone marrows, MRIs, bone scans, collapsed IV lines and surgeries. I remember the empty halls of Children's Hospital when Kate had surgery Christmas Eve. It was a big deal to get Kate home for three hours Christmas morning. And now she's out there throwing the high heater to Dave Valle in front of 34,501 at Fenway Park.

Life changed for Kate Nov. 26. It was the day after Thanksgiving, the day of the Boston College-West Virginia game. It was the day my wife and I sat side-by-side on a conference room couch on the sixth floor of Children's Hospital and heard Dr. Kenneth Cooke say, "Your daughter has leukemia."

Kate has standard risk, acute lymphoblastic leukemia. I'm told it happens to one out of every 1,580 Caucasian children under the age of 15. Kate is 8 and played her full soccer schedule last fall. At the end of the season, she complained of sharp lower back pain. We took her to our family health clinic. The doctor ordered a blood test and sent her home with Advil. Then there was a phone call, a trip to the emergency room at Children's, and, by nightfall, we knew.

Bad things happen to all of us. This is not fair to Kate, but it's something we've all had to learn to deal with. My wife and I are thankful we live in Boston, thankful it is 1994, and thankful for our families and wonderful friends. December and January were especially cold and scary, but I still get a warm feeling when I remember the love and care showered on our home in the days and weeks after Kate was diagnosed. Ever seen homemade lasagnas stacked like cordwood?

"It's just like the old days," Kate's grandmother would say after another neighbor put some food on our doorstep.

A week after she was diagnosed, Ted Williams called Kate in the hospital. Kate knows nothing about old-time baseball stars. She held the phone a few inches from her ear and said, "Daddy, there's a loud man on the phone, telling me I'm going to be OK."

She passed the phone to me and Ted Williams bellowed, "Dr. [Sidney] Farber used to tell me, 'Ted, we're going to find a way to cure these kids.' Sure enough, he did it. You tell your daughter she's going to be fine. Tell her I'll come visit her."

Ted Williams was the star of the Red Sox when the Jimmy Fund got rolling in 1948. When the Braves moved from Boston in 1953, Tom Yawkey made the Jimmy Fund the Red Sox' official charity, and Teddy Ballgame became keeper of the flame. Ted's only sibling, his brother Danny, died of leukemia in 1960. Ted never stopped working for his favorite charity. Meanwhile, Dr. Farber pioneered treatment of cancer in children.

It was the late Edward Bennett Williams who first told me, "The cure is worse than the cancer." In dramatic lore, it is known as chemotherapy, but the real names of some of the drugs are methotrexate, 6 mercaptopurine, vincristine, and dexamethasone. Some of this stuff is administered at home and its power and potency is underscored by the toxic spill kit that comes with the medicine. Kate is scheduled to have chemotherapy for two years.

Each Tuesday is Kate's Jimmy Fund clinic day, and the Red Sox are all over the place. John Harrington cut one of the ribbons this winter when

Photo by Jim Davis, The Boston Globe

the new clinic was dedicated. There's a Carl Yas-
trzemski treatment room. There's a Ted Williams
mural, and one of his silver bats—right next to the
Robert K. Kraft blood donor center. Former Sox
second baseman Mike Andrews is executive director of the Jimmy Fund, and Rose Lonborg,
wife of Cy Young winner Jim, volunteers her time
to make the clinic visits less painful and more fun.

One of our lasting impressions of this horrible
experience is the innate goodness of people. The
nurses of 7-West cared for our Kate as if she were

their own daughter. Kate's teachers, coaches and friends have done everything to make her feel comfortable and included.

Individuals who've been roughed up in this column have called and written to lend support. Dave Gavitt. Lou Gorman. Billy Sullivan. Jim O'Brien. Joe Morgan. Chris Ford. Cam Neely. Adam Oates. Glen Wesley. Mo Vaughn. Larry Bird. Bill Walton. John Blue. In the dugout before yesterday's first pitch, Butch Hobson came over with bubblegum for the whole family. Even me. These sports professionals are fathers and brothers and uncles. They know there is the stuff we do every day...and then there is the important stuff.

You should have seen the look on the face of the guy who drives the Federal Express truck when a large package arrived at our door from Katy, Texas. The driver saw the names "Clemens" and "Shaughnessy" and suggested we check to see if the thing was ticking. It was a giant white teddy bear. Kate calls her "Clementine."

And yesterday she stood on the mound where Roger Clemens stood Friday night.

There are no guarantees. We pray that Kate stays the course and someday is cured. We know there are many families far worse off than ours. But most of all we watch Kate, and enjoy the good days after so many bad ones. She is strong and smart and—without hair—more beautiful than ever.

She says she plans to be Charlie Brown next Halloween. I love that. Kate and Charlie Brown. Same pitching motion. Same haircut.

Lessons Learned

BY DAN SHAUGHNESSY

This was a difficult piece to write. My daughter, Kate, was diagnosed with leukemia on Nov. 26, 1993, and for more than a month I didn't write anything at all. During Kate's long stay in the hospital, there were times when I thought I might someday write about it, but the notion usually passed. It somehow seemed too personal and indulgent. Every family has problems. Why burden *Globe* readers with our Kate's illness?

I think many of us in this business have an instinctive aversion to the "I" word. Generally speaking, we are not the story. We are here to report the story. As a columnist, one is more likely to employ the first-person device and I think there's a danger to the practice. I have read columnists who I think may have been seduced by the sound of their own voices and fall back on first person too often. Done badly, first-person writing can be dreadful.

Eventually, Kate started to feel a little better and I started to write sports columns again. When the Red Sox asked her to throw out the first ball with another cancer patient on "Kids Opening Day," I felt it was time to tell Kate's story. My wife and I wanted to thank everybody who'd been so thoughtful, increase awareness of childhood cancer, and encourage New Englanders to give to the Jimmy Fund.

I wrote most of the piece before Kate actually tossed the ball. I knew the things that I wanted to say, and thought it might be too emotional to compose on deadline after she'd actually stepped out in front of 35,000 fans at Fenway Park.

The bulk of the essay was written on a Friday afternoon, two days before Kate threw the pitch. I wanted to explain what she'd been through, and tell everybody that there is a great deal of hope for her and other children like her.

My wife, Marilou, read the piece later that day and made a crucial edit. In the original piece, I'd written a tag line about having trouble reading my own computer screen because I "had something in my eye." Marilou said it was melodramatic. The story didn't need any extra sappiness. The line came out. Later that night, my agent and friend, Meg Blackstone, reviewed the essay. She suggested I delete a line about carrying Kate to the bathroom during the difficult days. It came out. Two good edits. In the days and weeks after the story appeared, many colleagues complimented me for "not being melodramatic."

Kate threw her pitch on Sunday afternoon, and I scrambled to the press box to update the column and send it to the *Globe*.

There tends to be more reader feedback after one writes first-person columns. After the story ran on the front page (accompanied by a spectacular photograph by the *Globe*'s Jim Davis), I received close to 200 letters and faxes from readers. The mail was extremely personal, emotional, and supportive. I heard from many families of children with cancer. I heard from many parents who had lost their children. I read the letters once, and put them in a box. They are difficult to read.

Kate was pretty happy with the story when it came out. She did not like the fact that I told people what she was going to be for Halloween (she wanted to surprise everybody), but otherwise said it was OK. She got mail from all over the country. Her picture was used as part of a blood drive. The Jimmy Fund received thousands of dollars in contributions in Kate's name.

I think using first person is valuable if there is a real story to tell. The beauty of first person is that it needn't be overwritten. Just tell the story.

As I write this I am happy to report that Kate is tolerating her therapy well and has a good chance to beat leukemia, but I know I will never relax.

For me, the lesson learned from this story is that people are good. People care deeply about a sick child, a child they do not know. It is a lesson that will stay with me forever, a warm thought to offset the chill that so often invades our lives.

Eye to I: Writing the personal essay

BY CHRISTOPHER SCANLAN

"We've got the O.J. 911 tapes," the disc jockey promised. "Coming up after these messages."

Like other commuters on this July morning, I was hooked. When the playback finally came over my car radio, I was sitting at a stoplight downtown. I heard Nicole Brown Simpson's voice —fed-up, frightened, resigned—but that wasn't what brought tears to my eyes. It was the voice in the background—the shouts of a man out of control, choking on contempt and rage, spewing abuse. I knew that sound.

I've heard it echoing off the walls in our house. I've felt the lump of remorse that screaming at the top of my lungs leaves in the back of my throat and the pit of my stomach. "I have to write about this," I thought. The light changed. I drove on. "But I don't want to."

Like most journalists, I feared the word "I."

I was warned off using the first person at the start of my career by a chorus of voices—a jaded competitor at my first paper, a fearsome city editor, skeptical colleagues. "Reporters don't belong in their stories. That's what bylines are for." They added, "Besides, nobody cares about your personal life. If it were really interesting, some reporter would be writing about you."

I don't need both hands to count the times I used the first person in 20 years of reporting: a deadline account about a stint volunteering at a mental hospital during a state workers' strike; a recollection of a year in the Peace Corps; a Father's Day message to my unborn daughter; a travel piece about the search for a soldier's grave in Europe; a brief stint as a fill-in columnist. But in all of these I stayed back, my presence little more than a personal pronoun.

Writing about yourself is often difficult for reporters and editors whose work focuses on others.

But writing about yourself, honestly, even painfully, can make you a better reporter and editor: more empathetic, more skilled, better able to spot the universal truth in the individual story. Unlike the column, which usually delivers judgment on others, or the feature, which focuses on someone other than the writer, or the op-ed essay, which explores an issue or situation, the personal essay is not detached. It trains its sights on the writer's own life and the writer's emotional, psychological, and intellectual reactions to the most intimate experiences. As Phillip Lopate says in his introduction to his anthology *The Art of the Personal Essay* (Anchor Books-Doubleday, 1994): "The personal essayist looks back at the choices that were made, the roads not taken, the limiting familial and historic circumstances, and what might be called the catastrophe of personality."

At a time when newspapers are increasingly fearful about losing their audience, personal writing, as most columnists know, generates enormous reader response. Donna Britt's columns about the emotional landscape of modern life for *The Washington Post* sometimes generate 70 letters a week. Mark Patinkin, a columnist for the *Providence Journal-Bulletin,* spent a month in Africa writing about famine and two months writing about religious violence in Belfast, India, and Beirut. "But a single column I did on how my parents met got more response than either of those two global projects."

I have gotten more reaction—letters to the editor, phone calls, personal comments—from personal essays than any single story in my entire career.

In the last year, writing a personal essay has been an integral part of seminars for professional and student reporters and editors and broadcast journalists at The Poynter Institute. With my colleagues Karen Brown, Roy Peter Clark, and Valerie Hyman, and visiting writers such as *Boston Globe* columnist Donald M. Murray, I have asked participants in our seminars to write a personal essay as well as coach another writer through the experience.

The result has been a small but growing collection of powerful essays and an enthusiastic response from editors and writers who confess that the prospect of exposing themselves on the page terrified them at first. By week's end, they are convinced of the value of writing "eye to I." Tina Ezell-Hull, a copy editor at *The Post and Courier* in Charleston, S.C., expressed a typical reaction:

"I thought, 'Write a personal essay? Are they nuts. I don't know these people.' And then: 'They want us to read OUT LOUD to the ENTIRE class. Are they kidding?' But by the end of the week, we'd all been up together at night getting this done and we all were a little punchy from lack of sleep, and I think most of us forgot to be scared. After all, we did something that's NOT easy. I guess what doesn't kill us makes us stronger."

In her case, the experience also produced a poignant tribute to her "90something great-grandmother." Ezell-Hull begins "Memories of Mama," published on Mother's Day, with a riveting blend of detail and emotion:

In my mind, I'm still in my tiny bedroom at 230 Miller St. Summer never ended. I never grew up. I never had to say goodbye.

The best friend I ever had is still there, too. Patent leather purse clutched to her side, three-strand pearl choker at her neck, she's clicking briskly up the sidewalk, switching her hips just a tad.

Mama's home. And I'm happy again.

FINDING YOUR SUBJECT

I couldn't put off writing about my temper any longer.

Don Murray, who has written hundreds of columns for *The Boston Globe,* had come to Poynter in July 1994 to teach in a summer program for college graduates bent on a career in journalism. The assignment: to write a personal essay.

"Make a list of what you think about when you are not thinking," Murray advised. "What makes you mad? What makes you happy? What past events were turning points in your life that you'd like to understand?''

It's here, at the beginning of the process, that I almost chickened out. My wife and I have three daughters, including a set of twins, who are always doing and saying cute things. I would write about being the father of twins, scattering my essay with funny anecdotes and the darndest things kids say.

I certainly wasn't going to write an essay that let anyone in on my dirty little secret, that I too often lost my temper with these three little girls. But how could I ask these students to bare their souls if I wasn't willing to take the risk along with them? And then I remembered my reaction to O.J. Simpson's shouting on the 911 tapes and I knew I couldn't keep my distance anymore.

The night before the class, I lay in bed with Murray's instructions beside me and filled two pages with a staccato of disjointed thoughts about the one thing I didn't want to write about but which I knew I should.

Temper, Temper.

911 tape in car...tears at stop light. I have been there. My voice too.

Temper school.

Male anger.

I had my subject. Or more accurately, it had me.

"The place you come from and how you remember it matters," says writer Robert Love Taylor. "It is your territory."

Writing the personal essay requires you to seek out the territory that is your life and to explore it as deeply and honestly as possible. For journalists, it means subjecting your own life to the same scrutiny that you train on your sources.

■ **Choose your subject.** This is the first and most important step. And if it's not close to the bone, keep looking. It's the willingness to explore something that is very personal and even painful that will serve you and the reader. I think it's best to write about something you feel deeply about but which you don't yet fully understand.

The stuff of everyday life, meticulously observed and described, is what sets the personal essay apart. At Poynter, seminar participants have written haunting, wrenching, funny, and inspiring essays about a 30-year-old prom dress, the minefield of personal relationships, a friend's suicide, the pain of racism, the trials of living with a pack rat, their children, their marriages, their parents' lives and deaths. "There are common human experiences, and journalists strike a chord when they write about them," says Ruth Hanley, an assistant city editor for *The Dispatch* in Columbus, Ohio.

In the past year, I have written essays about my pathetic boyhood athletic career and how it made me a non-sports watcher ("Stupor Bowl" in *The Boston Globe Magazine*); how my wife and I ask the parents of our children's friends if they have guns in their homes ("It's 10 p.m. Do You Know Where Your Guns Are?" in *The Christian Science Monitor*); and an account of the struggle with my temper (*Newsday* and the Sunday magazines of *The Boston Globe* and *The Detroit Free Press*).

Evelynne Kramer, editor of *The Boston Globe Magazine,* says she looks for writing "that plumbs a universal feeling that a reader can relate to on some level even though they might not have had that particular experience." Effective essays, she says, "explore universal themes although not necessarily experiences."

■ **Discover your story by writing it.** Melvin Mencher, a professor at the Columbia University Graduate School of Journalism, had a simple cure for writer's block: "Whenever you are blocked," he said, "just stop and ask yourself, 'What am I trying to say?'"

Last summer, I sat in front of a computer terminal with my students on all sides in a Poynter Institute computer lab, fingers frozen, until I asked that question and the first tentative words began to appear on the screen.

I do not want to write this. I love my kids,
but I have left my handprint, like a blush, on
the backs of their thighs.

I do not want to write this.

Don Murray had given us 45 minutes to produce a first draft. Like a child whistling by a cemetery, I spent it typing as fast as I could, writing without thinking, trying to discover what I wanted to say by talking to myself on the page as honestly as I could.

■ **Think small.** Essays are most effective when they are "a snapshot of an experience, not a panoramic view," says Mary Jane Park, who edits the Private Lives column for the *St. Petersburg Times.* A personal essay she published by Amelia Davis of her paper's Clearwater bureau, illustrates her point.

For four years, on Friday, Saturday, and Sunday nights, I had dated only one boy. He was a classmate and neighbor whose front gate was less than a quarter mile from my back door. His football jacket was my winter coat. My class ring hung on a chain over the rear view mirror of his old Pontiac. Everyone knew we were a couple.

■ **Recreate pivotal moments.** Lary Bloom, editor of *Northeast,* the Sunday magazine of *The Hartford Courant* and author of *The Writer Within: How to Discover Your Own Ideas, Get Them on Paper, and Sell Them for Publication,* puts the form to a rigorous test. "You don't have a personal essay unless you have a religious experience," he says. "Then it's the task of the writer to recreate that moment."

For me, that meant trying to recreate an unforgettable moment that occurred nearly 40 years ago and which I became convinced held answers to my own battles with anger.

I am no more than 9, and I am standing just outside our family kitchen. My father has come home drunk again. He is in his mid-40s, (about the age I am today). By now, he has had three strokes, landmines in his brain that he seems to shrug off, like his hangovers, but which in a year will kill him. He has lost his job selling paper products, which he detested, and has had no luck finding another. He and my mother begin arguing in the kitchen. Somehow he has gotten hold of her rosary beads. I hear his anger, her protests, and then, suddenly, they are struggling over the black necklace. (Has he found her at the kitchen table, praying for him? I can imagine his rage. "If your God is so good, why are the sheriffs coming to the door about the bills I can't pay? Why am I broke? Why can't I find a job? Why am I so sick? Why, dammit? Why?") Out of control now, he tears the rosary apart. I can still hear the beads dancing like marbles on the linoleum.

■ **Learn to self-edit.** Journalism is a craft that teaches writers to write quickly and concentrate more on accuracy and clarity than style or voice. Depending on the deadline, a reporter may only have time to try out a few leads and then forge ahead, making small changes as the writing is completed with an eye on the ticking clock.

Essay writing gives writers the luxury of time absent in most newsrooms. And it can teach invaluable lessons about good writing. Time is not the secret. The real key to writing success is learning how to read your manuscript with a discriminating eye—and ear. You have to discover what you want to say by writing it and then be willing to jettison it all when it doesn't work.

So I re-read what I wrote. I read it aloud to my wife. I choked back my usual disgust at my first draft. I rewrote. I jettisoned entire pages. I worked over paragraphs until just one phrase remained. I made my endings my beginnings. I added new material. I gave them to readers I trusted and asked their reaction. I listened to their reactions and cut and added and re-ordered and wrote again.

■ **Be ready to be judged,** says *Providence Journal-Bulletin* columnist Mark Patinkin. "When you use the letter 'I,' for every supportive letter you get from someone who related to your one-year-old having a scene at a restaurant, you'll get another from a reader tired of hearing about your kid."

Readers bring their own autobiography to each text they read, says Murray. "The better the piece of writing, the more it happens." "Good writing articulates their own fears, hopes, memories, psychological needs. The further the writer goes into his or her life, the further the reader goes into theirs."

After I wrote about my temper with my young daughters, several letter writers to *The Boston Globe Magazine* denounced me. "I am outraged that *The Globe Magazine* devoted space to a domestic-violence apologist," wrote one. "Temper tantrums are excusable for 2-year-olds, not for grown men," another agreed.

Their criticism was softened by other letters from parents who said they recognized their own family struggles with temper in my story. One mother from Maine planned to share the piece with her siblings "so they can tackle the trait sooner and hopefully more effectively." Another woman said she wished her father was still alive so he could read it.

WHY THE PERSONAL ESSAY?

"Writing that personal essay was extremely difficult for me," says Ruth Hanley, who explored a difficult relationship with a close relative. "One of the things that surprised me was the physical reaction I had—whenever I sat down to work on it, I squirmed. I was wired and tense. I was especially uncomfortable at the thought of digging so deeply into an experience that I still hadn't come to terms with personally."

Reporters and editors have more than enough to do covering their beats, making deadlines, planning coverage. So why bother?

■ **It can make you a better reporter.** "If you can't tell an honest story about yourself, you're a long way from telling an honest story about someone else," Walt Harrington, staff writer for *The Washington Post Magazine,* says in *The Com-*

plete Book of Feature Writing, edited by Leonard Witt (Writer's Digest Books, 1991). Rather than an ego trip, saying "I" in print was "simply another vantage from which to tell a story," Harrington says.

■ **It can make you a better editor.** The personal essay invites and allows editors to write and in writing they become better, more perceptive, more understanding editors. Editors are not reporters and writers, but they can report on their own world. Editors who never write get an opportunity to experience the terror of the blank page.

Kevin McGrath, an editor at the Munster, Ind., *Times,* says writing personal essays "gives me a better appreciation of what reporters go through each day, and it gives me a glimpse of the sort of thing our craft can accomplish when raised to its highest level. It inspires me to do better, and to help others do the same."

■ **It will connect you with readers.** Public cynicism about the media may never have been as pervasive as it is today. Writing personally gives journalists the opportunity to show readers they share the same joys and costs of being human.

"It's too easy to put a distance between them and us," says Maria Carrillo, an assistant city editor at *The Free Lance Star* in Fredericksburg, Va. Writing personally gives journalists the opportunity to "revisit your human side, the one journalism strips away little by little."

The feedback Carrillo received about her essay focusing on her ambivalence as a child about her Hispanic heritage and her hope as a mother that her children wouldn't leave it behind convinced her that "readers respond more to personal essays than any other kind of writing we do because it lets them make a connection."

At a time when connecting with readers has never been more crucial to the industry's survival, the personal essay gives the journalist a resonant form that links us with our audience.

By reporting on the central issues of the human condition—joy, loss, birth, anger, fear, death, hate, and love—they will give voice to the unspoken feelings and thoughts of their readers and draw each other into the human community.

■ **It will expand your writing skills.** "Personal essays also force us to communicate emotional values, a demand we too seldom face, or too seldom seek, in everyday newswriting," says Kevin McGrath. "Yet it is often the emotional center of a story that draws and holds the reader."

"You can't write a personal column without going to some very deep place inside yourself, even if it's only for four hours," says essayist Jennifer Allen in *Speaking of Journalism,* edited by William Zinsser (Harper Collins, 1994). "It's almost like psychotherapy, except you're doing it on your own. You have to pull something out of yourself and give away some important part of yourself...It's a gift you have to give to the reader, even if it's the most light-hearted piece in the world."

For me, writing about my temper led me to an unexpected insight—and a new peace—about my relationship with my father who died when I was a boy.

Whatever psychic wounds my father's death caused when I was 10 seem to have frozen over my recollection of him. I have few conscious memories; those I have are starkly-etched scenes of drunkenness, grief, and rage that left me with a reservoir of unresolved anger. This limitless supply feeds the frustrations of my own life, as do my templates of parental behavior that I, the loyal son, can re-enact with my own children. For many years, I thought that I hated the dimly-remembered stranger who was my father. I believed that I hated him for dying before I could learn who he was, for scaring me when he was drunk; but now I realize I hate him only because he left me before I could say "I love you."

Part confession, part travelogue of the soul, the personal essay isn't a form journalists will write every day, unless they write a column. In a typical career, a reporter or editor may produce a handful of essays. But these stories have the potential to teach them lessons they will use profitably in their reporting, writing, and editing. They may also become psychological breakthroughs that may make them not only better reporters and editors, but will change them in ways they could never imagine before they went "eye to I" with themselves. "Over the years," novelist Don De-Lillo says, "it's possible for a writer to shape himself as a human being through the language."

Annual bibliography

BY DAVID SHEDDEN

WRITING AND REPORTING BOOKS, 1994

Berentson, Jane, ed. *Dressing for Dinner in the Naked City and Other Tales From The Wall Street Journal's "Middle Column."* New York: Hyperion, 1994.

Besser, Pam. *A Basic Handbook of Writing Skills.* Mountain View, CA: Mayfield Publishing, 1994.

Botts, Jack. *The Language of News: A Journalist's Pocket Reference.* Ames, IA: Iowa State University Press, 1994.

Charlton, James, ed. *Fighting Words: Writers Lambaste Other Writers—From Aristotle to Anne Rice.* Chapel Hill, NC: Algonquin Books, 1994.

Clark, Roy Peter. *The American Conversation and the Language of Journalism.* Poynter Paper: No. 5, St. Petersburg, FL: Poynter Institute, 1994.

Gaines, William. *Investigative Reporting for Print and Broadcast.* Chicago: Nelson-Hall Publishers, 1994.

Garrison, Bruce. *Professional Feature Writing.* 2nd ed. Hillsdale, NJ: L. Erlbaum Associates, 1994.

Goldstein, Norm, ed. *The Associated Press Stylebook and Libel Manual.* Reading, MA: Addison-Wesley, 1994.

Itule, Bruce D. and Douglas A. Anderson. *News Writing and Reporting for Today's Media.* 3rd ed. New York: McGraw-Hill, 1994.

Lanson, Gerald and Mitchell Stephens. *Writing and Reporting the News.* 2nd ed. Fort Worth: Harcourt Brace, 1994.

Mencher, Melvin. *News Reporting and Writing.* 6th ed. New York: St. Martin's Press, 1994.

Rosenblatt, Roger. *The Man in the Water: Essays and Stories.* New York: Random House, 1994.

Scanlan, Christopher, ed. *Best Newspaper Writing 1994.* St. Petersburg, FL: Poynter Institute, 1994.

Schulte, Henry H. *Getting the Story: An Advanced Reporting Guide to Beats, Records and Sources.* New York: Macmillan, 1994.

Sloan, William and Laird B. Anderson. *Pulitzer Prize Editorials: America's Best Editorial Writing, 1917-1993.* 2nd ed. Ames, IA: Iowa State University Press, 1994.

Watts, Cheryl Sloan, ed. *Pulitzer Prize Feature Stories.* Ames, IA: Iowa State University Press, 1994.

Zinsser, William, et al. *Speaking of Journalism: 12 Writers and Editors Talk About Their Work.* New York: Harper Collins, 1994.

CLASSICS

Atchity, Kenneth. *A Writer's Time: A Guide to the Creative Process, from Vision through Revision.* New York: Norton, 1986.

Berg, A. Scott. *Max Perkins: Editor of Genius.* New York: Dutton, 1978.

Bernstein, Theodore M. *The Careful Writer: A Modern Guide to English Usage.* New York: Atheneum Press, 1965.

Biagi, Shirley. *Interviews That Work: A Practical Guide for Journalists.* 2nd ed. Belmont, CA: Wadsworth, 1992.

Blundell, William E. *The Art and Craft of Feature Writing: Based on The Wall Street Journal.* New York: New American Library, 1988.

Brady, John. *The Craft of Interviewing.* New York: Vintage Books, 1977.

Brande, Dorothea. *Becoming a Writer.* Los Angeles: J.P. Tarcher; Boston: distributed by Harcourt Brace, reprint of 1934 edition, 1981.

Brown, Karen, Roy Peter Clark, and Don Fry, eds. *Best Newspaper Writing.* St. Petersburg, FL: Poynter Institute. Published annually since 1979.

Cappon, Rene J. *The Word: An Associated Press Guide to Good News Writing.* New York: The Associated Press, 1982.

Clark, Roy Peter. *Free to Write: A Journalist Teaches Young Writers.* Portsmouth, NH: Heinemann Educational Books, 1986.

Clark, Roy Peter, and Don Fry. *Coaching Writers: The Essential Guide for Editors and Reporters.* New York: St. Martin's Press, 1992.

Dillard, Annie. *The Writing Life.* New York: Harper and Row, 1989.

Downie, Leonard, Jr. *The New Muckrakers.* New York: NAL-Dutton, 1978.

Elbow, Peter. *Writing With Power: Techniques for Mastering the Writing Process.* New York: Oxford University Press, 1981.

Follett, Wilson. *Modern American Usage: A Guide.* London: Longmans, 1986.

Franklin, Jon. *Writing for Story: Craft Secrets of Dramatic Nonfiction.* New York: Atheneum, 1986.

Gross, Gerald, ed. *Editors on Editing: An Inside View of What Editors Really Do.* New York: Harper & Row, 1985.

Howarth, William L., ed. *The John McPhee Reader.* New York: Farrar, Straus and Giroux, 1990.

Hugo, Richard. *The Triggering Town: Lectures & Essays on Poetry & Writing.* New York: Norton, 1992.

Mencher, Melvin. *News Reporting and Writing.* 5th ed. Dubuque, IA: William C. Brown, 1991.

Metzler, Ken. *Creative Interviewing: The Writer's Guide to Gathering Information by Asking Questions.* 2nd ed. Englewood Cliffs, NJ: Prentice Hall, 1989.

Mitford, Jessica. *Poison Penmanship: The Gentle Art of Muckraking.* New York: Knopf, 1979.

Murray, Donald. *Shoptalk: Learning to Write With Writers.* Portsmouth, NH: Boynton/Cook, 1990.

— *Writing for Your Readers.* Old Saybrook, CT: Globe Pequot Press, 1992.

Plimpton, George. *Writers At Work: The Paris Review Interviews.* Series. New York: Viking, 1992.

Ross, Lillian. *Reporting.* New York: Dodd, 1981.

Scanlan, Christopher, ed. *How I Wrote the Story.* Providence Journal Company, 1986.

Sims, Norman, ed. *Literary Journalism in the Twentieth Century.* New York: Oxford University Press, 1990.

Snyder, Louis L. and Richard B. Morris, eds. *A Treasury of Great Reporting.* New York: Simon & Schuster, 1962.

Stafford, William and Donald Hall, eds. *Writing the Australian Crawl: View on the Writer's Vocation.* Ann Arbor, MI: University of Michigan Press, 1978.

Strunk, William, Jr., and E.B. White. *The Elements of Style.* 3rd ed. New York: Macmillan, 1979.

Talese, Gay. *Fame & Obscurity.* New York: Ivy Books, 1971.

White, E.B. *Essays of E.B. White.* New York: Harper & Row, 1977.

Witt, Leonard. *The Complete Book of Feature Writing.* Cincinnati, OH: Writer's Digest Books, 1991.

Wardlow, Elwood M., ed. *Effective Writing and Editing: A Guidebook for Newspapers.* Reston, VA: American Press Institute, 1985.

Wolfe, Tom. *The New Journalism.* New York: Harper & Row, 1973.

Zinsser, William. *On Writing Well.* 4th ed. New York: Harper & Row, 1990.

— *Writing to Learn.* New York: Harper & Row, 1988.

ARTICLES 1994

Aregood, Richard. "...Writers (And Editors) Should Stop Grabbing Onto Every Writing Fad That Comes Along." *ASNE Bulletin,* October 1994, p. 29.

Armao, Rosemary. "Editors: Friends and Foes." *The IRE Journal,* November/December 1994, pp. 2–3.

Astor, David. "He Wants a Course in Writing Columns." *Editor & Publisher,* July 23, 1994, pp. 30–31.

Bartimus, Tad. "Writing and the Meaning of Life." *Workbench: The Bulletin of the National Writers' Workshop.* Vol. 1, 1994, pp. 8–11.

Boroson, Warren. "Copy Editors From Hell." *Editor & Publisher,* March 12, 1994, pp. 56, 46.

Clark, Roy Peter. "If I Were a Carpenter: The Tools of the Writer." *Workbench: The Bulletin of the National Writers' Workshop.* Vol. 1, 1994, p. 2.

Connelly, Caren. "Good Editing Means Involvement From the Start." *The IRE Journal,* November/December 1994, p. 6.

Davis, Foster. "Memo to Project Editors." *The IRE Journal,* November/December 1994, p. 12.

Fitzgerald, Mark. "Cottage Industry For Sportswriters." *Editor & Publisher,* January 22, 1994, pp. 9–13.

Fry, Don. "Help Your Writers: Invest Time Early." *ASNE Bulletin,* January/February 1994, p. 33.

— "What Do Coaches Coach Nowadays?" *The Coaches Corner,* December 1994, pp. 6–7.

Fry, Don and Roy Peter Clark. "Return of the Narrative." *Quill,* May 1994, pp. 27–28.

Garrison, Bruce. "Coaching Factual Short Stories." *The Coaches' Corner,* June 1994, pp. 6–9.

Gaultney, Bruce. "The Video Generation Expects Visual Writing." *ASNE Bulletin,* March 1994, pp. 8–9.

Gillies, Patricia. "Copy Editors Deserve Some Respect." *The Editor,* November 1994, p. 24.

Haas, Stewart. "Narrative Leads are not Created Equal." *ASNE Bulletin,* August 1994, pp. 26–27.

Hart, Jack. "Happy Endings." *Editor & Publisher,* December 10, 1994, p. 23.

Harvey, Chris. "Tom Wolfe's Revenge." *American Journalism Review,* October 1994, pp. 40–47.

Hoover, Erin. "Applying Lessons on Deadline." *Workbench: The Bulletin of the National Writers' Workshop.* Vol. 1, 1994, p. 4.

Hyman, Valerie. "What Newspaper Writers Can Learn From TV." *Workbench: The Bulletin of the National Writers' Workshop.* Vol. 1, 1994, pp. 6–7.

Kaminski, Dave. "How to Win with Every Story." *The Editor,* April 1994, pp. 12–15.

Klinkenberg, Jeff. "Writing About Place: The Boundaries of a Story." *Workbench: The Bulletin of the National Writers' Workshop.* Vol. 1, 1994, p. 3.

Laurent, Anne. "Workshop Notebook." *Workbench: The Bulletin of the National Writers' Workshop.* Vol. 1, 1994, p. 7.

Maier, Thomas. "Combining Journalism and Biography." *The IRE Journal,* September/October 1994, pp. 6–8.

Maraniss, David. "How to Stay One Step Ahead of Your Editors." *The IRE Journal,* November/December 1994, pp. 8–11.

Mills, Pat. "On Method and Madness: Teaching Writers to Write." *Journalism Educator,* Winter 1994, pp. 67–70.

Moen, Daryl. "Promises, Promises: Leads that Deliver." *The Coaches' Corner,* June 1994, pp. 10–11.

Nelson, Deb. "Going Beyond Anecdotal Reporting." *The IRE Journal,* September/October 1994, pp. 4–5.

Scanlan, Christopher. "The Clock is Ticking: Techniques for Storytelling on Deadline." *Workbench: The Bulletin of the National Writers' Workshop.* Vol. 1, 1994, p. 5.

Smith, Rex. "Editors Must Help Reporters Do Their Jobs Better." *The IRE Journal,* November/December 1994, pp. 4–5.

Spear, Michael M. "Americans Embrace Technology and Rush to Verbify Language." *Journalism Educator,* Winter 1994, pp. 71–75.

Underwood, Doug and C. Anthony Giffard and Keith Stamm. "Computers and Editing: Pagination's Impact on the Newsroom." *Newspaper Research Journal,* Spring 1994, pp. 116–127.

Winkelaar, Susan. "How to Give the Facts a Bit More Flavor." *The Editor,* September 1994, pp. 17–18.